MERCS

True Stories of Mercenaries in Action

MERCS

True Stories of Mercenaries in Action

Edited by

BILL FAWCETT

AVON BOOKS NEW YORK

AVON BOOKS, INC.
1350 Avenue of the Americas
New York, New York 10019

Contents

Mercenaries in History

If Greece were a rolling fertile land, the history of mercenaries would be very different. But Greece is a mountainous land whose stony fields were capable of supporting only a very limited population. The mountains meant that Bronze Age Greece was divided into city-states, called *polis*, and never unified from within. These cities were not the homes of philosophers and columned temples such as they are often portrayed today. These were small cities, often with far less than 100,000 residents, whose main concerns were simply to protect the crops and wealth of their populations. Almost all were ruled by a single strong man or family. While there was a tradition of oral composition that eventually gave us the *Iliad* and *Odyssey,* the great age of Democratic Athens came only at the end of this era. For a large part, the main occupations of the Bronze Age Greeks were farming and warfare. There was rarely a season when there wasn't a war occurring between the various *polis.* With comparatively small populations, virtually every free male was required to defend the city. This led to the development of an entire population of highly trained phalangites, soldiers trained to fight with a long pike in a tight formation.

As in all wars, there were losers. Often the homes or city of the losers were destroyed, creating a large number of unemployed and homeless but highly skilled soldiers. The Greek cities, with their own limited resources, could only absorb so many of them. Eventually, large numbers of men—skilled soldiers capable of fighting in what was that era's unstoppable formation, the phalanx—left Greece. Once in the richer kingdoms and empires to the east, these men sold the only real skill most had: their ability to fight. They became mercenaries.

This exodus of mercenaries continued for centuries. It became a part of the culture of Bronze Age Greece. There are records of Persian emperors, and pretenders, hiring units consisting of ten thousand Greek mercenaries as a group. The less educated, less sophisticated Greeks excelled at one thing—as shown by the ability of ten thousand Greek mercenaries, who, having been hired by the losing side in a Persian civil war, were able to literally march across Persia and defeat all opposition along the way.

Macedon was considered by the more sophisticated Bronze Age Greeks to be a "barbarian" country with illusions of being a Greek state. When a strong leader named Philip rose there, he imported Greeks to train his army and to educate his son. With this army, he unified a Greece weakened by centuries of internal conflict and two invasions by Persia. His son, Alexander the Great, fought against thousands of Greek mercenaries in Persian employ at every major battle he fought while defeating Darius and conquering Persia.

By this time, there was a thousand-year mercenary tradition. That tradition continues even to this day. In the pages that follow, you will see the evolution of the modern mercenary in a battle-by-battle history of the mercenary and his world.

Greek Mercenaries in Persia

The Anabasis, 400 B.C.

by William R. Forstchen

WHEN ONE CONSIDERS THE MODERN HISTORY OF STRATEGIC withdrawal, that most difficult of all maneuvers, history quickly points to the famed retreat of 10th Corps in North Korea during the bitter winter of 1950–51, the evacuation of Dunkirk in 1940, or, most remarkable of all, Manstein's retreat through the Ukraine after the debacle at Stalingrad. Yet these three modern campaigns, famous and heroic in their own rights, must stand in the shadows of the epic withdrawal of Greek mercenaries after the Persian civil war of 400 B.C., as recorded by Xenophon.

After nearly thirty years of bitter strife between the city-states of Greece, both in home waters and on distant fronts as far away as Sicily, a temporary cessation of hostilities had left tens of thousands of hoplites, the famed heavy infantry of the ancient world, unemployed. Hardened by a war that spanned generations, and knowing no other life, many of these men sought employment elsewhere and thus were recruited by Cyrus of Persia (not to be confused with the famed Cyrus the Great who had lived nearly two hundred years earlier) in an attempt to overthrow the rule of his older brother, Artaxerxes II. Cyrus turned to the Greeks to provide the core of his army and thus hired the famed Spartan general Clearchus.

Though Persia and the Greeks were traditional enemies, military agreements between them were actually rather common. During the Peloponnesian War, the Persians had adroitly played their old enemies against each other, lending aid to one side and then the other. Cyrus, as satrap of Lydia, became involved in Greek affairs and helped to turn the tide for Sparta by aiding them in the construction of a fleet that defeated the Athenian navy, forcing Athens to seek peace.

Marshalling an army of fifty thousand, of which thirteen thousand were Greeks serving under Clearchus, Cyrus launched his campaign straight into the heart of the Persian Empire. Leaving the coast of the Aegean Sea, Cyrus maneuvered his army through Anatolia and down into the open plains near Babylon, where his brother waited with a massive force of nearly one hundred thousand men.

Though outnumbered two to one, Cyrus deployed his army with the Greek phalanxes on the right. The Greek heavy infantry, armed with twelve- to fifteen-foot-long spears, formed their traditional battle array of heavy rectangular blocks, twelve to sixteen men deep and a hundred yards across. Advancing at a walk with spears lowered, the famed Greek infantry presented an imposing front. One of the fatal weaknesses of such formations was compression, the men piling close into each other during the heat of battle and thus losing the ability to maneuver. But these men were battle-hardened veterans, having fought for their own city-states in the long Greek civil wars, and now, as mercenaries, they knew their business and kept their formations flexible, ready to turn and maneuver as needed.

Crashing into Artaxerxes' left wing, the hoplites began to roll up the left of the Persian line. This was adroit maneuvering on the part of Cyrus and Clearchus, for in ancient warfare the left of any line tended to be weaker and more vulnerable due to the natural human instinct to maneuver to the right. The reason for this was the right-handedness of nearly all warriors; in close combat, men tended to move toward their weapon side and shy away from their shield side. This tendency to maneuver to the right would often result in two armies of equal strength pivoting during a battle, sometimes even finishing the action 180 degrees from their starting position. Thus, as Clearchus and his mercenaries smashed into the enemy's left, Cyrus held his own left of the line and attempted to keep the overwhelming numbers of Artaxerxes at bay.

The superior fighting skills of the Spartan-led Greeks soon told, and the Persian left collapsed into confusion. The Greeks then pivoted to roll up the entire line of Artaxerxes, and the battle was all but won. It was at this moment that Cyrus, caught up in the joy of battle that had carried him to within grasping distance of the imperial throne, charged into the fray. As happens a number of times in history, the random course of an arrow laid low all the plans of men. Cyrus tumbled from his mount . . . dead.

If ever there was an "oh . . . damn" moment in history, this was it, at least for the Greeks. Hired to put a rival claimant on the throne, they had carried him to all but certain victory, only to see him die in a reckless charge. Not only had they lost their paymaster; they were also very much alone on that field of action. The thirty thousand or more Persian troops, hearing of this sudden change of fortune, took the quickest route out of there and headed for the hills—for, in Persian civil wars, losing armies could rarely expect mercy. The only thing that saved any of them was the fact that Artaxerxes' army was all but defeated and fleeing in panic. For the Greeks, defeat had been snatched from the jaws of victory.

The Greeks quickly pulled back from the battlefield and took stock of the situation. The only hope now was to put on the best possible face, argue that they were, after all, merely professionals following orders, and suggest that there were no hard feelings.

To their surprise, Artaxerxes offered to discuss terms, and Clearchus, along with all his senior generals, accepted the flag of truce and went into the camp of the general commanding Artaxerxes' all-but-defeated army. As soon as they were in the camp, Clearchus was seized and killed, his staff and lieutenants overpowered. Dragged before Artaxerxes, all were beheaded. The terms offered the army: slavery or death.

The situation was grim. The entire upper command was gone, the victorious army of Cyrus had melted away, and the emperor was in the mood to teach a lesson to the damnable Greeks who had nearly cost him his throne. Beyond that, he wanted a clear message sent back to all of Greece: that the internal dynastic struggles of the Persian Empire were not to be trifled with.

The meeting of the junior officers of the Greek mercenaries after the death of Clearchus must have been one of the most remarkable officers' meetings in history. It had been Clearchus who had welded the army together out of the various rival factions after the end of the Peloponnesian War. The men who had come to him had not been professional mercenaries who just happened to have served different employers, but were in fact men who had fought each other for nationalistic reasons. That war had been a long and bitter one, and one hundred years of hatred between the Athenians and the Spartans had all but destroyed Greece. With Cyrus, their acknowledged leader, gone, there must have been a moment when all the junior officers looked at each other with doubt and suspicion.

There was little to discuss regarding what to do with Artaxerxes. Surrender wasn't even an option, for they all realized there would be no ransom offered by their home cities and Artaxerxes was in a killing mood. There was little time for debate as well, since, even as they met to ponder their course, the emperor was marshalling his forces for the hunt. Though former enemies, all realized that if there was any hope of getting out, they would have to learn to trust each other and work as a team.

A joint command of officers was established, one of them being Xenophon, a young Athenian veteran. Rolling out the map, they considered their options. A direct march back through Anatolia was ruled out as too treacherous. There was only one other choice—to strike north and head for the Greek colony of Trapezus in modern-day Armenia. There was only one drawback: it was over a thousand miles away, through mountainous territory, most all of it hostile.

Thus began the March of the Ten Thousand. Stalling the approach of Artaxerxes' avenging army, they headed up into the mountains of what is today Iraq, blocking the passes and shaking off the pursuit of his infantry . . . and five months later, six thousand surviving Greeks marched into Trapezus.

They had fought across a thousand miles of hostile terrain, not only battling the forces of Artaxerxes but enduring sandstorms, debilitating heat, icy mountain passes, torrential downpours and numbing cold, each of the men burdened with at least fifty pounds of armor and weapons. Without any logistical support, they had survived off the land, foraging as they advanced while at the same time holding enemy forces at bay. There were no modern roads, depots, medical support, communications, or any hope of relief. What awaited them on the other side of each mountain range was not known until they arrived. The only thing that was certain was the death bearing down on them from behind.

Most miraculous of all was the fact that this army, made up of once-bitter rivals, had forged itself into an effective combat team, fighting innumerable actions, delaying the enemy, clearing the roads ahead, and sweeping up the daily rations needed to survive. Even the most cohesive of modern forces would find the strain of such an extended operation all but impossible to endure; the fact that these men had changed from soldiers of rival states into an alliance of professionals stands as one of the most remarkable feats of arms in history.

Reaching Trapezus, the army gained transport back to their native cities and then dispersed. Tragically, many of these men would one day serve on the same field again, facing each other in battle as the civil wars of Greece exploded once more. One cannot help but wonder how these survivors of the long march felt, knowing that comrades in arms they had learned to trust and rely upon were once again enemies.

There are two interesting postscripts to this campaign. The first is that one tradition has not changed all that much across twenty-four hundred years . . . and that is the book deal. Xenophon penned an account of the campaign that became an acclaimed best seller throughout Greece. One can almost imagine the warrior-turned-author out on the autograph circuit.

Second was the impact on history. Some sixty-odd years afterward, a young prince received a copy of this book and later claimed that throughout most of his life he slept with the book under his pillow alongside a copy of Homer. When this prince came to power and proposed to invade Persia with his small army, many of his veteran generals were hesitant. The prince then proclaimed that if but ten thousand Greeks could fight their way from one end of Persia to the other, think what his army could do fighting their way in . . . and thus did Alexander the Great begin his campaign.

Hannibal in Italy

The Battle of Lake Trasimene, 217 B.C.

by William R. Forstchen

THE DISTINCTION BETWEEN ARMIES OF MERCENARIES AND NA-
tional armies in the ancient world is at times a difficult line to
draw. Nations and city-states might maintain small standing
armies, but in times of crisis levies would be raised, allies
called upon, and, as in the case of the Greek forces glorified
by Xenophon, outside professionals called in. It is in the distinction between allies and mercenaries that we can run into
difficulties regarding definitions. If money is exchanged for an
"alliance," is the army then a mercenary one? One could say
"no" if the alliance also serves to directly advance the political goals of the "hired" nation or tribe; otherwise, the standard of mercenary might better apply. Thus, when we look at
the army of Hannibal that poured out of the passes of the Alps
in 218 B.C., we see a force that is both allies and mercenaries.
This unique force was, without doubt, the most dangerous foe
Rome would face across nearly a thousand years of history.

At the close of the First Punic War (264–241 B.C.), Carthage
had been forced into a peace of exhaustion. Carthage had entered the war, which was fought for control of the strategic
island of Sicily, as the predominate naval power in the western

Mediterranean, while Rome was the major land power of the Italian peninsula. The first war ended with Carthage ceding Sicily and also dismantling its naval forces. Shortly after the close of the war, Carthage made an expansionist move into the Iberian Peninsula, retaking colonies that had rebelled during the First Punic War.

It would be this expansion to the western flank of the Mediterranean that would trigger the next conflict with Rome. Hannibal, son of Hamilcar Barca—who was a general in the First Punic War—came to command all Carthaginian forces in Spain in 221 B.C., at the age of twenty-six, when his father fell victim to a Celtic assassin. Trained to believe that the current peace with Rome was merely a temporary respite, Hannibal provoked an incident with Rome the following year, an action backed by the Carthaginian government. Soon afterward, war was declared.

A comparison of forces would lead one to believe that Hannibal's chances were slim at best. Hardened by twenty years of combat, the Roman army was the army of a republic. Its citizens served in defense of their land, a high motivator for soldiers in any period of history. At this point in history, there were still tens of thousands of small landholders in the Italian peninsula, the type of men the founding fathers of the United States viewed as ideal stock for a citizen army. In addition, there were the various allied and subject cities of Italy, at least some of them willing allies. It is estimated that the total population of the Italian peninsula might very well have been close to six million, a significant population base for the mobilization of massive armies.

Carthage, in turn, was a small trade nation that had lost significant territorial holdings in the last war and now had only a very small population of free citizens to draw upon. The situation is, in some ways, parallel to the one faced later by the medieval Italian city-states. As centers of trade, they might have limited manpower for armies, but their surplus of wealth could be used to hire mercenaries to fill out the ranks.

This was precisely what Hannibal set about doing in preparation for war. Numidians, other groups in Africa, and the native population of Spain were recruited to stand alongside the small contingent of true Carthaginians. The mercenary auxiliaries provided light infantry, slingers, archers, and mounted squadrons. With this light infantry and his mounted formations, Hannibal's army stood in direct contrast to the traditional heavy infantry of the Romans. This contrast would significantly shape Hannibal's tactics on the battlefield.

Hannibal was a master of the psychology of soldiers, particularly how to mold his polyglot army into a unified fighting force. These men were not bound together by that single greatest bond for an army—the need to defend one's homeland—nor were they united by a political or religious creed. Granted: throughout history, mercenaries have almost always been motivated by professional pride, the simple need for a job, and the hope for loot; but to throw such an army against a highly disciplined defensive force, and to win, required far more. Hannibal repeatedly assured his troops that loot would be divided fairly, then made the audacious announcement that any slaves who marched and fought with the army would earn their freedom with just compensation for their masters. He appealed to the Spanish, Celts of Gaul, and Transalpine Celts of northern Italy to resist the grasping expansionism of Rome, while promising that Carthage would provide far better financial rewards and would not occupy their territory once the fighting was done. This tactic would be repeated in the conflict between the French and English in eighteenth-century North America, where both sides appealed to the native populations for warriors; the French usually won with the argument that wherever the English went, they tended to stay, while France was interested solely in trade.

As Hannibal moved across southern Gaul and crossed over the Alps, he was forced to fight local tribes but succeeded as well in incorporating some of them into his ranks. Having crossed the Alps late in 218 B.C., he descended into the upper Po Valley and there was confronted by a Roman Army. He soundly defeated them in two battles.

Hannibal's brilliance was clearly evident in the second action, the Battle of Trebia, where he routed a superior enemy force but did not follow up with an attack on their reserved fortified positions, an inaction that might have resulted in a serious reversal. The Celts of northern Italy, who had stood on the sidelines, now rallied to his cause and swelled the ranks of his depleted army from a low of roughly twenty-five thousand back up to forty thousand.

There is a legend about how Hannibal brought the Celts of northern Italy into his ranks. As Hannibal's army poured out of the passes of the Alps, skirmishes were fought with the locals and prisoners were taken. The tradition of the time was to hold prisoners for ransom or enslave them. Hannibal brought a group of prisoners together, produced two sets of armor and finely crafted weapons, and offered a challenge: two of the prisoners could fight to the death and the winner would keep his new weapons and gain his freedom. Being Celts, all clamored for the chance to show their prowess and win their freedom. The fight was staged, and the winner strutted off with his new armor. Hannibal now drew an analogy, saying that his struggle with Rome was the same; if the Celts allied with him, they too would be able to leave the battlefield with all they could carry and the glory of their names enhanced. Thousands of Celts rallied to his standard (and Hannibal made it a point to put these wild men in the forefront of the attack, thus sparing the small contingent of his fellow countrymen).

In 217 B.C., Hannibal moved south and crossed over the Apennines, a passage almost as dangerous as the crossing of the Alps since the trail on the reverse slope descended into swamps infested with malaria, a disease that afflicted Hannibal and most of his army. The Romans, learning of the advance, deployed two armies. The stronger, over forty thousand men under Flaminius, advanced to the west of Hannibal. The second force, twenty thousand men under Servilius, moved up the valley near present-day Assisi.

Hannibal's rapid onset threw the Romans off balance, and the Carthaginian general, with an army of approximately thirty thousand men, almost all of them mercenaries, carefully laid his trap. Pushing between the two enemy forces, he turned east, moving quickly and skirting the western and then northern shores of Lake Trasimene. His intent appeared to be a drive on the smaller force of Servilius. Flaminius came on fast, tagging along behind Hannibal's army, but was kept at bay by the continued skirmishing and delaying actions of the light Numidian and Spanish cavalry. Hannibal soon noticed that

Flaminius showed an almost reckless aggressiveness and desire to close for battle.

Encamping for the night along the northern shore of the
lake, Hannibal baited the trap. He let the Romans see him go
into camp, his skirmishers holding the enemy back until dark.
This writer recently visited the site of the battle, and, even to
an untutored eye, the lay of the ground and its tactical advantages are obvious. The level of the lake is believed to be somewhat lower than it was twenty-two hundred years ago;
nevertheless, even today the passage is narrow. At this narrow
point, it is less than fifty yards from the lake to the face of a
cliff that slopes at an angle of at least forty-five degrees. Just
east and west of this narrow point, the ground opens out
slightly but even then presents terrain that is usually less than
a hundred yards across before soaring up hundreds of feet, and
the hills ringing the north shore are so steep as to be impossible for a heavily burdened foot soldier climb, especially
while trying to fight.

Hannibal now blocked the road on the northeast side of the
lake with his light infantry, most likely as a precaution in case
Servilius, with his large cavalry force, should attempt a forced
march during the night, pinning Hannibal in a trap. Next he
deployed his heavy Carthaginian and African infantry across
the eastern end of the defile and then sent light infantry, archers, slingers, and, surprisingly, his cavalry up along the steep
ridges, the cavalry moving back westward along the reverse
slope of the steep ridge to position themselves above and behind the Roman camp. All settled down now to wait in the
dark, campfires and movement forbidden.

In the chill of early morning at that time of year, a heavy
mist would often rise off the lake before dawn. On this fateful
morning, nature seemed allied with Hannibal in much the
same manner that the fog of Austerlitz would serve to conceal
Napoleon's fatal surprise.

Flaminius, aggressive as ever, pushed forward at dawn, eager to come to blows, perhaps expecting that Hannibal would
offer a delaying action in the narrow defile, maybe suspecting
as well that it would be nothing more than a light force facing
him while the rest of the Carthaginian army continued east.

The heavy marching column of the Romans occupied at

least half a dozen miles of road as it set out, the legions tightly packed together, moving at their usual disciplined pace. The fog was so thick that visibility was down to less than the range of a javelin, the legionnaires barely able to see a dozen ranks ahead. A light force moved ahead of the column, but skirmishers were not deployed to cover the left flank since the ground was far too steep and maneuvering skirmishers up to sweep the hills would rob Flaminius of valuable time—he feared that Hannibal might be escaping.

The head of the column, after passing into the narrowest part of the defile, ran into what was suspected to be the rear guard of Hannibal's army. Weapons drawn, the legionnaires attempted to deploy in the narrow pass and form their traditional, and deadly, battle lines.

A column on the march can be compared to a long line of cars moving at high speed during rush hour, all of them bumper-to-bumper. As long as the lead car keeps moving at the same rate, all is well; but if it should ever slam on its brakes, a chain-reaction accident would start, especially in heavy fog.

As the first maniples in line attempted to shift from marching column to battle line, Flaminius's entire formation came to a stop. Marching discipline in the Roman army was usually exacting and well maintained, the units carefully spaced so that in a crisis they could swiftly shift from road column into line, facing whichever way the formation was threatened. But Flaminius had been pushing hard, and in the heavy fog it was difficult to see what the next legion was doing, let alone the next maniple in column up ahead.

As the front of the first legion in column collided with Hannibal's blocking force, the rear of that legion continued to march until the men were packed solid in the road. The second legion on the road now came up hard against the first, and so on back down the line. The sound of battle could be heard up ahead but was muffled by the thick cloak of fog.

Atop the heights dominating the north shore, the situation was far different. Morning fog burns off the top first, and chances were that the mercenary forces deployed up on the ridge were standing in light mist or perhaps even air that was already clear, while the narrow valley and shoreline below were cloaked in heavy mist, out of which rose the metallic clatter of forty thousand men on the march. The trick was for the Romans to completely stick their necks in the noose. As the sound of battle erupted to the east, the ambushing forces waited a few more minutes.

Flaminius, still most likely thinking he had hit a delaying force, tried to batter the defenders aside. As is usual in such a situation, the troops farther back, blinded by the fog, would edge forward, driven by curiosity and eagerness.

Suddenly, a man in the ranks, hundreds of yards back from the main action, screamed and collapsed, struck down by the first arrow or slinger's stone. Then a clattering roar, like the sound of hail striking a metal roof, erupted as thousands of stones and arrows slashed into the packed column. In the gray light, no one could see more than a few dozen feet, so there was no sense of what was truly happening. All the average Roman soldier knew was that someone above and to his left had cut loose with a volley of javelins, arrows, and slinger's stones. Men started to go down, helmets crushed in by rocks, arrows driving through exposed arms, throats, and faces. In the heavy fog, there was no hope of seeing the incoming rounds and blocking them.

Centurions and tribunes screamed orders, attempting to get their men to turn left and raise interlocking shields overhead. But in those first moments there was no sense of the magnitude of the attack, that it was not just a few raiders striking their one maniple but rather a concerted attack by over ten thousand men deployed on the heights above them.

As the shower of death rained down on the packed ranks, the first seeds of panic started to spread. Individual units, attempting to get out from under the blows raining down from the invisible foes above, shifted along the road to the east or west. In so doing, they added to the confusion, slamming into other units who were attempting to move as well. Meanwhile, for those at the far western end of the narrow pass, a new terror emerged out of the fog. Numidian, Spanish, and Celtic cavalry came charging out of a concealed valley and cut across the westward line of retreat, then wheeled and started to drive east. The cavalry that had been protecting Hannibal's retreat the day before had, during the night, moved up over the steep mountains (a remarkable feat, considering the terrain they had to pass over in the darkness) and were now attacking the rear of the Romans.

The cavalry now started to herd the Romans eastward, pushing the rear of the column into the slaughter pen of the defile. The wild screaming of the trapped Roman columns echoed the maddening battle cries of the Celtic infantry serving under Hannibal's banner. Faces painted, helmets adorned with twin horns, man-sized swords flashing in the dim light, the Celtic warriors, who preferred a wild and undisciplined charge to disciplined lines, came sliding down the steep slope. Against a solid line of Roman infantry, such a charge was suicide—but this was different. Their morale already shattered by the unending rain of destruction pouring down from above, the Roman legions began to panic at sight of the demonlike apparitions leaping out of the fog.

The Celtic swordsmen slashed into what was quickly disintegrating into a terrified mob. There was no place for the Romans to form and no open ground to rally upon; the road was narrow, with the rocks above and the lake behind them. Slashing into the Romans, the Celtic swordsmen cut bloody swaths. It was in this charge that Hannibal suffered most of his casualties, but the warrior spirit of these men could not be contained. A small force of Romans did manage to break through the line of heavy infantry deployed to cover the east end of the defile, but for the vast majority there was no place to flee except into the cold waters of the lake. Thousands of men burdened down by armor sank to the muddy bottom and drowned. The cavalry cutting in from the west added to the carnage, swinging out into the water, hunting down fugitives, and hacking them apart.

Entire formations threw down their arms and pleaded for mercy, a commodity hard to find as the enraged attackers swarmed through the confusion. Finally, as the fog lifted roughly three hours after the start of the battle, Hannibal was able to survey his victory. Of the forty thousand Romans who had entered the defile, over three-quarters were dead or captured. The approximately six thousand who had managed to cut their way through the eastern end of the trap were surrounded later in the day and forced to surrender. The few who had eluded capture by stripping off their armor and swimming far out into the lake or managing to slip into the fog-shrouded hills staggered back to Rome or into the camp of Servilius, spreading terror about the approach of Hannibal.

Hannibal's victory had come remarkably cheaply. Over thirty thousand Romans dead or captured at a cost of only several thousand of his own forces, most of them the wildly impetuous Celts who had charged into the seething mass of the panic-stricken enemy. As for loot for his mercenaries, there was more than enough to go around. The triumphal forces were burdened down with captured swords, armor, money, baggage, and even thousands of Roman camp followers. In a shrewd move, Hannibal held captive only citizens of Rome; those men from allied states and subject provinces were soon set free with the explanation that he had come not to conquer them but rather to set them free from Rome.

After the battle, the limitations of Hannibal's army became evident: it was simply too small for the grandiose dream of taking Italy, and it lacked the heavy siege train necessary for the storming of a major city such as Rome. Though he had successfully used his lighter forces against the heavy Roman infantry, any hope of storming the extensive fortifications of that city was out of the question.

After Trasimene, Hannibal pushed back Servilius and then settled into camp. Still ravaged by malaria, the army needed to rest and refit, giving the Romans time to regroup and raise another army that he would meet the following year at Cannae in the south of Italy.

Though the battle of Cannae is often held up as the quintessential victory of Hannibal due to the famed double envelopment of the Roman army, it was Lake Trasimene that set the stage. Trasimene was actually a double envelopment as well, in some ways far more masterful than Cannae, with its cunning use of terrain and weather, and uncanny reading of an opponent's intent. The victory also forged a divergent group of mercenaries into a well-disciplined fighting force imbued with elan and an unshakable belief in a commander who could bring them loot and victory.

Even after these twin victories, Hannibal could not take Rome. His hope had rested from the very beginning on the premise that his mercenary army would trigger a war of rebellion on the part of the various cities of the Italian peninsula that had fallen under Roman domination. This hope never fully materialized, in part because of the brutal response offered by Rome to any city that, in their opinion, had turned "traitor." Thus Hannibal's campaign was doomed from the start. It would be the general Scipio Africanus who would finally develop the strategy to unseat Hannibal. Striking into Spain and North Africa, he wiped out the base of Hannibal's mercenary forces with the invasion of their homelands. Hannibal's army started to melt away as men deserted to return home. Finally, the Carthaginian government recalled Hannibal to defend their home city. Defeated at Zama, Hannibal finally advised peace, and in 202 B.C. the Second Punic War came to an end, with Rome imposing a harsh and restrictive peace. Hannibal was forced to flee Carthage when Rome demanded the personal surrender of the feared Carthaginian general. Seeking refuge in Anatolia, he eventually committed suicide rather than surrender to his lifelong foes. Generations later, the Roman writer Livy would declare "of all that befell the Romans and the Carthaginians, good or bad, the cause was one man and one mind—Hannibal."

Hannibal, perhaps more than any other general in history, showed what could be done with mercenary troops, welding an almost impossible diversity of national groups into a unified whole and using them effectively to further a national cause. The effect was made even more remarkable by the fact that they were facing a nationalistic and highly disciplined foe. Trasimene and the Battle of Cannae the following year stand as two of the finest victories ever gained by mercenary forces.

The Fine Art of Contract Negotiation

The White Company and the Battle of Florence, 1364

by William R. Forstchen

IF EVER THERE WAS A "GOLDEN AGE" FOR MERCENARIES, IT was in Italy from the late thirteenth century until the French invasion in the 1490s. The north of Italy at this time was in many ways similar to ancient Greece: small city-states deriving their wealth from trade, bitter and intense rivalries for control of that trade, and grasping rulers ever eager to wage war. Like Carthage, these city-states did not have the significant manpower to field large armies, but they did have the wealth to pay for them. Thus the rise of the *condottieri*.

The word is rooted in the Latin *conducere*, from which comes the Italian noun *condotta*, which at that time meant a contract between a government and a freelance commander. The English noun *freelance*, usually applied to writers, traces itself back to the mercenary, the "free lance" ready for hire if the price is right (and then, as now, it rarely is!).

In Italy, the freelance companies, or *condottieri*, were initially seen as a means of extending power in the bitter intercity rivalries, such as the classic struggles between Pisa and Florence, or Milan, Genoa, and Venice. In time, they became the scourge of the Italian peninsula, a remarkable extortion and protection racket in which cities paid not for services rendered but to avoid being "serviced." Commanders sought titles and crowns. Soldiers who served Florence today might in mid-stride break contract and serve Pisa tomorrow. The wolves were truly loose among the sheep with a certain professional courtesy to their peers not unlike that of lawyers. An enemy might be a friend tomorrow, and thus those who were paying for the services often complained about battles that raged for hours with a lot of smoke, dust, and fury, but not a single casualty inflicted—a situation that might remind some of a professional wrestling match. But when it came to unleashing their fury on a city that did not pay promptly, the condottieri could be implacable.

Yet some of these mercenary bands, especially those of the fourteenth and early fifteenth centuries, fought well and honored contracts, breaking them only after due notice was given. The greatest of these was the White Company of Sir John de Hawkwood.

Born in 1320, in the final years of the reign of the dissolute Edward II, Hawkwood was the son of a prosperous tanner and came of age near Colchester, England. According to tradition, he went off to the wars in France, following the standard of the Black Prince, and fought at that greatest of fourteenth-century battles: Crécy, where the famed Welsh bowmen shattered the chivalry of France. In these campaigns in France, Hawkwood won his spurs and gained a mastery not only of how to command men, but also of the new method of combined arms on the battlefield.

The old paradigm that had dominated the battlefields of Europe for over five hundred years, the mounted and heavily armored knight, had been laid low at Crécy. A new weapon had emerged out of the forests of England and Wales: the longbow. From five to six feet in length, the English longbow had a draw of over forty inches and a pull that could be in excess of one hundred pounds. Mastery of the weapon took years of training. An accomplished bowman could loose six aimed shots a minute, dropping an unarmored horse at two hundred yards and driving an arrow through chain mail—and even through plate armor at fifty yards' range. The longbow arrow, fired by a well-trained yeoman, was the Maverick missile of its day.

The English who fought in the opening campaigns of the Hundred Years War soon learned the correct usage of combined arms. When possible, infantry armed with spears would deploy across the center of the line and, if given enough time, would use sharpened stakes to make a barrier and would dig entrapments forward of the line to break up a charge. Archers would be interspersed between the spearmen and in block formations on the flanks. A small mounted force would be on the flanks as well, in order to protect the bowmen first and then to sweep the field once the enemy charges were broken.

This well-oiled machine consumed all before it until the Treaty of Brétigny in 1360 brought about a temporary cessation of hostilities between England and France. As was typical of most treaties in medieval and early modern Europe, the royalty of both sides feasted each other, with dukes and barons shaking hands and exchanging pleasantries about the adventures they'd had while facing each other; then they returned to their manors. But for the ordinary soldiers of both sides, such treaties were usually a disaster, especially after a lengthy conflict where men had come of age with warfare their only trade.

The armies of both sides dispersed, but what to do next? Former enemies now found a common bond, and soon Welsh, English, Gascons, and Bretons banded together, many of them drifting southward down the Rohône Valley. The legendary wealth of French Avignon acted as a magnet. The French Pope (whether false or not, depending on one's orientation toward the French or Italian claim to the Papacy) retained some for his own service but quickly maneuvered to shoo these troublesome forces out of France and into Italy, where promise of employment by the various warring city-states awaited them.

Within a year of Brétigny, we first see records regarding a ''White Company'' in Italy, the name supposedly a reference to the highly burnished armor worn by the unit. It was made up primarily of English longbowmen, a mixed force of English and French footmen, and a mounted contingent. In actuality, the unit would have more closely fit the modern description of mounted infantry, with even the longbowmen riding to the field and dismounting before going into action.

Even for those times, it must have been a tough mix of men, battle-scarred from hard years of campaigning in France, survivors of the years of the Black Death. The backbone of the unit were hardy veterans of Crécy and Poitiers, men who had stood in rank behind the legendary Black Prince and now were practicing the only craft they knew in a distant exotic land of mountain fortresses and opulent, warring city-states.

The city of Pisa, long at war with its nearby neighbor Florence, saw potential in this new alien band of warriors and quickly retained their services. So redoubtable was their reputation that the Pisans, in order to throw a scare into the Florentines, snuck a number of citizens out of town, dressed them up in burnished armor, then had them parade back in the next day while rejoicing citizens lined the walls. A nearby Florentine force quickly withdrew in terror. The real arrival of the White Company, however, sent a nervous shudder through Pisa. In short order, those who could afford to do so sent wives and attractive daughters to other towns, and the city elders resorted to an endless series of false alarms and then dispatched their alleged defenders on these wild-goose chases. As for closing with Florence and destroying it, the White Company did not seem in any great hurry. After all, the pay was regular, the food good (though one could argue that, for an Englishman, any food to be found in Italy would be deemed exceptional), and the few women available were at least exotic and different. Thus was the state of the White Company when, in 1364, Sir John de Hawkwood wandered into Pisa and hooked up with the unit.

There must have been something remarkable about Hawkwood—charisma, intelligence, or warrior skill—that made him stand forth, for shortly after his arrival, the men of the White Company insisted that he take the banner of captain-general. His fellow professionals were right. Soon Hawkwood became the embodiment of the true warrior, and perhaps the finest mercenary captain who ever lived.

Rousing his new command to action, Hawkwood intended to honor the contract, and early in 1364 he moved against Florence. His opposition was a large contingent of German mercenaries under the command of Henri de Montfort. Out-numbered at the start of the campaign, the White Company came off poorly in the opening skirmishes. The Pisans, forced to outbid the Florentines, doubled the size of their mercenary army by hiring six thousand Germans and Swiss under the command of Annechin Bongarden. The combined force pulled a tough flanking march through the high Tuscan mountains and came down onto the Fiesole Heights, a high range of hills on the same side of the Arno River as Florence and less than two leagues from the center of the city.

The splendor of Florence, without a doubt one of the most beautiful cities of Europe, lay before them. Though the famed *duomo* that now dominates the skyline of Florence was still two hundred years off, the city was nevertheless already re-nowned for its palaces, high towers, and wealth.

Barricades were already going up in the suburbs of the city. The term *suburb* had a somewhat different distinction then than it does today. The *urb* proper was that part of the city contained within the city's walls. This security came with a higher price in taxes, and many seeking a lower bracket built their villas outside the walls. Now they were open to attack.

Hawkwood surveyed the defenses and decided on a strata-gem, postponing attack until May Day, which in the Middle Ages was a festival day celebrating the start of the summer season.

At dawn on May 1, 1364, the White Company stormed out of the hills, lances and archers intermixed to provide mutual protection. The primitive barricades ringing the suburbs, made up of upturned carts, wagons, barrels, and scrap lumber, were swept clear by high-arcing volleys of arrows. Storming the barricades, the White Company burst into the suburbs. Henri de Montfort, feeling obliged to honor his own contract, led a spirited defense and was seriously wounded in the fray and carried off the field of action.

The men of the White Company now encountered an old traditional foe, Genoese crossbowmen deployed along the main walls of the city. The archers of Wales had met them before, on the battlefield of Crécy. Then, the Welsh had proven their superiority, but that had been an open field fight. This was a battle of snipers, with the Genoese having the advantage of height. The Genoese also had the advantage of the cross-bow, which did not have the range of the longbow but which could be fired in a flatter trajectory due to its higher "muzzle velocity." In the narrow confines of a fight in a medieval city, the crossbow was easier to maneuver and aim.

Archers and crossbowmen waged a day-long fight, one that as professionals they most likely saw as an interesting contest of skill that later would be used as proof regarding which weapon was superior. While the archers sniped at each other, Hawkwood "demonstrated" against the city of Florence, marching his troops in full military muster, but had no real intention of trying to storm it. Even if they had managed to gain the walls, throwing a precious mercenary force into an opponent's city was an invitation to disaster since even wealthy citizens could be induced to fight and kill if cornered. A mercenary force could perhaps take a city, but the cost in lives would not have been worth the effort. Also, if Florence was actually looted and eliminated, that would almost certainly mean unemployment.

At the end of the day, Hawkwood ordered a withdrawal. For the White Company, the entire action must have had a partylike atmosphere. They had taken a wealthy suburb at little cost and there was loot aplenty—stashes of gold and silver "coaxed" out of house owners unlucky enough to be captured, ransoms for prisoners, heavy tapestries of gold thread, glasswork, leather, armor, rich brocades, barrels of fine Tuscan wines, and food enough to provide for the evening feast. Setting the suburbs on fire, a final act of vandalism sure to delight his troops, Hawkwood pulled back to his encampment, his men undoubtedly jeering the defenders with a delightful mixture of English and Italian invectives.

That evening, the White Company threw an uproarious party that eventually became legend. According to a contemporary chronicler, several leaders were knighted for the day's work. Thousands of torches were lit and the men marched about, juggling the torches and drinking themselves senseless while parading just outside crossbow range and shouting insults at the good citizens of Florence. As a practical joke, they sent several drummers and trumpeters around to the southeast gate of the city and had them give the signal for the attack.

This threw the Florentines into a panic, so fixed were they on watching the demonstration on the other side of town. The terrified defenders now believed that the drunken parade had been a ruse and a real attack was under way. The entire city was roused, defenders rushing through the city to the threatened point. The joke revealed, Hawkwood's men laughed themselves senseless, the two sides finishing off the night with exchanges of curses and obnoxious pantomimes.

For the next week, Hawkwood's men drove the Florentines to distraction with feigned attacks, midnight alarms and general rioting, while groups of raiders swept the surrounding countryside clean of any valuables worth carting off. After years of marching and fighting in the damp, bare fields of northern France, this campaign must have seemed like paradise for the veterans of the White Company. To add insult to injury, they vandalized the crops, tore up vineyards, and chopped down olive trees.

Driven to desperation, the Florentines counterattacked, using the classic approach that if you can't beat a mercenary force, bribe them.

The rulers of the city offered a flag of truce and sent a delegation to Hawkwood's camp. The proposal was straight and to the point: sacks full of gold florins if the White Company would go away or, better yet, switch sides. Bongarden, commander of the German/Swiss contingent, jumped at the chance. Taking nine thousand florins for himself and thirty-five thousand for his men, he quit the field. Half the Pisan army had just disappeared. The shrewd Florentine negotiators now turned to the White Company.

It was at this moment that Hawkwood rose above the pack and set himself on the path of legend. He flatly refused any Florentine inducements to quit the campaign, declaring that a contract was a contract and he would never break his word of honor to the Pisans. A truce for both sides was acceptable, but he would never leave his employers.

Hawkwood's rise to captain-general had been decided by the various contingents of the group, but it was now evident that the previous commander, Albert Sterz, a German who knew English and had first guided the men of the company into Italy, was not happy with the choice. Here was his chance to reassert control. The Florentines were offering tremendous wealth if the White Company would leave, and even more if they switched sides. Sterz took the money to switch sides, and the famous White Company fell apart, with all but eight hundred men agreeing to follow their first commander and the gold he now offered. The Florentines spent a hundred thousand florins to break the most famous of mercenary bands—a remarkable sum, especially in those times.

Hawkwood and his loyal eight hundred withdrew, announcing that they would continue to fight for the employer who had hired them. Henri de Montfort recovered from his wounds and returned to the field of action, turning the war around and raiding right up to the gates of Pisa, with Hawkwood now on the defensive. As for Bongarden and Sterz, they combined their old units into a new command, the Company of the Star. Within months, they broke contract with Florence and went to Siena, another of Florence's traditional enemies. For ten thousand florins, they raided Florence once again. After this double-dealing, the Company of the Star drifted south.

As for Hawkwood, his career was made. In a world of back-stabbing, lies, and broken contracts, he had done something rather remarkable—he had kept his oath. Word of this remarkable feat spread throughout Italy, and Hawkwood continued on to become the most famous and respected condottiere of them all.

The Game of Survival

Sir John de Hawkwood at Borgoforto, 1367

by William R. Forstchen

FALLING BACK TO PISA AFTER THE COLLAPSE OF THE WHITE Company, Hawkwood fought a valiant defense and actually managed to keep the superior forces of Florence at bay until a settlement was reached. Hawkwood, however, was still without pay, while his former comrades who had accepted the bribes of Florence were rolling in cash and heading south. Giovanni Agnello of Pisa finally took it upon himself to see that Hawkwood and his company were paid by going to Milan and seeking a loan from Bernabò Visconti, the ruler of that city. On the surface, this might seem like good citizenship, but Agnello threw into the loan a clause that he must become doge of Pisa upon receipt of the money. Fearing that Hawkwood and the remaining troops might walk out, the city elders agreed. This payment eventually resulted in Hawkwood's taking his sword north to Milan when Pisa loaned out their top mercenary during a period of relative peace. This second "loan" brought Hawkwood into the employ of the ambitious and self-serving Visconti, who was about to have a confrontation with the Holy Roman Emperor Charles IV.

Visconti's appetite for life was legendary, even for those times, and is the envy of many a political figure today. He fathered at least fifteen children with his wife, Beatrice, and, according to one historian, had thirty-six additional children. At one point, eighteen different women were pregnant with his children at the same time. When not out procreating, he indulged in his obsessions—boar hunting, politics, and war.

Throughout the medieval period, northern Italy had been loosely defined as owing allegiance to the Holy Roman Emperor. A few emperors of strong will had actually managed to bring the various city-states to heel, but most simply made believe that the city-states were part of their territory and let it go at that. Visconti decided to challenge the authority of Charles IV, who had come down out of Germany with a sizeable contingent of troops in an ostentatious display and required the various princes to swear allegiance to him. The emperor's effort was supported by Visconti's rivals, who desired to see the overbearing prince of Milan humbled. Thus the stage was set for another legendary victory for John de Hawkwood, a coup that was won without even drawing a sword, but rather by wielding a spade.

Coming out of the Alps, the emperor's army would be forced to cross the Po River. Visconti decided to block that crossing by constructing fortifications at Borgoforto, located just south of Mantua and across the river from Milan. Visconti almost lost the war before it had even started when he sent a contingent of Italian mercenaries to increase the garrison of the fort. There was an immediate falling out between the Italians and the German and Burgundian mercenaries already stationed there. In stepped John de Hawkwood, the one commander whom nearly all mercenaries looked upon with respect.

Arriving at Borgoforto, Hawkwood took command and rallied the mercenary army. He needed unity, for the battle shaping up around Borgoforto could very well prove to be a clash of epic proportions. By this point, the emperor was in a rare alliance with the Avignon pope, who threw in his forces on the imperial side. The result was an army of over twenty thousand mercenaries hailing from Germany, Poland, Serbia, Bohemia, and all of France.

For Hawkwood, the fight also had a touch of a personal nature to it. Twenty-two years earlier, Hawkwood had stood at Crécy in the ranks of the Black Prince, and on that field, the young Charles IV, fighting on the side of France, had been seriously wounded and carried from the field.

The spring of 1367 had been a wet one, and now, in early May, the Po was a raging torrent as the winter snows melted off the Alps. Deployed with their backs to the river, Hawkwood's forces were in a precarious position. If they were overwhelmed by the emperor's forces, retreat might prove to be impossible.

The emperor maneuvered his massive army down to the Po, placing his vastly superior force between Hawkwood's fortifications at Borgoforto and Mantua. Apparently, the emperor was considering flanking Hawkwood, for galleys were dragged up the flooded river and heavy rafts were constructed. The situation for Hawkwood looked grim. If he attempted to abandon his position now and retreat across the river, he could be caught in midmaneuver by the emperor, and smashed. Stand and fight, and mere numbers alone might tell. Hawkwood, however, saw a third way, one that must have appealed to the latent practical joker who had been revealed in front of the walls of Florence.

The emperor, with all his elaborate preparations, had forgotten one simple force: gravity, and its effect on water. He was downstream from Hawkwood, camped next to a flooding river that was contained only by ancient dikes. Hawkwood simply waited for the emperor's army to go into camp and, under cover of darkness, led downstream a contingent of troops who set to work tearing the dike apart. The men created a small breech, and once the dike was cut open, the Po River began to slice through the old earthen walls like the proverbial hot knife in butter, tearing the dike wide open.

The emperor was awakened by cries of alarm from the sentries upstream. In those first seconds, he undoubtedly thought that Hawkwood was attempting a dangerous night attack, compelled to do so in order to offset the superior numbers of the enemy. Then the wall of water slammed into the camp.

The rude shelters of impoverished footmen, high-walled tents of knights, and brocade-hung pavilions of the princes and the emperor collapsed as the wave swept through the camp. Men, tumbling out of soaking cots, suddenly found themselves swimming in the frigid torrent, any thought of retrieving armor and weapons forgotten.

Within minutes, the entire imperial army was in rout, knights desperately trying to save their precious mounts, infantry scrambling in every direction, all semblance of order lost in the chaos. By dawn, the muddy, waterlogged mob of the emperor's army staggered into the city of Mantua, the high hopes of conquest and humiliating Visconti forgotten. One can easily picture the legendary mercenary Sir John de Hawkwood standing on the banks of the Po, roaring with childish delight.

The humiliation along the Po was too much for poor Emperor Charles IV, and he struck an understanding with Visconti to leave the territory of Milan in peace. Instead, Charles wandered off to the south to pay a visit on Hawkwood's nominal employer, Agnello of Pisa. It seems that Charles brought bad luck with him wherever he went. While waiting to receive Charles at the gates of Lucca, a city under the sway of Pisa, the platform Agnello was standing on collapsed, and the doge and his companions fell to the ground in a heap, Agnello breaking his thigh. At that time, most anything could be the cause of a coup, and Agnello's rivals seized the moment, galloped back to Pisa, and overthrew the government. Agnello, bound in heavy splints, fled to Milan and sought refuge with Visconti.

As for Hawkwood, the next ten years would find him serving Visconti and briefly taking service with the worst of his employers, Pope Gregory XI, who cheated Hawkwood at every possible turn. At one point, Hawkwood was reduced to kidnapping a cardinal as a guarantee of payment. Not even this worked, and Hawkwood finally let the cardinal go when the pope made the token offer of giving Hawkwood a couple of run-down estates. While Hawkwood was in service to the papacy, an incident occurred that placed one stain on his honor: the massacre of Cesena.

Hawkwood was lured to Cesena with the promise of pay by a papal legate who had already tricked the city into surrendering but was angered by the continued sullen resistance of the citizens. Once in the city, Hawkwood and his men were bluntly informed that the city had to be punished severely for their disloyalty. Hawkwood tried to argue that he could talk to the town leaders and persuade them to do whatever the legate wanted, but this was not enough. The Breton mercenaries of the papacy, already in the city, were unleashed upon the populace, and the massacre began. Hawkwood's men were told to find their back pay in the city or to get out with empty pockets.

Given the long period of poverty, Hawkwood most likely could not have stayed in command of his company if he had simply led them away without payment, but even at that murderous moment, he still tried to find some way of redeeming his honor. A chronicler later reported that Hawkwood and his men saved more than a thousand women of the city by rescuing them from the sack, taking them out of town, and setting them free.

After this incident, Hawkwood quit the employ of the corrupt Gregory in disgust. The legate who instigated the massacre would later rise to be installed as Clement VI, the first of the so called antipopes of Avignon.

Hawkwood returned to Milan in 1377 and joined with the Visconti family by marrying one of the illegitimate daughters of his old employer. The relationship, however, was an uneasy one as the Visconti family moved toward a confrontation between the domineering Bernabò and his intellectual and soft-spoken nephew, Gian Galeazzo. At first, Gian was dismissed by many as a lightweight, but he would prove to be far more cunning and grasping than his legendary uncle.

At this stage, Hawkwood attempted to retire to the life of a country squire on the estates given to him by the pope. But he could never stay out of action for long, and we shall finally see him in the employ of Florence, standing against the family of his wife in the greatest battle ever fought by the mercenary warriors of Italy.

Mercenaries Triumphant

The Battle of Castagnaro, 1387

by William R. Forstchen

AFTER HIS MARRIAGE TO ONE OF THE MULTITUDE OF BER-
nabò Visconti's illegitimate daughters, Sir John de Hawkwood
gradually disengaged himself from the service of Milan,
spending as much time as possible tending to his estates. He
was, after all, nearly sixty years old. He had survived the great
plague, bouts with malaria, and innumerable campaigns. The
mere fact that he was still alive is a testament to his hardiness.

He finally came to the attention of a city he had once fought
against, Florence, when he entered into a bit of negotiation
worthy of the intriguing world of fourteenth-century Italy. Part
of the reason for Hawkwood's success (and his ability to avoid
assassination) was his extensive network of contacts and informers. Through one of these mysterious contacts, it came to
Hawkwood's attention that a plot was brewing against the rulers of Florence.

An envoy from Florence hurried to Sir John's estate, and
Hawkwood entered into a shrewd bit of negotiating. For fifty
thousand florins, he would reveal the entire plot, naming
names, but would be given the right to extend protection to
six of the plotters (most likely old business associates). If fifty
thousand was too much, there was a bargain-basement package

for twenty thousand florins, which would reveal enough of the plot that the city elders could protect themselves, but names would not be named. Yet again, we see the old mercenary's code shining through—he was willing to help out a city for profit, but he would not take blood money to give up the lives of friends.

The negotiating dragged on for days with the envoy and Hawkwood locked away, haggling over price and levels of information. Finally, a deal was struck for the discount package with a payment of twelve thousand florins. In a darkened room, the informer was brought in, his identity hidden from the envoy, and the discounted story was told.

The envoy hastened back to Florence; the plot was uncovered and the ruling government saved. Hawkwood's reputation with the government of Florence was enhanced, and in short order, a contract was offered for his services. He bailed out of Milan just in time. Shortly after he left, Bernabò Visconti fell to his nephew and soon thereafter died of "natural" causes in prison. This was a family affair for Hawkwood: a father-in-law murdered by a cousin-in-law, and one that could have destroyed him. An attempt was made on one of Hawkwood's innumerable brothers-in-law, but again Hawkwood's network of informers came through, enabling the old mercenary to warn his wife's kin not to eat a less-than-healthy meal.

Late in 1386, another war began to brew north of Florence, this one between the old traditional enemies Verona and Padua. Florence loaned Hawkwood out to fight for Padua since Verona was backed by Florence's traditional enemy, Venice. Hawkwood marched out of Florence with five hundred men-at-arms and six hundred mounted English longbowmen, most of them veterans of more than twenty years of combat in Italy. He was immediately offered command of Padua's army, though for protocol's sake he would first review his plans with Francesco Novello, the son of Padua's ruler and a man who went on to a twenty-year career as a noted soldier before being strangled by the Venetians. The army under Novello and Hawkwood had eight thousand troops and the five hundred mounted archers, a sizeable force for that time but still less than half of what Verona would pit against them.

Initially deployed forward with the intent of besieging Verona, Hawkwood was forced to withdraw due to logistical problems, retiring back to his base of supplies. On the evening of March 10, 1387, he stopped at Castagnaro, just short of his logistical base. The forces of Verona, smelling the opportunity for an overwhelming victory against an inferior force, came on fast with nearly nine thousand men-at-arms, twenty-five hundred crossbowmen and pikemen, thousands of civilian militiamen, and a contingent of artillerymen.

The late fourteenth century was unfolding into a period of transition in the technology of war as gunpowder was slowly introduced onto the field of battle. Such early periods of technological innovation often produce bizarre results, and the prince of Verona, who had a penchant for wild engineering schemes, produced one of the most interesting guns in history. It was an early attempt at a machine gun—an excellent idea when it comes to murdering one's opponents wholesale—but this one didn't quite live up to expectations. The gun consisted of one hundred and forty-four barrels stacked a dozen barrels across and twelve rows high. Given the primitive metallurgy of the time and the tendency to overcast gun tubes as a precaution against bursting, this monstrosity was over ten feet across and stood twenty feet high. Weighing several tons, it was mounted on a heavy cart and required a team of four draught horses. The idea was to push the weapon up to the front, aim it at the enemy—who, of course, would willingly remain in the line of fire—then light the fuse and run like hell. This endeavor being a government contract job, not one but three of these gigantic weapons were dragged along with the army of Verona. Since it was designed by the prince of Verona, there was no way the army's commander could ditch the machines, and thus the advance was slowed.

On the evening of March 10, Sir John surveyed the ground his army had occupied, and undoubtedly memories of Crécy and Poitiers came to mind. Both of these famous fights had been operationally defensive, and Sir John felt he had at last found some "good ground" upon which to turn and make his stand.

Directly in front of his position was an irrigation ditch, the fields beyond the ditch soggy from the early spring rains. To his left, the ground sloped off into a boggy swamp. His right was protected by a canal. The one drawback was that his back was to a river, but more than once in history had a mercenary general chosen such a situation, for with retreat cut off, all men realized that the only path to survival was total victory.

Sir John ordered his army to be well fed and rested. At dawn, he was up, maneuvering his units into position like so many chess pieces. His main front, arrayed behind the irrigation ditch, was set up as two lines of battle. Each line was broken into three units. A third line, a single battle group, was deployed behind the two lines and would remain mounted. His personal headquarters company was mounted and positioned here as well. The small contingent of crossbowmen and the few pieces of artillery were sent to the right flank and positioned along the canal, while his own English archers stayed in reserve and were mounted.

In modern terms, this would be a brigade front of three battalions, with three battalions as a secondary line and a battalion of mobile infantry in reserve. The reserve would also consist of the headquarters company and mobile artillery (the archers) with a screening force of light artillery (crossbowmen and bombards) deployed along the right flank.

This deployment caught the enemy by surprise, since it was assumed that the retreating Paduan army would cross the river during the night and avoid contact with the vastly superior force. The army of Verona, therefore, took its time coming up into range. Observing the irrigation ditch in front of the Paduan position, the army was ordered to construct bundles of wood called fascines, which could be tossed into the ditch by the advancing troops and thus provide a somewhat dry and level crossing.

Hawkwood, to boost morale, had several of his commanders knighted prior to the fight. This might seem a reversal of usual procedure, but it was a shrewd move, because the knights were now obligated to show their worth. Since their fee for ransom would increase as well, there was also the additional incentive to avoid capture.

By late afternoon, the Veronian army moved to attack, deployed in a massive rectangle formation covering the entire front of the Paduan army. There was no chance to overlap the Paduan line, due to the swamp and canal anchoring the two flanks, so it would be a straightforward frontal assault. The first lines of troops approached and threw hundreds of fascines into the ditch, filling it up.

The charge now pressed in. With thousands of spears lowered, the Veronese army swarmed over the ditch. The Paduan battle line lowered spears as well, and the two sides collided. The sound of the two sides slamming into each other resounded across the battlefield, thousands of men screaming, iron spearheads striking against shields, trumpets braying, the hoarse commands of officers lost in the confusion. The onset of the attack staggered the Paduan line, causing it to recoil backward. Hawkwood ordered the second line into the fray, and the three second-line "battalions" charged into the crush, pressing in behind their comrades.

A modern observer entertained by such bloody spectacles as *Braveheart* might assume that within seconds the battleline would be a charnel house of blood, severed limbs, and decapitated bodies. He would be surprised at how little blood was spilled in the opening stage of a medieval fight. Rather than a wild, slashing confusion, such battles bore a closer resemblance to a pileup at a rugby match, when both teams swarm about the ball, trying to push back the other side.

No matter how brave these men were, after all, charging headlong like a maniac into a wall of leveled spears just wasn't good business sense. As both sides approached to within a few feet of each other, the pace slowed to a near standstill. The back ranks, however, continued to push, driving the leading ranks forward whether they were eager to advance or not. Opposing spears overlapped and then slammed into heavy shields, and if a weapon did not slip through and find its mark, it was diverted upward, passing over the heads of the enemy. If a spearman had been alone in an open field, it would have been simple for him to just step back, lower his spear, and try again. But on a crowded battlefield, it was all but impossible to step back, and, beyond that, there were thousands of others waving their ten- to fifteen-foot lances about in front, on the flanks, and in the rear. Thus spears became tangled together, clattering, the battle sounding like a giant had gone berserk in a lumberyard and was throwing piles of two-by-fours about.

In this way, the opposing sides compressed in on each other, men pressing against each other shield to shield, pushing and

shoving. Those without spears would have their swords out—
but without room to swing, they were reduced to waving their
weapons up high, trying to brain their opponents, who would
block the blows with their shields. In case a shield did not
block a strike, the helmets of the time were designed like the
modern armor of tanks, with sloping surfaces to deflect blows.
There were no free-swinging heroics as displayed in a Hol-
lywood epic, and for the moment the biggest danger was for
a fighter to lose his footing and be trampled under. When men
did go down, others would tumble over the fallen, adding to
the pileup.

The battle surged back and forth along the irrigation ditch,
spears tangled together, swords and daggers flashing, men
shoving, cursing, and screaming. All semblance of formation
was lost on both sides as the tightly packed ranks tumbled
against each other. There was no room for mounted knights
or famed captains to maneuver in one-on-one fights, which
would enhance their reputations (and also gain them significant ransom money), so it was senseless to wade into the fray,
risking one's own life as well as that of an expensive mount.
As for the mob of foot soldiers, the nearest modern analogy
would be the sense one has when trapped in a huge crowd
surging to get into a concert or sports event—it was nearly
impossible to move except to follow the flow of the crowd.
There would be the occasional kill as a dagger slipped through
a helmet visor or under an armpit, or when a man numb with
exhaustion, who could no longer hold up his shield, fell and
others tripped and piled up around his body. For those not
directly on the front line, the scope of battle was limited by
the narrow view slits of their helmets, usually not more than
an inch wide and several inches across for each eye. Thus, all
they could see was the helmet of the man in front, with occasional glimpses of spear points, banners, and perhaps an
errant arrow or rock flashing past.

Given this limited view and the instincts aroused by being
trapped in a crowd, most men simply ducked their heads down
and shoved indiscriminately forward. The lines thus surged
back and forth, men literally picked up off their feet and carried half a dozen feet forward, then a dozen feet back, then
forward again as the thousands pushed and shoved. What

made it even worse was the noise. The heavy helmets distorted sound, compounded by the ringing of blows, so that everything was reduced to a roaring cacophony. Only the best-trained troops could be expected to hear and respond correctly to signals issued by trumpets or the shouted orders of commanders.

This is not to say that a medieval battle was not bloody. The slaughter, however, came when one side finally broke, usually due to exhaustion or the superior weight of an opponent, or if a flank was turned. Once an army broke and men turned to flee, the cavalry would be unleashed to ride down the panic-stricken enemy. A fleeing soldier was exposed, with back turned, so there was no chance for the modern system of suppressive fire and leapfrog withdraw.

Thus the two sides struggled back and forth along the edge of the irrigation canal, the Veronese pouring in the last of their reserves with the intent of bowing back the Paduan lines and cracking them open. Unfortunately, at least for the perversely curious, the monstrous Veronese machine guns never even made it into action, having become bogged down in the mud. It would have been interesting (at least from the sidelines) to see whether the darn things would work or not.

Both armies had with them, as their command center, a curious rallying point unique to Renaissance Italy: the *carroccio*, or war wagon. This was a huge cart usually drawn by a team of oxen and bedecked with banners, bunting, and the colors of the city. It was the Italian equivalent of an imperial eagle or standard of a legion and thus a prize that both sides struggled to take. The cart was also something of an oxen-drawn APC, loaded down with archers and crossbowmen and even sporting wheels covered with razor-sharp blades. Hawkwood, standing atop his *carroccio* finally judged that the moment had come and passed command of the main battle line to one of his lieutenants.

Mounting his charger, the aging knight waved his baton of command, signaling for his headquarters company, mounted reserve battalion, and mounted archers to follow. Swinging behind the battle line, he raced to the right flank, ordering the crossbowmen and artillerymen deployed there to follow. Prior to the battle, he had carefully reconnoitered the canal covering the right flank. We are not certain whether he located a shallow crossing or laid fascines beneath the water prior to the fight, but, regardless of how it was done, Hawkwood led his men across the canal, raced around the left flank of the Veronese army, and then crossed the canal again, coming in on their flank and rear.

The Veronese army, focused on punching through the center, had paid scant heed to their left flank, assuming that the canal was impassable. The commanders were focused on the center, and in the heat of battle, their vision blocked by thousands of waving spears, most could not see more than a few dozen yards. The Veronese on the extreme left saw the flanking force swarming around to their rear and started to raise the alarm, but their cries were lost in the confusion. Thus, for the vast majority of the endangered force, their first indicator that something was wrong was when arrows started shrieking in from *behind* them.

Defensive armor was designed to protect the front of a man. It is the same type of trade-off that tank designers wrestle with today—the fine balance between frontal, side, and rear armor versus the engine size (or strength of the warrior) needed to move that armor on the battlefield. Given the constraint of just how much metal a man could wear and still fight, the back was protected with just some chain mail or perhaps nothing at all, so that emphasis could be placed on forward shielding. Suddenly, men in the rear ranks started to go down as Hawkwood's mounted archers raced in close and, with their deadly longbows, slammed arrows in from just a few dozen yards away. At this range, the heavy, forty-inch shafts struck with the impact of a high-velocity bullet, pinning men to the front of their armor.

As men turned and saw what was behind them, instant panic set in. In the tight-packed confusion, it was all but impossible to turn ranks around and lower spears. As for the volunteer militia of Verona, a clear demonstration was made as to why most medieval generals tried to keep such levies as far away from the action as possible . . . most of the militia panicked, some breaking for the rear, the others racing headlong into the ranks of their own mercenaries and throwing them into confusion.

Standing tall in the stirrups, Hawkwood now threw his golden baton into the enemy ranks, a clear signal that he fully expected to recover it and that the man who did so was certain to receive a prize. Hawkwood's lieutenant in command of the main battle line cried for his trumpeters to signal the charge. The exhausted line pushed forward one more time, just as the confusion on the left of the Veronese line and at their rear was spreading across the front. Men at the front of the Veronese line now knew that something was dreadfully wrong. The sound of battle was behind them, men were screaming and arrows were winging down and slamming into their ranks from the rear. This final push by the Paduans cracked the Veronese line, sending it reeling.

To be caught in the panic-stricken retreat of a medieval army must have been terrifying. One second your line is holding, perhaps even surging forward toward victory. Within seconds, the ranks behind you start to melt away, the pressure to move stops, and the enemy surges forward, their morale soaring while yours plummets. Suddenly, a man breaks to one side or the other, screaming that the battle is lost. With your flank exposed, all you can do is break as well . . . and within seconds, thousands of well-disciplined troops turn into a mob.

The Veronese forces tried to escape from the noose closing around them as Hawkwood surged forward, his charge smashing into the Veronese *carroccio* and seizing it, along with the three hundred men posted as guards. The enemy commander fell prisoner, as did most of the other lieutenants. After all, they were professionals and knew when a cause was lost.

Some of the militia, imbued with patriotism for their city, refused quarter and were slaughtered, but for most of the Veronese army, there was now only one thought, and that was to get the hell away from Castagnaro as quickly as possible. Men, burdened down with armor, staggered across the muddy, bloodstained field. In desperation, hundreds cast aside their expensive armor while the Paduan host pressed the attack on into the evening.

As darkness closed down around them, the pursuit finally ended. Sir John de Hawkwood, greatest of the mercenaries of Italy, had won his crowning achievement. Almost every leader of Verona on that field had been killed or taken prisoner, along with more than four thousand men-at-arms and nearly a thousand other troops. The precious *carroccio* of Verona would be taken back and paraded through Padua with an impressive take of booty, including the entire supply train of the enemy, their entire camp, thousands of cast-off sets of armor, dozens of banners and pennants, twenty-four bombards, and, yes, the three machine guns that were found stuck in the mud, their crews having sensibly abandoned their futuristic weapons and fled.

Nearly eight hundred dead were recorded on the side of Verona, while Hawkwood counted less than a hundred lost. As far as modern slaughter matches go, this might not seem impressive, but for the standards of warfare of that time, it was a bloody and resounding defeat for Verona.

As for the fruits of the victory, perhaps the only permanent result was the capping off of a remarkable career for Sir John de Hawkwood. The war between Verona and Padua was, in fact, a game within a game. Milan had stood waiting in the wings, and in the power struggles between Milan, Venice, and Florence, the two combatants of Castagnaro were merely minor players. In less than a year, Verona, crippled by the defeat, fell to Milan, followed shortly thereafter by Padua as well.

Sir John remained in the employ of Florence throughout the closing years of his life. In 1391, Florence conferred on Hawkwood the highest honor that could be offered to one not born of the city—honorary citizenship, with the privileges of citizenship to be passed on to his descendants.

His declining years were typical of those of most old soldiers who had loyally served a country—his earnings were eaten up by taxes. Yet Florence was not ungrateful, even offering significant dowries for Hawkwood's daughters and helping with the wedding expenses, for the Italian tradition of a costly wedding was as alive then as it is now.

Early in 1394, at the age of seventy-four, Sir John de Hawkwood sold off part of his estates and announced his desire to return to the land of his birth. This adventure was stopped by the one adversary the legendary mercenary had faced throughout his life but in the end could not beat—Hawkwood died of a stroke on March 16, 1394.

Florence offered him a state funeral, his body given the honor of resting in the famed Baptistery and being buried near the altar in the new cathedral then under construction. A request then came from no less a personage than Richard II of England, asking that the great warrior be returned to his native land. Thus the tanner's son came back to rest in the parish church where he had been baptized. The tomb is now lost. All that remains is the niche in the church wall where he was buried and the image of a hawk carved above it.

The Hessians in America

The Battle of Trenton, 1776

by William R. Forstchen

THE EMPLOYMENT OF THE SO-CALLED HESSIAN TROOPS IN THE American War of Independence, or, as we more commonly call it, "the Revolution," was significant, both militarily and politically. It can be argued that the mere presence of the German troops went far toward galvanizing American public opinion against the British crown and might very well have created the turning point in public support of the revolutionary cause.

The Revolution was, if anything, an accidental war triggered by miscalculation on both sides. The famed British march on Concord was not intended as a *causa belli* but rather as a police action to seize illegal weapons from a group of wild-eyed militia fanatics. Mistakes were made; the mysterious discharge of a musket on the Lexington Green ignited a firefight, and, by late afternoon on that fateful April day, thousands of enraged militia were pursuing a retreating British column. For the colonials, it was yet to be fully perceived as a revolution with the intent of forming a new country. Rather, it was a protest by Englishmen, protecting the rights of Englishmen.

The political situation was made far worse by what happened two months later at Breed's Hill, when over a thousand

44

British troops were killed and wounded in a foolish frontal assault. When the casualty lists reached England, the die was cast. The perception had been created that all of the colonies were in mad, wild-eyed rebellion.

Then came the fateful decision to employ the "Hessians." Though the English king George III perceived that the colonists were in direct rebellion against his rightful authority, opinion in Parliament was divided. There were in fact some MPs who actually agreed with the colonists, declaring that by standing against royal authority, the rebels were defending the rights of all Englishmen. Remember, this occurred only 130 years after Parliament had overthrown a king for what they believed was a usurpation of their rights, and then beheaded him.

Throughout the late summer and fall, George III forged ahead with plans for the suppression of the rebellion. It was quickly realized, however, that the standing forces of the British army were inadequate to the task. Estimates ran that a field force of over fifty thousand would be needed. Given the lack of solid support in Parliament, and from the British populace in general, George III turned to other sources for troops. It must be remembered as well that the Hanover line of kings that ruled England in the eighteenth century was in fact German. Given his German background, the king decided to turn to his family, as it was, for military support, and negotiators were sent to the minor German states in search of troops for hire.

Germany at this time was divided into dozens of small countries and principalities, the dominant ones being Prussia and Bavaria. Massed armies had been raised throughout Germany during the turmoil of the Seven Years War, but, except for a minor skirmish in Bavaria in the late 1770s, these armies were now standing idle. For the smaller German states, their armies could, in fact, be viewed as a valuable export product. Service in the small professional armies of the German states was usually a long-term enlistment. Whether fighting or sitting idle in garrisons, defending the homeland, or campaigning five thousand miles away, such men still had to be paid, clothed, and fed. Since they were not citizen soldiers but rather paid professionals, the prospect of leasing them out for profit struck many a ruler as a good deal.

Thus an arrangement was born. George III needed troops. Going to Parliament with the request of raising new troops to fight was politically embarrassing and might prove difficult. Appealing to the middle and lower classes for support to go fight in the distant jungles of America in a campaign that many saw as a war against fellow citizens wasn't going to work, either. And the German troops were available at bargain rates. Over the next seven years, approximately thirty thousand professional soldiers from the small states of Hesse-Cassel, Hesse-Hanau, Brunswick, Anhalt-Zerbst, Waldeck, and Ansbach-Bayreuth were hired.

When word of this decision reached the colonies early in 1776, it was George's political undoing. Except for a few radicals, most of the Revolution's supporters still perceived themselves as Englishmen protesting for their rights against an overbearing king. Historically, they looked back to the Glorious Revolution of 1688 and the civil war of the 1640s as their legal precedents. Some even hoped that Parliament itself would finally come to their side, block the actions of the king, and acknowledge the rights of fellow Englishmen who lived on the other side of the Atlantic. George's decision to hire mercenaries was a visceral blow, striking at the xenophobic streak in Englishmen (and in Americans to this day) when it came to foreign involvement in issues regarding their rights. George III had changed an argument between cousins into a fight against foreign invaders unleashed by a reckless king who wasn't even really English.

This was one of the major issues that helped to bring about the Second Continental Congress and the move to declare independence well over a year after the firing of the first shots at Lexington. An examination of that Declaration of Independence will show in the second part of the document, which outlined our grievances, that there is the direct denouncement of the king's decision to transport foreign mercenaries to our shores.

The German troops, who would be known as Hessians since a majority of them came from that province, first arrived in the Americas as part of Howe's army, which landed on Staten Island late in the summer of 1776. From the surviving diaries and accounts of the troops, most of them felt—at least initially—that, as troops loyal to their princes and kings, they were going where duty sent them to serve. Their performance in most actions was at least as good as that of the English troops and in some instances was far superior. The legend of American riflemen fighting in the Revolution is oftimes overblown; what are usually forgotten are the feared jaeger companies of German riflemen who, on many fields of action, proved to be just as deadly.

Thousands of Hessians deployed out with Howe's army and fought in the battles of Long Island, Manhattan, and White Plains, and the seizures of Forts Lee and Washington. Fort Washington was primarily a Hessian fight, with the surrender of over two thousand American troops received by Colonel Johann Gottlieb Rall.

The involvement of Hessians in the disastrous campaign of 1776 served to create an undying resentment toward the foreign mercenaries as the American forces recoiled from an unending string of defeats. This was an army of foreign despoilers who fought with a frightful machinelike precision. The armies of the smaller German states were, in general, reflections of the famed Prussian military system of Frederick the Great. Trained with brutal discipline, they were unmatched in the violent and frightful system of linear warfare. Yet again, one of the myths of the American Revolution is of the wily Americans using natural cover and terrain to devastate the incredibly stupid and foolish British and Hessian armies. This is pure fabrication created by early-nineteenth-century historians. A simple examination of the record will show that, throughout most of the campaigns in the Mid Atlantic states, the forces of the king almost always triumphed, for the settled villages and open farmlands of Connecticut, southern New York, New Jersey, and eastern Pennsylvania were all but custom-designed for the requirements of linear combat. Colonial militia and the barely trained troops of the continental line could not hope to stand against the crushing four volleys a minute delivered by the machinelike German troops.

It is forgotten as well that this was also a civil war between rebel and loyalist. As Washington's army disintegrated under the repeated hammer blows of Howe's British/Hessian army, the hopes of loyalists in New York and New Jersey soared, while those who were sitting on the fence tucked away their colonist banners and brought their old British flags out of the closet for display. After being kicked out of New York and falling back into New Jersey, Washington made a desperate appeal to the men of New Jersey to rise in support—and not one man came to his ranks.

Since this was a civil war, barn burning, looting, and denouncements of disloyalty now came to the fore. It is here that the Hessian troops gained their reputation as pillagers and looters. It seems clear that they engaged in these activities no more than did the British troops or colonials, but it was the fact that they were foreigners doing this that made them so noticeable. This only helped to serve the propaganda point that foreigners had been unleashed by the king and were now despoiling the land.

Meanwhile, Washington's broken rabble continued to fall back across New Jersey. He was routed out of Newark with barely a shot being fired. At New Brunswick, his withdrawing column was saved only by the burning of the bridges across the Raritan River, the demolitions team nearly driven back by sniper fire from jaeger riflemen.

Given a temporary and fateful breather by Howe when the British general decided to call off pursuit due to the advent of winter, Washington fell back across the Delaware River with less than fifteen hundred men left out of his army of nearly twenty thousand that had attempted to hold New York less than five months before.

Howe had succeeded beyond his wildest dreams. Initially, he had hoped merely to take New York and perhaps extend his operations into northern New Jersey. He now made the decision to fling a forward picket line out to the Delaware and thus secure central New Jersey for forage and protect the loyalists living there. A line of garrisons were set up, with a base of operations established under Cornwallis at New Brunswick. The best of the Hessian troops were deployed forward with a main garrison established at Bordentown. A smaller garrison of three regiments of Hessian infantry, a battery of artillery, and a company of jaegers—a total of fourteen hundred men under the command of Colonel Rall, the victor of the Battle of Fort Washington—was established at Trenton.

Rall and his command quickly settled into winter quarters. The colonel appropriated a large home and entertained himself and his staff by staging parades with the regimental bands and the trooping of the artillery battery. Rall knew that Washington's army was somewhere on the other side of the river but dismissed them as a broken rabble who would completely collapse and go home once winter had set in . . . in short, the war was all but over.

Thus there was no need to ring the town with fortifications, and the sending of patrols to keep an eye on the fords and river crossings north of town was a waste of energy. Contrary to the mythical stereotype of the hard-driving German commander who was impervious to the needs of his men, Rall felt that his troops had behaved well throughout the summer and fall campaign and were now deserving of a little R and R. The suggestion by one of his staff to keep forward patrols out was waved off as a waste of time.

On the other side of the Delaware, Washington had not given up, but he clearly saw a dangerous deadline looming. Appeals for reinforcements had temporarily boosted his command to approximately five thousand men, but most of those would leave when their periods of enlistment ended on December 31. If something was not done to raise the spirits of the revolutionary forces, the army might very well disintegrate during the winter, never to be reborn. He also saw the opportunity for a major strategic thrust, a maneuver that would move the front line back from the Delaware and perhaps bring it all the way back to the Hudson River.

Thus was started the planning for Washington's audacious offensive against the Hessians at Trenton. The fact that they were Hessians played no smaller part in his thinking. A victory over the hated foreign mercenaries could show that the frightful machinelike quality of these troops could be overcome. And a key point of his plan was the knowledge of just how much the Germans enjoyed their Christmas party.

On the night of December 25–26, Washington launched his offensive. A diversionary column was sent south to demonstrate near Bordentown while a second column was deployed to cross the river just south of Trenton. They were to serve as an anvil for the hammerlike blow coming down from the north.

In a dramatic night crossing, lashed by sleet, freezing rain, and snow, Washington transported several thousand men and nine artillery pieces across the river nine miles north of Rall's partying troops. By three in the morning, they started a march south. Washington hoped to have his army deployed for a predawn strike, but he was already behind schedule. He realized that a predawn strike was now impossible but forged ahead anyhow, fully expecting to meet a German force deployed and ready for action. Washington, at this moment, had heroically thrown the dice for an all-or-nothing victory.

Rall's Christmas party had been a brilliant success. From colonel down to lowest private, the celebration had been non-stop. One of the three regiments was supposedly on duty for the night, but it is evident that they had joined in the celebrations as well. Huge quantities of beer, wine, grog, rum, and whatever else was handy were consumed. The war was all but over. The campaigning (at least for the officers) was an exciting experience that had enhanced their professional growth, and the whole adventure was seen as some damn good training at little cost for the troops. In fact, they had turned a profit for their countries. A bit of blooding in this distant colonial war was perceived as a good exercise to train the ranks in case another war ever flared up back in the homeland. As for the homeland, rumors were flying through the ranks that operations might very well be over by spring, and all would return to Germany by the following summer, where the men, now veterans, could strut about the garrison towns and boast of their experiences in the exotic jungles of America to wide-eyed *Fräuleins*.

The festivities were briefly interrupted when a report came in of a skirmish north of town. Several companies were run north to the outpost on the edge of the village, but the attackers had disappeared into the storm. There is no historical record as to who these attackers were. Chances are, they were some local citizens, a bit drunk on Christmas cheer, who decided to take a few potshots at the hated mercenaries—the eighteenth-century equivalent of a group of good old boys in a pickup doing a drive by shotgunning of someone's home. The fun-filled raid almost changed the course of the war. One of Rall's staff, made alert by the incident, suggested pushing some scouts up the road, just to double-check. Nothing came of the suggestion. After all, it was Christmas night, the storm was vicious, and any sane man, including Washington, was most likely curled up by a warm fire nursing a hot buttered rum or schnapps. If the patrol had gone north, they would have run smack into Washington's column struggling along the icy road.

Washington's plan was a complex one. Having already split his army into three sections, he again divided his main column in half, sending them on parallel roads. The eastern column was to swing around Trenton and box the Hessians in on their eastern and southern flank, while the main column slashed into town from the north. The line of retreat to the west was blocked by the Delaware River. In addition, the attacks were supposed to hit at exactly the same time. This dividing of forces, in the dark, with the intent of then striking simultaneously, was all but suicidal and, if discovered, would have left Washington's army open to total destruction. Washington then ordered a halt to eat breakfast before going in. When the columns set off again, officers and NCOs were forced to shake and kick awake many of the men. Malnourished and worn-out, they had collapsed into exhausted sleep on the slushy and ice-covered ground. The columns continued to stagger through the snow, their trail literally marked by blood as unshod men, with rags bound around their feet, forged ahead on the rutted, icy roads.

As if fate were trying to give Rall another chance, a loyalist farmer appeared at Rall's headquarters, asking for the colonel. Apparently the language barrier now came into play. The farmer was denied access to the colonel, who was playing cards in the next room. In desperation, the loyalist farmer wrote out a note declaring that Washington's entire army was crossing the river and would attack at dawn. The anonymous farmer then disappeared into the night. One of Rall's servants handed him the note. He stuck it into his pocket (history doesn't tell us if he tried to read it and gave up, or just simply ignored it) and then returned to his party.

At least one officer, however, was anxious. Lieutenant Andreas Weiderhold, responsible for the picket forces on the north side of town, sent an additional nine men up to the outpost and personally went up to join them.

Dawn broke into a dark, gray morning with the storm still continuing. Weiderhold, anxiously keeping watch, stepped outside of the house that served as his outpost to stretch. Through the swirling mist and snow that blanketed the road, he saw a shadowy movement that materialized into a detachment of troops and a forward sentry running ahead of the Americans, screaming the alarm.

Weiderhold roused his men, who poured out of the house and managed to get off one ragged volley. With lowered muskets, the Americans charged. About to be overwhelmed, Weiderhold pulled back to the company of Captain Alterbockum, which had been roused by Weiderhold's volley and was attempting to deploy. Visibility was approximately two hundred yards, and Alterbockum saw that he was about to be swarmed under as hundreds of American troops came storming out of the gray, many of them already spilling around his flank and rear. He ordered his men to break and run back toward the center of town.

On the east side of town, the second American column, which had swung around to flank the village, now started to drive in the Hessian pickets. As near as can be ascertained, both columns struck at nearly the same moment in a brilliant coordinated attack.

In the center of the village, Rall's adjutant, awakened by the rattle of musketry and the first blasts of artillery as American gunners swung their pieces into position, pounded on the door to Rall's house. The hungover colonel leaned out the second floor window, still wearing his nightcap, asking what was wrong. The adjutant pointed toward the edge of town, shouting that they were under attack. Rall, moving quickly in spite of the early morning and the undoubtable aftereffects of the all-night party, was outside and mounted within a few minutes.

Surprisingly, the Hessian units were not caught entirely

asleep. Officers and NCOs spread the alarm, men poured out of their quarters, and part of Rall's regiments managed to form in the center of town. The Americans, however, already had the advantage. Driven forward by cold, hunger, hatred of the foreign enemy, and sheer desperation, the ragged army came on with grim determination while the Hessians, confused and surprised, came staggering out of warm beds into a swirling storm from which a wall of mad, wild-eyed enemies were charging.

A regimental flag, snatched from Rall's headquarters where it had hung as a decoration during the party, was carried to the front, and Rall's own regiment attempted to advance. The forward movement had barely started, though, when a volley of solid shot, fired at close range by the American artillery, slammed into their ranks. At nearly the same moment, scathing fire developed on their left flank as yet more Americans came pouring into the town.

Caught in front and flank in the narrow village streets and house lots, the regiment managed to get off only two volleys before breaking apart in the confusion. A stand-up fight, on a clear field, with heads clear as well, was one thing; this surprise attack, delivered at dawn after a night of partying, was something entirely different. There was another factor at play as well. The Hessians were used to seeing the ragged American lines breaking and running, oftimes even before they had advanced to within range of musket fire. These Americans, many of them without shoes, feet bound with rags, were storming down the icy, slush-filled streets with muskets lowered, screaming wildly. Perhaps some of the stereotyping fear of the Americans as a bunch of frontier savages now came to the fore . . . this was certainly no European army advancing with drums beating, flags flying, and bewigged officers riding astride their splendid mounts. At close quarters, the fight was visceral, the Americans already smelling victory, the bitter frustration of months of defeat now unleashed against a hated foe.

Rall's regiment disintegrated and broke for the rear, slamming into a second regiment that was attempting to form. This second regiment broke apart as well. Rall tried to move up his artillery, and the battery, which was quickly hitched up, galloped toward what Rall assumed was a stabilizing front. The advancing Hessian battery ran straight into the aimed fire of the American guns. Before they could even swing around to unlimber, men and horses were going down in bloody heaps. It is a tribute to the training of the Hessian artillerymen that they followed orders and did not immediately break for the rear as well. Unlimbering while under a galling fire, they actually managed to fire several rounds from each gun before they were overwhelmed, with over fifty percent casualties. The survivors broke, abandoning their pieces and running for cover.

The weather was playing a major part in the battle beyond that of concealment. In the driving sleet, the muskets of both sides quickly fouled, often after just one shot, as the flints and firing pans became wet. Therefore, the battle was mainly one of artillery, the sword, and the bayonet. Normally the Hessians would have had the advantage here as well, but the battle had disintegrated into a confused street brawl, fought by isolated clusters of men in alleyways and backyards, and along the streets. The Battle of Trenton, at this moment, resembled a humongous barroom brawl more than a formalized battle, and as such, perhaps here as well, something uniquely American came to the fore.

Driven back to the edge of the Delaware, Rall was stunned and confused. One of his staff pushed the colonel to either reorganize the regiments and go back in or attempt to flee southward over a bridge spanning Assunpink Creek, a small stream that ran east to west and emptied into the Delaware on the south side of town.

Rall decided to counterattack and snatch victory back from the jaws of defeat. Forming two of his regiments, he had the colors brought to the front. One of the regimental bands started to play, and the regiments marched back into the center of town. They were torn apart. Scores of Americans had broken into the houses lining the streets, dried their flints and flash pans, and were now poised by windows and doorways. Their fire slashed into the regiments at close range while massed artillery swept the advancing columns with grape and canister. A surprise charge came storming out of an alleyway on the left flank of the advancing columns, and the Hessians broke yet again and went streaming to the rear in panic.

But the route of retreat over Assunpink Creek was now sealed off. While the regiments had advanced back into the center of town, American forces had snuck around the rear of the column and seized the bridge. American artillery was now rolled closer and continued to slash into the milling crowd of frightened soldiers. Rall, still mounted, attempted to rally his companies of grenadiers, most likely to form a spearhead for one final breakout attempt, when he was mortally wounded by two bullets in the side.

The two regiments that had formed around Rall now tried to move through the backstreets and alleyways to a rallying point: an orchard on the southeast side of town. Cut off and surrounded, they finally surrendered. A third regiment met the same fate near the orchard as the men desperately raced back and forth from one flank to the other, trying to find a way out of the ever-tightening circle.

By nine in the morning, after approximately an hour and a half of combat, the Battle of Trenton was over. Roughly five hundred Hessians had managed to escape in the confusion. No organized units got out, other than a small detachment of British dragoons who had hastily mounted and galloped south out of town as soon as the battle started, abandoning their German allies to their fate. The freezing refugees staggered into Bordentown throughout the rest of the day, spreading panic and alarm that Washington was loose in New Jersey.

Nine hundred Hessians were either killed, wounded, or captured, along with all their weapons, a full battery of artillery, precious supply wagons loaded down with matériel, fifteen stands of colors, and even the instruments of the bands. Total loses for Washington's army: one officer and one private KIA!

After resting his army till midafternoon, Washington withdrew northward and recrossed the Delaware. By the end of the day, some of the men had not only fought a pitched battle but had marched well over thirty miles in a driving storm. On the return march, three men died from exposure; the following day, close to a thousand men were reported as unfit for service due to exposure and exhaustion.

Nevertheless, the affect on army morale was stunning. Washington now offered a bounty to any man who would sign on for six months and made personal appeals to his troops. Those actions, combined with the renewed spark generated at Trenton, convinced a precious five thousand men to stay with the colors until the end of spring.

In yet another audacious move, Washington again crossed the river into New Jersey and flanked Cornwallis, who was advancing down from New Brunswick with the intent of pinning Washington against the Delaware. The Americans fought a brilliant flanking and then rearguard action at Princeton and stormed northward, at last coming to a halt at Morristown, New Jersey, where the army went into winter quarters. Ending within a day's march of New York, this deployment northward was one of the most audacious and brilliant of the war.

Trenton is cited by many as the psychological turning point of the Revolution. Though the bitter winter of Valley Forge and the hard-fought campaign at Saratoga were still a year in the future, Trenton proved that the enemy—and especially the Hessians—could be not just beaten, but routed. More wholesale surrenders of German forces were yet to come, especially at Saratoga, Bennington, and Yorktown. Close to half of all Hessian forces deployed in America would become POWs, some held until the end of the war, others repatriated and exchanged for colonial prisoners. Hundreds of these men stayed, coming over to the American side and seeing in the Revolution a cause they could believe in as well.

Hessian forces, in general, fought with courage in every theater of operations, struggling through the choking tropical heat of South Carolina and enduring the arctic cold of Canada and upstate New York. As mercenaries, they were admirable, disciplined, and well trained. But as to their overall impact on the Revolution, they were a disaster for the cause of the Crown, arousing in Americans a sense of outrage over the fact that foreign mercenaries had been unleashed to suppress the rights of free men. It was this rage that undoubtedly drove the freezing men of Washington's army forward through a stormy Christmas night and onward to the first true victory for a new revolutionary nation.

Faithful unto Death

The Massacre of the Swiss Guards, 1792

by William R. Forstchen

A COMMON MISCONCEPTION TODAY IS THAT THE FRENCH Revolution of 1789 immediately resulted in the overthrow and execution of the king, Louis XVI. In fact, for over three years the revolutionary government was a compromise effort modeled in part after the British system of constitutional monarchy. It wasn't until 1792 that the Jacobin radicals finally made their move, overthrowing this compromise government, sending the king to his death, and igniting the Reign of Terror. The first group of victims killed in this holocaust was a mercenary regiment: the famed Swiss Guards.

Several monarchies, including the papacy, had turned to the tough mountain folk of Switzerland to form the backbone of their personal guard. Since the use of German guards by the Caesars, monarchies have often found that the importation of a foreign elite guard was far wiser than recruiting locally; while locals might be moved by the various political factions, a foreign regiment could be kept above such intrigue. As professional soldiers, the Swiss have always been ranked among the best.

In 1792 the Swiss Guards of the Bourbon dynasty become a target. Highly visible in their distinctive red uniforms, perceived as a pampered elite, and viewed as a constant reminder of the *ancien régime*, the Swiss increasingly became a focal point of hatred to the Paris mob.

Rumors of a coup against the king and the Assembly had been brewing in Paris throughout the hot summer of 1792, the situation inflamed by Austria's declaration of war and the incredibly stupid manifesto issued by royal refugees which declared that anyone who did not foreswear the revolution was now a traitor and would be dealt with accordingly. The Revolution was becoming a war of annihilation, and the vast majority of moderates were now forced to choose sides.

By the evening of August 9, 1792, it was evident to the king that a mob was preparing to storm the Tuileries, the palace in Paris where he had been a virtual prisoner since his removal from Versailles. Throughout the night, the Swiss Guard prepared their defenses, barricading doors and windows and deploying artillery to sweep the courtyards. Mingled in with them were units of the National Guard, few of whom were eager to die for their hated king. Individual appeals were made to the Swiss to defect and a few, seeing what was about to happen, stripped off their uniforms and slipped through the gates into the ever-increasing mob surrounding the palace. The vast majority—750 officers and men—stayed at their posts.

On the morning of August 10, Louis addressed his troops, exhorting them to serve him loyally. The Swiss mercenaries cheered this final address of the king, but the National Guard troops jeered, broke ranks and drifted to the gates where the mob, which now numbered in the tens of thousands, prepared to storm the palace.

The speech might have been a good one, but here was a moment when the king did not live up to the honor of the men who served him. Shortly after the speech, the king and his family fled the palace, going across the courtyards to where the Assembly was in session.

There was some early confusion amongst the revolutionaries as to the intentions of the Swiss Guard, but it didn't last long. When a National Guard unit loyal to the revolution approached the palace, a volley cut down more than a hundred men. The revolutionaries retreated, and the battle/riot was on. This first volley showed that the Swiss were not just overdressed toy soldiers but highly trained professionals who knew how to aim low and fight with discipline.

Mixed into the mob were revolutionary battalions that had been marching into the city over the past several days, National Guard units, and even a sprinkling of old soldiers from the prerevolutionary days. Nearly fifty pieces of artillery were deployed and opened up while the various regiments poured tens of thousands of musket rounds into the building. The Swiss, showing remarkable skill and courage, mounted a sally, storming out of the palace and seizing several guns, which they dragged back into the palace and then used to keep the thousands at bay.

The size of their defensive perimeter was, however, simply too much for the 750 mercenaries and the several hundred court retainers, servants, and minor nobility who joined the ranks. Repeated charges against the palace were met by scathing volleys and blasts of canister fired at near-point-blank range, but the mob was still increasing in size beyond the gates. Worse, however, was the simple lack of preparation for the defense. Most of the Swiss carried only the ammunition that was in their cartridge boxes, and there was no reserve stockpile. After several hours, nearly all the men were out of ammunition and reduced to defending with the bayonet—yet here again we see their skill, for even with bayonets alone, they managed to hang on for several hours, keeping the mob at bay.

In the midst of the battle, a detachment of Swiss broke out of the palace, running a gauntlet of musket and artillery fire and reaching the Assembly. The King, concealed in a stenographer's booth, had been listening to the rambling and spineless debate of the few members present as to what to do next. At the approach of the bloodied and battle-stained soldiers of the guard, there was a panic, the Assembly members assuming that in all that confusion, with a battle raging literally under their windows, the guard was now staging a countercoup. Apparently the Guard went there with the intent of finding the king and trying to cut their way out. The king, however, refused to leave and ordered the guard to surrender itself to the mob!

His defenders would later claim that this was an act of compassion and that he truly believed the surrender would be accepted and the lives of his men would be spared. Those on the other side declare that he was so cowed that his only thought now was to surrender and, if need be, give his loyal guard over to the mob and thus divert their blood lust.

Here stands yet another remarkable moment in the history of mercenaries. One could charitably say that their employer had ''let them down''; a cynic would say that the king had sold them out—but, regardless of this, the vast majority of the Swiss Guard obeyed his command. These men were realists; they knew what was coming, but nevertheless many did ground arms as ordered and march out of the palace. The mob fell upon them, and the massacre began. Men were dragged down, garroted, stoned, and impaled, their mutilated corpses literally torn to pieces in the bloody frenzy that followed.

Not all the Swiss were so blindly obedient. Some did retain their weapons and went down fighting, while the more pragmatic, seeing that their terms of employment were over, stripped off their uniforms and tried to escape. The mob, however, was in such a frenzy that apparently no one escaped. Anyone who looked suspicious was cornered, and if he spoke French with an accent or, worse yet, could not speak French at all, his fate was sealed. With resistance collapsing, the mob stormed into the palace, hunting down anyone associated with the king, and murdered them all. At the end of the day, a bonfire was lit in front of the palace, and what scraps of bodies remained were consigned to the flames.

So ended the Swiss Guards of the Bourbon dynasty, a mercenary band far more loyal to their employer than he was to them. Fittingly, Louis XVI would outlive his guards by only five months.

Death With Honor

The Battle of Camerone, 1863

by William R. Forstchen

The French, being a thrifty and practical people, have always been eager to let any available foreigners assist them in any necessary bleeding and dying for la Patrie.

JOHN ELTING

ONE OF THE SIDE EFFECTS OF THE AMERICAN CIVIL WAR WAS the bizarre and ill-fated Maximilian affair in Mexico. With the advent of hostilities in the spring of 1861, the United States was forced to turn its attention inward and the loudly proclaimed Monroe Doctrine was left on the sidelines. First and foremost, Lincoln's foreign policy sought at all cost to avoid providing an excuse for European intervention. This policy of avoidance now left the road open for one of the strangest military/political affairs of the nineteenth century: the invasion of Mexico by the combined forces of France and the Hapsburgs.

Napoléon III, nephew of the famed Corsican, presided over nineteenth century France with a rule marked by desire to revive *la gloire* of the legendary days of the empire. The trumped-up excuse for his New World adventure was the issue of unpaid debts by Mexico and the political chaos in that nation. The underlying political cause, which would unite former foes France and Austria, was the mystical belief that it was their sworn duty to defend the Catholic faith, which they claimed was threatened by the Juárez revolution that had successfully seized power in the aftermath of the war with America. After the republican forces of Juárez seized power, wealthy conservative Mexicans sought refuge in Paris and there gained the ear of Napoléon III's wife, a devout Spanish Catholic. Of course, support of this counterrevolution would not only preserve the faith but also would fulfill Napoléon's fantasy of creating a new French empire in the Americas.

So France saw in Mexico an opportunity for imperial expansion. Austria saw the chance to be heralded as defender of the faith, in this case against the alleged anticlerical forces of Juárez. Belgium, as part of the old Hapsburg empire, threw in support as well.

Landing an expeditionary force at Veracruz, the combined Austrian, Belgian, and French army (including a couple of companies of troops recruited from Egypt) embarked on a full-scale invasion of the country, an invasion that for many would bear an unsettling resemblance to Napoléon I's campaign in Spain. The expedition, lacking any clear-cut mission statement other than the suppression of a widespread and popular rebellion, was plagued by disease and increasingly harassed by the implacable "little war" waged by the locals.

Napoléon III, in a bizarre move, agreed to support the crowning of Maximilian, a Hapsburg duke, as emperor of Mexico. He then propped up his position with the bayonets of the French army. But the unpopular dynasty could only last so long. Eventually, the French withdrew in failure, and Maximilian, who had set himself up in Mexico City, was captured and beheaded by the Mexican people.

Paradoxically, though the campaign in Mexico proved to be a total disaster, it served as the salvation of the French Foreign Legion. Organized in 1831, the Legion was mandated with providing a military force for operations outside of France. Basically, it was a mercenary body that could fulfill the needs for overseas service without having to draw on troops from home. Initially, its primary theater of operations was Algiers, but by 1861 serious campaigning in that region was all but finished, and some felt that the Legion had outlived its usefulness. One regiment was disbanded, and recruitment for a second was suspended; those foreigners who were ''short timers'' were induced to resign early. However, the Mexican adventure changed that, and the quixotic campaign that followed created one of the most enduring legends in the history of mercenary forces.

Initially deployed to Veracruz in 1863, the Legion suffered devastating losses from *vómito,* the dreaded yellow fever. Approximately one-third of the Legion troops deployed to Mexico died of the disease within twelve months. The decision was made to move the bulk of the troops supporting the supply head at Veracruz sixty miles inland, to the highland town of Córdoba, which, at twenty-eight hundred feet above the fever-ridden coastal plains, was considered relatively safe. The major problem with this redeployment was the need to maintain a secured line of communication back to the coast. Patrols and supply convoys moving along this corridor increasingly became the targets of hit-and-run guerrilla raids. It was the patrolling of this vital corridor that set the stage for the epic last stand at El Camarón, or Camerone, a battle that for the Legion is of the same mythical proportions as the Alamo or Thermopylae.

An expedition of sixty-two legionnaires and three officers, under the command of Captain Jean Danjou, started a patrol near Palo Verde, forty miles southwest of Veracruz, at one in the morning of April 30, 1863. (At exactly the same time, fifteen hundred miles to the north, Robert E. Lee's veteran army was moving into position just outside of Chancellorsville, Virginia, for what would prove to be Stonewall Jackson's last battle.)

Captain Danjou was already the stuff of legend in the Legion. A hero of the war in Crimea, he had lost a hand to an exploding musket while serving on a topographical expedition in Algeria. Eccentricity and flamboyance have always been part of the makeup of a mercenary, and in the Legion, Danjou stood out by replacing his missing hand with a beautifully carved wooden replica.

With the coming of dawn, Danjou's patrol stopped for breakfast. They deployed in a clearing, and Danjou posted sentries while the rest of his men gathered wood to cook breakfast. Before the meal had even started, a sentry on the western edge of the perimeter reported a large body of mounted troops approaching. Danjou ordered his small detachment to form a square.

Though rarely used at this point by American armies due to the drastically increased range of rifled weapons, the Legion still used the infantry square as a standard defensive deployment when facing mounted troops. Given the small size of the detachment, Danjou most likely formed them into a single-rank formation with a small reserve in the center, thus presenting a block formation approximately ten yards to a side.

The advancing Mexican troops attempted to charge, but a single volley of rifle fire, delivered at one hundred yards, broke the attack, and the enemy pulled back out of range. Danjou redeployed a hundred yards to the east, seeking better ground, and repulsed a second charge as easily as the first.

He was now faced, however, with a serious dilemma. His small force was cut off and isolated in enemy territory with no hope of immediate relief. On foot and facing a mounted force, there was no chance of breaking off the engagement and withdrawing back to the safety of their main base.

This dilemma revealed the startling inadequacies of the European forces and their ignorance regarding the tailoring of unit formations to fit the tactical and operational requirements of the mission. In the first months of the campaign in Mexico, the Legion had developed a dismissive disdain for the Mexican forces confronting them. Their attitude toward the hit-and-run raids was typical of those of regular forces confronting guerrilla operations—the enemy were opportunistic cowards who refused to come to blows in a fair fight. Complacency regarding their enemy took hold, resulting in the sending out of patrols like Danjou's without regard for what might happen if a determined foe was encountered.

The situation was exacerbated by the fact that the Mexicans were almost always mounted while the European forces were primarily infantry. What was ignored by the distant architects of this mad campaign was that the enemy could move as they pleased, picking the point of battle and almost always choosing that point when it was to their advantage. As in nearly any guerrilla war throughout history, the locals retreated when pressed, harassed when possible, and closed for the kill when it was to their advantage. Camerone proved to be the classic example of a small infantry force cut off by an overwhelming force of guerrillas. In minature, it was a foreshadowing of another legendary Legion battle nearly a hundred years later at Dien Bien Phu.

Word of the isolated French patrol had spread through the countryside during the night and early morning. Various guerrilla bands, which had rarely coordinated efforts in the past, now rushed in for the kill. Eventually, they were reinforced with several battalions of infantry so that, by the climax of the fight, Danjou's tiny force of sixty-five men was outnumbered by over thirty to one. Watching with dismay as more cavalry started to close in, Danjou moved his force into the Hacienda de la Trinidad, which was on the road to Palo Verde and just east of Camarón. The *hacienda,* typical of farmsteads of the region, was actually a miniature fortress, approximately fifty yards square with ten-foot-high adobe walls. Living quarters stretched along the north wall, with smaller detached sheds and outbuildings ringing the inner perimeter. The central courtyard was open and exposed to the blazing tropical sun.

Danjou set his men to work preparing the defense, barricading the doors and entryway into the *hacienda* and cutting firing ports. The drawbacks to the position were the difficulty of getting clear fields of fire; the higher ground beyond the *hacienda*, which allowed for plunging fire to rake the central courtyard; and, perhaps worst of all, no source of water inside the compound. Already, the day was oppressively hot.

An NCO, a Polish sergeant named Morzicki, climbed up to peer over the wall and reported that he could see hundreds of wide-brimmed sombreros and that more reinforcements were coming up and dismounting, with the horses being sent to the rear.

Eventually, the Mexicans approached the *hacienda* under a flag of truce, offering quarter if the legionnaires surrendered at once. More was at stake, however, than their lives. The honor of the Legion had to be upheld, and to Danjou the thought of surrendering to a motley band of raiders was an act beneath contempt . . . even if the odds were thirty to one. The offer of surrender was dismissed.

Danjou now ordered his small command to gather in the central courtyard. Reminding them of their gallant heritage, the extolled them to fight with honor and promised them immortal glory. Together he and his company raised their right hands and swore a solemn oath that they would fight to the death.

The attack started and the defenders rushed to their posts. The ground about the *hacienda* offered the opportunity to pour a steady fire over the walls and into the backs of the defenders deployed along the opposite wall. Several attempts were made to storm the position, but the legionnaires held fast, constantly encouraged by Danjou, who flamboyantly walked about, waving his wooden hand and cheering his men on.

The rate of fire plunging into the beleaguered position was murderous. Most of the Mexicans were armed with short, smoothbore carbines, a weapon barely capable of hitting the broad side of a barn at fifty yards, but in this situation that didn't matter—they had an entire *hacienda* to shoot at. They knew their enemy was trapped, and, at the height of the battle, thousands of rounds a minute must have been pouring into the position, a rate of fire equivalent to that of a modern-day Gatling cutting loose. In that insane fusillade, men were bound to be hit.

The black powder-smoke created a blinding curtain. The visibility dropped to a matter of feet. The situation was made worse by the fact that the buildings inside the *hacienda* caught fire, most likely ignited by muzzle blasts from the French rifles. The combination of smoke and heat created a hellish atmosphere for the French troops burdened down in their heavy uniforms. Though they were armed with superior rifled weapons, the smoke made it all but impossible for the French to fight back effectively.

The defense had a wild, desperate *élan* to it, which is sometimes displayed by troops who are surrounded, hopelessly outnumbered, and have reached that point where it is simply a matter of "taking as many of the bastards with me as I can." They continued to hold throughout the morning, cheered on by Danjou, who at times strode along the walls of the *hacienda* in a reckless display of courage. The tens of thousands of musket balls smashing into the *hacienda* could not be stopped by *élan* alone, however, and throughout the morning Danjou's ranks were thinned.

In the early afternoon, Danjou's number finally came up, and a heavy musket ball smashed into his chest. Collapsing, he died in the courtyard. The power of his presence, however, lived on, and his men refused to give way, struggling to return fire.

The end, though, was inevitable. Gaining the walls at last and breaking into the courtyard, the Mexicans fought it out with the five survivors: Lieutenant Maudet, Corporal Maine, and Privates Cattau, Constantin, and Wenzel, a German.

Down to their final round, Lieutenant Maudet ordered the men to fire one last volley, and then, with bayonets lowered, they charged headlong into the enemy host. The Mexicans fired a volley back. Private Cattau threw himself in front of his lieutenant . . . and was hit nineteen times. Lieutenant Maudet and Private Wenzel were also hit, though Wenzel struggled to regain his feet. Maine tried to lead the charge forward, but the Mexicans closed in, ringing them with poised bayonets. It would have been over at that moment, but a Mexican officer intervened, knocking up the bayonets of his men while shouting for the survivors to surrender.

With the panache one would expect of a legionnaire, Corporal Maine did not throw down his weapon but instead clung to his rifle and demanded to negotiate, insisting that the Mexicans give aid to Lieutenant Maudet and that he and his comrades should be allowed to retain their weapons, otherwise the fight would continue! The Mexican officer, moved by this display of courage, agreed. Offering his arms to the wounded Maine and Wenzel, he helped them out of the *hacienda* while ordering up a stretcher for the lieutenant. When this small band of survivors was presented to the senior Mexican commander in the field, the awed colonel could only exclaim, ''These are not men. They are demons!'' The few survivors were eventually repatriated back to the Legion. Though they had not died as they swore they would, Maine's demand to negotiate, even when ringed with bayonets, preserved their honor. The survivors, as well, were able to bear back the story of Danjou's heroic stand, thus ensuring the birth of a legend.

As for Napoléon III's efforts and the ill-starred rule of Maximilian, the cause was doomed from the start. All was predicated on the disintegration of the United States and a favorable post–Civil War response from an independent South. Even if the South had won, chances are that the Confederate government would have been as aggressively opposed to European imperialists at their back door as the Union would prove to be. In fact, during the Civil War, some Northern Peace Democrats even suggested that the North and South set aside their differences, unleash their combined forces into Mexico, kick the Europeans out, and then claim Mexico as a new slaveholding state in order to reestablish political balance in Congress. For those who enjoy speculation regarding alternate history, the thought of an all-out fight between the Legion and the Confederate infantry is an interesting one.

Immediately after Appomattox, General Phil Sheridan, with over fifty thousand men, the vast majority African-American combat veterans from the Army of the Potomac, were dispatched to Texas. Sheridan made it clear that he desired nothing more than to cross into Mexico in order to pick a fight. Support and shelter were given to the followers of Juárez, and, from enclaves along the Texas border and from within the United States, the revolutionary forces reorganized and pressed back into the fight. Direct American intervention, though threatened, never materialized as Napoléon III finally backed down and abandoned Maximilian to his fate.

After Sheridan's forces started to demobilize in late 1865, a number of black Union army veterans crossed over the border, joined the Juárez forces, and fought against the French-Belgian-Austrian army. Some of these men can be viewed as mercenaries, others as patriots who had fought for their own freedom and now wanted to fight for the freedom of others. Several of these men became officers and stayed on in Mexico after the war.

The promise offered by wealthy Mexican exiles in Paris—that the peasantry of Mexico would fight to the death to be freed from the liberal Juárez so that they might again be enslaved by the upper class—proved to be a mad pipe dream that ultimately cost the lives of thousands of European troops. By 1866, Napoleon wanted out, and within the year nearly all European troops had evacuated Mexico. The Legion left nearly two thousand men buried in Mexico.

As for Camerone, the battle was all but forgotten for many years; the campaign in Mexico had witnessed a number of similar actions where small detachments were cut off and wiped out. According to tradition, Danjou's wooden hand was recovered from the battlefield by a relief column that arrived two days after the fight (though some records, which are bitterly denounced by Legion purists, claim that an Austrian soldier purchased the hand from a local farmer as a souvenir when passing through the area of the battle a couple of years later).

Perhaps if the battle had served an overall strategic purpose (as supporters of the Alamo assert with the claim that the heroic defense gained valuable time for the Texan army to form) or been part of a successful campaign, Camerone might have been nothing more than a footnote. However, the facts that the battle was senseless, that the campaign was illogical, and that the entire ill-fated war was doomed to failure catapulted Camerone to legendary status within the Legion and amongst mercenary forces in general.

April 30 is now the high holy feast day of the Legion. The account of the battle and the names of the fallen are read at the headquarters of the Legion in solemn ceremony, and Danjou's hand is paraded before the troops as a holy relic. It is not a relic of victory, or even of the heroic defense of a noble cause. Rather, it is a relic of defiance. It is the willingness to fight for no other reason than that it is your job and that honor requires you to stand against impossible odds that makes the Battle of Camerone the stuff of legend.

Twentieth-Century Mercenaries

As you have learned, the historical mercenary is for the most part a man of heroism and honor. But, as always, there are exceptions to the rule. Consider the brutal, often cowardly, Swabian troops in the pay of the First Minister of France, Cardinal Richelieu. These hired soldiers looted and tormented the populace of the directories given to the cardinal by King Louis XIII for the prosecution of the Thirty Years War. Later, their attempts to isolate and discredit the queen became notorious. Such is the stuff of romantic adventure novels, like the Dumas books about the Three Musketeers.

Then there were the hirelings who laid waste to half of Germany and part of Austria while in the pay of ambitious archdukes and dukes, sovereigns over their own petty principalities.

Akhenaton hired brutal foreign soldiers to "protect" the workers on the temple of Amon-Ra at Luxor. In a later dynasty, Numidian troops fought for Ramses II in Egypt against the Hittites. Darius the Great employed Greek mercenaries against their brother Greeks. Balearics and Aegeans served as mercenaries in the legions of Rome. Nubians fought for Claudius in Britain and broke the charge of the Picts.

Through the Dark Ages, the Renaissance, and the period of European colonialism, mercenary soldiers played major roles in the armies of Europe—so much so that St. Bernardino of Siena labeled them as "locusts who leap here and there." Consider the Hessians and Prussians who fought for King George III in the American Revolution. The fact that many of these men were conscripts who fought so that their sovereign could line his pockets with the coin of the realm—and who often lined their own pockets with stolen loot—left a bad taste in the mouths of most people.

Yet, in contrast, not all mercenaries were malicious in their prosecution of their commissions. Reflect on the youthful Marquis de Lafayette, Baron von Steuben, Thomas Conway, Johann Kalb, Tadeusz Kościuszko and Kazimierz Pulaski, who fought against the

British, on the American side, in the Revolutionary War. They are not the sole examples of good mercenaries, confined as they are to the past. Like these brave men, the modern mercenary is a bird of a far different plumage.

In large part, this is due to the quantum leaps taken in equipment, tactics, technology, and weapons since the turn of this century. Granted, there are still a lot of mercs who fight for money. Still others enter the fray for fame or because of a lust for adventure. Yet the number of those motivated by a cause or a sense of "righting a wrong" has grown and is still growing.

Some fight as individuals; others, in organized units, often in the armies of other nations. Again, not all of them are "good guys," nor is there a guarantee that all "lived happily ever after."

Anyone who has read *MERC: American Soldiers of Fortune*, by Jay Mallin and Robert K. Brown, is familiar with the authors' cogent argument for the use of the term *"Soldiers of fortune"* rather than "mercenaries." We feel that their proposition is a good one. In the following pages, we will introduce you to some of these modern soldiers of fortune.

Combat in a Strange New World

The French Foreign Legion in World War II

by Mark Roberts

PRIOR EVEN TO WORLD WAR I, THE MACHINE GUN BEGAN TO alter the mission and tactics of one of the world's biggest standing mercenary forces: the French Foreign Legion. At the conclusion of the "War to End All Wars," the airplane had proven itself, as had tanks, armored cars, rapid communication by field telephones, and, by the mid-1920s, the "wireless" radio-telephone. More adaptable than the formal, rigidly traditional French army, the Legion quickly embraced the changes.

In the twenties, the Legion served in the desert of Morocco, enforcing colonial fiat over the natives from sixty-six border outposts. Facing them were the impressive forces of Abd el-Krim and his Riffian tribesmen, who numbered around one hundred thousand effectives. The Riff War ended in victory for France on May 26, 1926. For the next thirteen years, the Legion bided its time, patrolling a chain of outposts and making a show of the French flag over the desert sands. Then, in 1938, when the clouds of war again gathered on the northern horizon, the French government found new employment for the Foreign Legion.

For a while, it appeared that the Legion would not do much

75

fighting in the impending conflict. The Abwehr (German Intelligence) had infiltrated the French government and found it wary of sending any of its units into action against the German army. A sort of compromise followed in which the French war ministry authorized the use of three "foreign" regiments, to be raised inside France and trained and led by Foreign Legion officers and noncoms. The units were sent to the Maginot line to serve alongside regular French regiments. Once there, they idled their time.

When the possibility of combat finally came, it was not in *la belle France* but in the frozen northlands. The civilian pundits of the French government decreed that the legionnaires would be part of an Anglo-French expedition sent to aid the Finns in their conflict with Russia. Before they could arrive, however, the Red Army crushed resistance in Finland, and the Germans invaded Denmark and Norway. The Legion was hastily rerouted to take part in the battle for the key Norwegian port of Narvik. German hatred of the Legion dated back to World War I, and their impending presence only served to exacerbate it.

When the German commander at Narvik, General Edouard Dietl, learned of the Legion's arrival, he exclaimed, "The Alpine *Chasseurs,* that's fine. But the Foreign Legion—those international thugs. The British should be ashamed to use them against us."

Although their combat experience had been gained in the desert, these "international thugs" performed excellently in the frozen north. They made a major contribution to the Allied retaking of Narvik and went on to chase the crack German mountain troops (*Alpen jaeger*) to within a thousand yards of the Swedish border. This astounding victory would turn out to be France's single triumph in the early years of World War II.

In a matter of weeks, a Nazi *blitzkrieg* stormed through France, Belgium, Luxembourg, and the Netherlands. Just returned from Norway, the Legion went into bivouac outside Brest and immediately made preparations to fight. Accounts of the time record that when a young French officer urged the commander of the Legion detachment to surrender and not "cause trouble for us," the Legion colonel shot him dead on the spot.

To the south, Legion regiments in the Maginot line fought valiantly while regular French units crumbled and demoralized soldiers fled in disarray. Equipped with substandard weapons, their training in defense of fortified positions woefully lacking, these brave men, infused with the Legion doctrine of death before surrender, stood against the German onslaught of tanks, artillery, and Stuka dive-bombers.

"Why fight?" whined demoralized French common soldiers.

"The Legion dies on its feet!" a Belgian legionnaire heatedly replied.

Time and again, the Legion drove back ferocious German assaults. When these subsided, the Legion launched counterattacks. The losses continued to mount.

Eventually, even the legionnaires were driven from the Maginot line and forced to fight the German advance in the hit-and-run style of the Riff War. Astonishingly, several hundred finally managed to get back to Africa. Others reached England, where they met their comrades who had survived the *blitzkreig* in Belgium. There they endured a formal review by an obscure French brigadier who had suddenly become the rallying point for those Frenchmen who wanted to continue the resistance against the Germans: Charles de Gaulle. Those who wished to return to Africa might do so, he informed them. The men who wanted to remain in England would join with the Free French and work for the day they would return to France.

With all of Gaul truly divided, the Legion found itself in similar straits. Some served as Free French; others labored under the banner of Vichy. This division would prove even more tragic when the two factions—each honoring the flag of France—faced off during the Allied effort to take Syria in 1941.

The British invaded Syria on June 8, 1941, from Iraq. Two brigades under the command of Henry Maitland Wilson formed the spearhead. In addition, the Seventh British Division moved up the coast from Haifa toward Beirut. The Thirteenth Demi-Brigade, part of the First Free French Division, crossed the Syrian border at Dera along with the Fifth Indian Brigade, and marched for Damascus.

Early on the morning of June 19, the Thirteenth joined in an assault on one of the peaks that commanded the approaches to the village of Kissoue, which constituted the key to the southern defenses of Damascus. It was a short, vicious battle that left thirteen legionnaires dead and several wounded. The same evening, the Thirteenth continued its advance on Damascus.

Ever present in the minds of officers and common soldiers alike was the fear that the First Free French Division would encounter the French Foreign Legion unit now fighting for Vichy France. It was not an idle fear. On June 20, legionnaire met legionnaire on the field of battle when advance elements of the Thirteenth Demi-Brigade encountered a unit of the *Seizième Étranger* in occupied Kadam, a southern suburb of Damascus.

On the eve of the decisive campaign, the Vichy legionnaires of the Seizième Étranger under command of Colonel Fernand Barre, presented arms to their brothers while buglers on both sides played the *Boudin*. In the morning, the bloody battle was on. The Vichy Seizième fought stoically, incurring 128 killed and 728 wounded. On June 21, thirteen days after the invasion of Syria began, Damascus fell to the Allies. Three weeks later, the Vichy commander surrendered. So, while the Legion could rightfully add another victory ribbon to its regimental flag, it also ironically added a smirch to its escutcheon.

The Legion went on to many more victories as part of the Allied forces. Serving as a spearhead combat unit, it did more than its share in raising from the ashes the prestige of the French army following the fall of France. The list of their major engagements is impressive: the Legion helped the British take the Sudan and Eritrea from the Italians; it stood firm at Bir Hakeim in Libya, blocking for over a month a drive on Tobruk by the legendary Erwin Rommel; they fought at El Alamein, in Tunisia, and in the Italian campaign. At last came that glorious day—August 16, 1944—when the Legion landed in southern France, to return the *tricolore* in honor and defend its homeland. When France was finally liberated, the Legion was there . . . and rightfully so, for it had almost single-handedly vindicated the honor of French arms.

A Meeting of Honor

Bir Hakeim, 1942

by Mark Roberts

Of all of the engagements in World War II, Bir Hakeim most exemplifies the courage, determination, and superiority at arms of the Free French units of the Foreign Legion. It is there that the Thirteenth Demi-Brigade earned its unchallenged place in history and in the hearts of loyal Frenchmen. The three-month-long campaign was called the Battle of El Gazala by the Germans. Its pivotal point was Bir Hakeim.

On January 20, 1942, Field Marshal Erwin Rommel attacked the British south of Benghazi in Libya. His Afrika Korps pierced the British positions in three separate columns and drove the survivors back toward Egypt. In an effort to stabilize the front, the British began to prepare a series of defensive positions that stretched inland from El Ghazala. The southernmost point of that line was anchored by a triangle of moles and pillboxes at a place called Bir Hakeim. Once this new line had been established, the decision was made for the Legion, as part of the "First Free French Brigade Group," to replace the 150th Indian Brigade at Bir Hakeim. Two battalions of the Thirteenth Demi-Brigade, commanded by Colonel Pierre Koenig, arrived on February 14. The men saw nothing more than a sand-blown plateau, adorned with a few scraps of pale vegetation that looked more dead than alive. An abandoned Italian desert outpost that stood beside a dry well at the juncture of a number of desert tracks, Bir Hakeim presented a depressing vista. Combined with the blistering heat of day and frigid nights of wind-driven sandstorms, it was enough to make the strongest suicidal—a condition written about by several survivors.

But other concerns took priority with the officers and noncoms of the French Foreign Legion. What remained of the so-called defenses was in such poor condition that it would be impossible to hold out against determined attack of camel-riding Berber tribesmen, let alone the Afrika Korps. It took three months for the 957 legionnaires to improve the fortifications. They reinforced bunkers with stone and sandbags, laid mine fields, and practiced detached motorized recon patrols, known as "Jock columns" after the British general Jock Campbell.

On May 26, Rommel attacked the Allies in earnest. He feinted a frontal assault at the center of the Gazala line while swinging his main force in a southward arc to outflank the British positions . . . and ran into Bir Hakeim. An assault by Italian tanks early on the morning of May 27 met with disaster. Stopped cold by the Legion, the Italians lost thirty-two tanks with ninety-one prisoners taken.

"All the men and especially the anti-tank [gunners] were terrific," Lieutenant Gabriel de Sairigne wrote in his diary. So many tanks were abandoned, he wrote, that several German and Italian trucks drove into the French position, believing it to be an Italian fortress.

Encouraged by this victory and the evident confusion of the enemy forces, Colonel Koenig decided to run guerrilla-style strike-and-withdraw raids against Rommel's overextended supply lines around Bir Hakeim. Within a few days, the Axis attack ran out of impetus, and an Allied victory appeared likely. And then, on May 31, the Italians breached the British lines to the north of Bir Hakeim.

Immediately, the Panzerarmee of Erwin Rommel moved to widen this gap. By June 2, Bir Hakeim became an island of resistance in a rising tide of advancing enemy forces. In retrospect, it appears that Rommel had become obsessed with Bir

Hakeim. The First Free French, and their British allies led by Colonel Koenig, had stopped the Afrika Korps cold on five occasions in the last days of May. Determined not to leave this hindrance at his rear, Rommel decided to reduce the bastion to rubble if necessary. To this end, Rommel directed that a message be delivered to Koenig promising honorable treatment of the Free French as "official combatants." This was important because Germany was no longer at war with France and the legionnaires of the Thirteenth Demi-Brigade could be considered as "irregulars," not subject to protection under the Geneva Convention. Koenig did not receive the message, but he did hear from two Italian officers who came into camp under flags of truce on June 3 and 5 to demand the surrender of the French. They left with Koenig's cold refusal.

Immediately thereafter, Rommel launched what he hoped would be the final assault on Bir Hakeim, perhaps in part because he believed there were abundant supplies and water within the compound, items that were in short supply for the Panzerarmee. The initial German assault was fiercely repulsed, as were the second and third. Rommel appealed to the Luftwaffe for maximum effort. Over the next several days, the beleaguered legionnaires were under constant bombardment from German artillery and bombers. The result was the loss of fifty-seven German aircraft.

From the outset, Rommel had greatly underestimated Bir Hakeim. It would prove a costly error. By the eighth of June, Rommel had made no appreciable advance. He ordered an increase in artillery and air bombardment, incorporating occasional probes with tanks and infantry. On the ninth, a German attack threatened to penetrate the southern defenses at Bir Hakeim. It was repulsed at the last minute by a counterattack led by half-tracks. Water and munitions were dangerously low, and Rommel showed no sign of ending his tenacious attack.

The tenth dawned to a hellish artillery barrage. Far more serious to Koenig was the improved counter-battery fire of the Germans. It threatened to curtail the most effective part of his defense by preventing his own guns from firing. A resolute German attack came at three that afternoon. Not only did the Germans press against the weakened southern face of the camp, they also threatened the scarp to the northwest. *Panzergrenadiers* poured over the French pillboxes, taking several legionnaires prisoner before being repulsed.

To Colonel Koenig, the end had come. Out of water and ammunition for the 75mm cannon, he ordered a breakout. Each battalion was given detailed orders on its role in the effort, but there was no time to organize the intended movements. As a result, even under the cover of darkness, the breakout rapidly deteriorated into a rout. The legionnaires and others in the garrison charged the German and Italian positions with half-tracks, their Bren guns blazing. The Germans illuminated the black desert sky with flares while tracer rounds wove a spiderweb of death over the sandy hills. Koenig's escape soon proved to be the most costly engagement of the entire battle.

During the siege, the Legion had lost only fourteen dead and seventeen wounded. In contrast, eleven legionnaires were killed in the breakout, with thirty-two wounded and thirty-seven known to have been taken prisoner. One hundred fifty-two men were listed as unaccounted for.

Bir Hakeim was unquestionably the high point in the history of the Thirteenth Demi-Brigade, and for the Legion in World War II. Later, Radio Londres (Radio London), the Gaullist voice in exile, called Bir Hakeim a "meeting of honor" and a symbol of the spirit of Free French patriots, comparable to Verdun in the First World War.

The German *blitzkrieg* had been unstoppable, and the fall of the Maginot line inevitable, given the high mobility of modern warfare. Despite their early failures, the performance of the Thirteenth Demi-Brigade of the *Legion étrangère* was exemplary. Their courage and tenacity in the campaigns cited earlier made a major contribution to the Allied successes in the North African campaign, in Italy, and in France itself. Even before hostilities concluded, a new respect existed among professional military men regarding the Foreign Legion.

In the years following World War II, the ranks of the French Foreign Legion were swelled by former members of the Waffen SS. For the record, the soldiers of the Waffen SS *were not* depraved concentration camp guards. Rather, they were competent, courageous, highly trained, elite combat troops who served with distinction on the eastern front. They should not be confused with the Siecherheitdienst (the SD or Tottenkopf Brigaden—Death's Head Brigades), who indeed *were* concentration camp guards and extermination squads. So different were these two units, that calling a Waffen SS soldier to his face a member of the SD was to invite, at best, severe physical punishment and, at worst, a fatal encounter.

These Waffen SS soldiers served the Foreign Legion well, with courage and determination. After a change in policy that allowed foreigners to become officers in the Legion, many gained commissioned rank, although none would rise above captain. They fought in Chad, French Indochina, Zaire, and Algiers.

The Lost Cause

Dien Bien Phu, 1953

by William R. Forstchen

WHEN IT COMES TO THE FRENCH MILITARY, THERE SEEMS, AT times, to be a perverse compulsion to seek out defeat—and for the French Foreign Legion in particular to embrace this compulsion and then go blindly to their doom. Most military systems tend to pick the date of a glorious victory as their most holy of feast days, but the Legion celebrates the Battle of Camerone, a disastrous defeat in a senseless war. At least at Camerone, though, the men of the Legion were not aware that they were heading into a trap. At Dien Bien Phu, the trap was of their own making—and, lemminglike, the French army raced to their annihilation.

The wars of Indochina were the two great defeats of Western democracies in the post–World War II era. Both conflicts evolved out of miscalculation, arrogance, and hubris. For both the French and the Americans, the wars caused a bitter divide at home, a generation of self-doubt afterward, and a sense of betrayal within the military establishment. One could argue, though, that if the first war had been averted or, at the very least, fought intelligently, the second debacle could have been avoided.

The origins of the French war in Indochina are still a bitter

84

source of historical controversy but in general can be traced to the catastrophic collapse of France to the German invasion of 1940. Nearly all French colonies, including Indochina, aligned themselves with the Fascist Vichy government. This policy continued until it became obvious that the other side was going to win. Thus, in 1941, when the Japanese moved to occupy Indochina, the French administrators found themselves occupied by a nation that was, indirectly at least, an ally. This move, and the resulting oil embargo imposed by the United States as a response, set the clock ticking for the war between Japan and America.

Throughout four years of occupation, the French openly cooperated with their new Japanese overlords, except for an abortive coup in the last months of the war. On the other side, American OSS agents gave support to the Vietnamese nationalist leader Ho Chi Min, and it was the stated policy of the Roosevelt administration that French Indochina should be free of foreign rule once the war ended, this policy being a response in large part to French collaboration with the Japanese in the East.

After the collapse of Japan at the end of World War II, there was a brief period of British occupation and control that lasted for several weeks until forces of the new de Gaulle–led French government landed in order to take control. Here was the great ironic turning point that set the stage for a thirty-year war. Ho, supported by his OSS allies, declared a free Indochina. The new Truman administration, bowing to French nationalistic pressure, moved to a neutral stance. Most ironic of all, the French actually rearmed Japanese POWs held in Indochina and used them to reestablish "control." This was a direct slap in the face to Vietnamese patriots who had resisted the Japanese for four bitter years. Within a year, the French had moved to eliminate Ho's Vietminh, thus negating a brief period of semi-autonomous rule—and negating as well a free election that had put Ho in control of a legitimate coalition government.

By 1949, Indochina was ablaze in a war of national liberation centered primarily in the Tonkin region, an area that would later be known as North Vietnam. Ho, having lost American support, increasingly turned to the old traditional enemy, the Chinese, for logistical support. Since China was now Maoist, the French, in turn, cast their war not as an attempt to hold onto a colony, but rather as a fight against Communism. This stance duped the American government and public opinion into support for the French effort.

For those familiar with the American campaign in Indochina and unfamiliar with the French effort, one can find a number of parallels. The beginnings of both saw a tendency to be dismissive of the staying power of the enemy, a misdirected effort of attempting to apply "heavy" World War II–style tactics, a growing demoralization and disenchantment by troops who felt that the enemy was not fighting "fairly" and that public opinion at home had abandoned them, and finally the seeking of a negotiated way out while, at the same time, continuing to fight an enemy who merely had to hang on in order to win.

This failed French strategy reached its bloody climax in the debacle at Dien Bien Phu. By the middle of 1953, French forces had already lost control of most of the countryside in the Tonkin region and were faced with a growing effort by the Vietminh to push their war of liberation into the rest of Indochina, i.e., the regions later known as Laos, Cambodia, and South Vietnam. Since the French were unable to increase the manpower commitment that had already reached several hundred thousand, their tactics had evolved to the development of airstrip bases, identical to the later American "fire base" system, and fortified zones from which attempts would be made to pacify the surrounding countryside. From these defensive bases, troops would move into the countryside in an attempt to come to grips with the enemy and annihilate him, but, increasingly, the fortified zones were armed encampments where everything beyond the wire was enemy territory.

Dien Bien Phu, a base established early in the war, sat astride the main access route between the Tonkin region and northern Laos. Abandoned early by the French, it was reoccupied late in the fall of 1953. Out of this occupation, there evolved the strategy of using it as bait to lure the Vietminh into a climactic showdown and battle of attrition.

The French high command believed that the establishment of a major base at Dien Bien Phu would force Ho and his already famous field commander Giap to abandon their tactics of evasion and mount a traditional full-scale assault. The reasoning behind this was that the Vietminh absolutely needed the road that passed through Dien Bien Phu and that they would fall for the bait of a force that appeared to be under-strength but in fact wasn't. Once the forces were engaged, superior French artillery, relentless air strikes, and rapid air-lifting of additional troops into the fight would annihilate the Vietminh forces, deal a major psychological blow to the enemy, and turn the tide of the war.

The only problem was that every calculation on the French part was based on either ignorance or arrogance—or, in some cases, downright stupidity. The Vietminh had fought for years without need of major roads, having already mastered the transport of vast amounts of supplies without trucks or roads. If a required route was interdicted, they simply cut another one, concealed under the jungle canopy. This lesson would be lost during the American multibillion-dollar effort to bomb the "Ho Chi Minh trail," approaching the task as if attempting to knock out Hitler's *autobahn.*

As for the bait of a supposedly understrength French force that was not, the reality was that the force was indeed under-strength, with less than half the numbers needed to hold the perimeter of fortifications that ringed the valley. Beyond that, the defensive perimeter was laid out on the valley floor, with higher ground—within artillery range—looking down on the position. Dien Bien Phu was the bottom of a sack with insufficient numbers inside it to keep the drawstring from being pulled shut. The illogic of this insane position was explained away with the statement that the Vietminh didn't know how to use artillery and had little, if any, heavy ordnance in their possession.

As to the fortifications, no attempt was made to camouflage them—in fact, the forest was completely cut away so that all positions stood out clearly, in order to establish fields of fire. Unfortunately for the French, these open fields also offered an excellent opportunity for enemy forces in the surrounding mountains to pinpoint every one of their targets and to walk artillery fire in. Revetments, sandbagging, and bunker building were at a minimum, and the French artillery was fully exposed, with polished gun barrels jutting up like flagpoles.

The airfield was fully exposed as well and easily within

artillery range of the nearby mountains—but the French high command felt that this at worst would be a temporary problem, for once the Vietminh had shown their hand, artillery and air strikes would pin the enemy while mobile forces maneuvered for the kill.

Giap gleefully rose to the challenge. The Vietminh did own artillery, mostly 105mm American-made howitzers captured by the Chinese in Korea, along with 120mm mortars. Close to a hundred thousand labor troops were marshaled to build well-camouflaged roads into the region; the artillery was then broken down and literally carried, piece by piece, over the rugged terrain along with thousands of shells. As Giap's forces infiltrated the region, French patrols found it increasingly costly to move outside the perimeter; insanely, the French decided to stop nearly all forward patrolling as too dangerous, the logic being that they knew the Vietminh were coming, so let them come.

As for the Legion, they were heavily committed to Dien Bien Phu. Since the start of the Indochina war, Legion troops had participated in nearly every major action, and there were more than twenty thousand legionnaires in the field. The Legion of this post–World War II period was a fascinating polyglot of troops. Many of them were soldiers who had come of age during the Second World War and knew no other profession but arms. There was a liberal sprinkling of Czechs, Romanians, Poles, and Russians as well as troops from French Algiers and Morocco, and even some Vietnamese. Over seven thousand Germans served in the ranks as well, their past forgotten once they had taken the oath.

At Dien Bien Phu, the legion committed six regiments, one-third of the total force of sixteen thousand men. The most exposed position was strong point Beatrice, located on a small hill a mile and a half away from the main perimeter encircling the airfield. The purpose of Beatrice was to deny the Vietminh a firing position north of the airstrip, but it lacked tactical support and a secured connection back to the main base. It was held by a battalion of only 450 men of the Legion.

On March 13, 1954, Giap played his first card. Having deployed his troops on the highlands surrounding the valley, he had nearly fifty thousand men in place. The Legion troops, somewhat more battle-savvy than the other forces in the valley, knew that the storm was coming but were nevertheless caught completely unprepared when, early in the afternoon, a virtual hurricane of artillery fire slammed into Beatrice. Within several hours, the fortress was a shambles, bunkers collapsed, wire entanglements pierced, and the battalion command post taken out by a direct hit. This alone showed the ill-prepared nature of the defense, with bunkers unable to withstand a hit from a 105mm shell. With the lack of camouflage, the Vietminh on the encircling hills simply had to drop their fire on the obvious targets.

Thousands of Vietminh swarmed into the position in wave after wave of bloody suicidal charges. Meanwhile, back at the main base a mile and a half away, all attempts at support went awry. Within minutes after the opening of the battle, the airfield was all but inoperable as mortar and artillery fire slammed into the strip, taking out parked aircraft that did not even have adequate revetments.

French artillery batteries, their guns exposed, were soon under a hail of counter battery fire, the Vietminh guns so well concealed that no targets were visible for reply. Radio communication to Beatrice was hampered by the loss of the battalion headquarters, and it was soon impossible to offer an effective counterstrike since the Vietminh were already through the wire. Those planes that tried to scramble were bracketed by deadly antiaircraft fire, yet another weapon the Vietminh were not suppose to own. In the ensuing weeks, pilots who were combat veterans of World War II would claim that the antiaircraft fire was far more deadly than anything they had encountered over Germany. By the end of the first day, the airstrip was out of action, severing the only supply line for the French. Giap had, within the first hour, completely destroyed the entire French battle plan.

The last communiqué from Beatrice announced that the base was falling and called for fire to be dropped in on top of the position. Only a handful of legionnaires managed to cut their way out to safety. By dawn the following morning, the Vietminh held Beatrice and, with it, a clear and open field of fire straight down onto the airstrip and the other strong points that ringed the main position. Within two days, two other outlying posts, Gabrielle and Anne-Marie, fell to the same type of assault. The Vietminh were now firmly dug in on high ground looking straight down at the main camp.

Morale in the main fortress collapsed, the rest of the garrison expecting annihilation in a matter of hours—but the attack did not materialize, for Giap had suffered grievous loses in the three assaults that had also consumed most of his artillery ammunition. Though the Vietminh supply system was a miracle of tenacious ingenuity, it was nevertheless slow and limited. Individual artillery rounds had to be backpacked across hundreds of miles of rugged terrain. As for manpower, Giap was forced to draw on many of his logistical support troops to fill out the ranks.

Unfortunately for the French, their high command remained paralyzed and did nothing to exploit the brief hiatus. This was the moment for the stinging counterstrike that had been the foundation of the battle plan: the use of a massive barrage of air and artillery strikes to counterblow the Vietminh, followed up by direct infantry assault. Or if the perception was that the battle was already lost, a means to evacuate should have been developed and executed. The French high command did neither.

As for supplies, the garrison needed between 150 and 200 tons a day. But with the airstrip shut down, the French were reduced to parachute drops. On average, 120 tons a day were dropped, of which roughly 100 tons fell into the camp. So, indirectly, the French were helping to supply the Vietminh as well. In addition, desertion started to take its toll, with thousands of French colonial troops breaking out of the camp and moving into nearby caves. They became such a problem, racing both the French and the Vietminh to recover supplies that fell outside the wire, that for a while the French considered striking to knock them out as well.

During the two-week slowdown, Giap adopted the ancient tactic of siege lines. Every night, Vietminh sappers labored to ring the camp and then push traversing lines closer to the French position. Again, the high command was paralyzed. When position Isabelle, to the south of the main camp, was cut, legionnaires of the *Premier* BEP counterassaulted, annihilating a battalion of Vietminh but losing over 150 dead and another 70 wounded. The ratio of dead to wounded alone demonstrates the ferocity of the fight. Such casualties so intimidated the high command that further offensive operations were curtailed. The garrison of Dien Bien Phu was now reduced to the position of a scared rabbit watching as the serpent gradually encircled and started to squeeze.

On March 30, Giap resumed offensive operations. Battalions of Vietminh troops rose out of the approach trenches without warning and stormed the fortresses of Eliane and Dominique, which were a little more than a half mile to the east of the airstrip. The attack hit with such speed and surprise that by the time defensive artillery fire was called in, the Vietminh were already inside the wire and on top of the French positions. A Legion mortar company was totally annihilated. The Algerian troops who made up the majority of the defenders in these two positions broke, many of them fleeing outside the compound to the hidden caves where thousands of deserters already lingered.

Vicious counterattacks by Legion paratroopers finally retook part of Eliane and all of Dominique, but with heavy casualties for both sides. Giap finally stopped the battle and pulled his forces back. This was a crucial moment in the fight, not unlike the situation with Tet in 1968. The Vietminh had gained psychological mastery of the field and the political front, but at that particular moment they were tottering on the edge of losing the fight due to massive casualties inflicted by the bitter resistance offered primarily by Legion troops. If the French had concentrated forces outside Dien Bien Phu and moved aggressively to lift the siege, it might have been a turning point, since Giap had lost nearly thirty thousand men by this time and was forced to pull up cadres of young recruits who had yet to be trained.

The French, however, were morally drained and perceived the fight now in purely defensive terms. There was, however, a political development that would have a profound impact on the future: the French turned to America for direct intervention. A French proposal, which was tentatively accepted by Eisenhower, called for the United States to launch massive air strikes against the surrounding Vietminh forces from American carriers already positioned off Hanoi. There was even talk of employing tactical nuclear weapons. Eisenhower, however, backed away when senior members of Congress, led by Lyndon Johnson, offered little support for the scheme.

As for the willpower of the French government to counter-strike on their own and lift the siege, talks were already pending in Geneva between the French and the Vietminh, and the decision was reached to simply maintain the status quo on the battlefront. As was the case with America in the 1970s, negotiating a way out became the policy; thus, the forces trapped in the valley were abandoned to their fate by the country that had sent them there.

Throughout April, Giap re-marshaled his forces, pulling in reinforcements and continuing the painstaking task of rebuilding his supplies, a job that became increasingly easier as his trenching system tightened the noose and more and more air-dropped supplies landed within his lines.

On April 9, the *Deuxième* BEP of the Legion went through the harrowing experience of airdropping in on the base while under antiaircraft fire. They immediately became part of a renewed fight for Eliane, which they took. Unfortunately, the survivors of that assault were all but annihilated when they were thrown into an attack on fortress Huguette, which was swarmed under on April 23 with only a few isolated outposts hanging on. Huguette was retained by the ever-entrenching Vietminh, and by the end of April the airfield was cut and occupied. Complicating the defense was the advent of the spring monsoons, which turned the entire battlefield into a soupy quagmire, collapsing many of the ill-prepared French positions.

By the first of May, the end was in sight. Well over 75 percent of the garrison was dead, wounded, or captured. Now started one of the truly bizarre aspects of the siege—the airdropping of Legion reinforcements. As if mesmerized by the glory of heroic defeat, Legion battalions outside Dien Bien Phu started to form volunteer battle groups that were airdropped in at night. At this point, the perimeter was so tight that many floated down into Vietminh positions and were dispatched on the spot, and the few who did make it down inside the wire were often cut apart before they could find safety. Yet still they came, one battalion proudly announcing that it had sent over a hundred men into certain death. It is as if the memory of Camerone and its yearly celebration had created a cult within the ranks of the Legion, compelling both enlisted men and officers to fulfill a pact with death.

By May 4, the few surviving Legion paratroopers within the Huguette perimeter were annihilated. Three days later, the final attacks swarmed in on the remaining defensive positions around Claudine and Isabelle, isolated outposts several miles to the south. The commander sent out a dramatic final message declaring that they would never surrender and would fight to the last man. Several hours later, he was taken prisoner in his dress uniform. The battle of Dien Bien Phu was over and, with it, the French occupation of Indochina.

Like Tet, this engagement could actually be claimed as a tactical victory for the French. Giap had won a Pyrrhic battle that had bled his army white, as he would at Hue fourteen years later. The casualties, however, were not the point; it was the psychological victory that counted. Elite French forces had been cut off and annihilated; the morale of the army collapsed, and the government's desire to continue the struggle evaporated. The French government negotiated a cease fire and abandoned Indochina.

Within the year, French Indochina would break into four independent countries: Laos, Cambodia, South Vietnam, and North Vietnam. In spite of the losses, Dien Bien Phu had been the victory sought by Ho and Giap.

As for the prisoners, more died on the infamous death march to the prison camps and in the subsequent months of captivity than in the actual fight. To this day, France, like America, is scarred by the fact that thousands who were taken alive never came home, and haunted by rumors that there are men still being held.

Across eight years of the first Indochina war, the Legion deployed more than twenty thousand officers and enlisted men, and sustained more than ten thousand casualties—losses higher than those they suffered in the First or Second World War.

The twin debacles that the Legion experienced in the 1950s, in Indochina and later in Algiers, shook the much-vaunted band to their core. It would be more than a generation before the Legion recovered its old esprit and heroic aura. Dien Bien Phu was the twentieth-century Camerone of the Legion, but it was a battle without glory—which is, after all, the true reality of war.

Mercenary Knight of the African Skies

Count Carl Gustav von Rosen (1909–1974)

by Mark Roberts

BORN IN 1909, THE SON OF A WORLD-RENOWNED ADVEN-
turer, Carl Gustav von Rosen led a life full of jeopardy. He
was no doubt inspired by events that he witnessed early in
life; at the age of eleven, for example, Carl Gustav was present
in the family castle at Rockelstad, Sweden, when his father
was flown home through a ferocious snowstorm by a World
War I flying ace—Herman Göring. Carl Gustav was to meet
Göring again, as we shall see later in this account.

Young von Rosen had a rather tempestuous childhood and
youth. Around five years after Göring's visit to Rockelstad,
von Rosen managed to get himself thrown out of a very proper
private school for various rules violations, including fighting.
This precipitated a fistfight with his father. Embittered, the
young man left home. Still in his teens, he became a motorboat
racer. When the thrills became routine, he turned to flying.

He had found his home. By the time he turned twenty-three,
he had reconciled with his father and become an outstanding
pilot, having achieved one of the first five certificates issued
in Sweden for flying instructors. He began to perform aero-

batics in a single-engine aircraft, a Heinkel, over astonished audiences in the folk parks in Swedish rural centers and the larger towns. Von Rosen and his partners developed a spectacular finale for their air shows. It revolved around a mock battle with an "enemy," consisting of his assistants on the ground. Von Rosen fired a battery of practice rockets from racks mounted on his airplane. Following the final pass, he was "shot down" by blanks fired from simulated antiaircraft guns. Von Rosen would throw his Heinkel into a spin, cut the engine, and glide down with wobbling wings, as though he were about to crash, then glide down until he was out of sight of the crowd, restart the engine, and fly off to land at a distant field. The spectators loved it. Von Rosen continued his air shows until 1935.

In that year, while still working the park circuit, von Rosen became aware of the terrible losses incurred by the Ethiopians during the brutal invasion of Mussolini's Fascist army. At a lecture he attended, von Rosen became so incensed over the plight of the Ethiopians that he immediately volunteered to go to Ethiopia to serve in the mountains at field hospitals operated by the Swedish Red Cross.

In no time, he was piloting a small Fokker between the mist-enclosed peaks of Ethiopia, landing in clearings where primitive tribesmen roamed at will. His mission: to ferry medicines and doctors to the beleaguered defenders.

On one such flight, von Rosen came under fire by Italian antiaircraft and was barely able to escape destruction by employing his old air-circus stunt. He cut his engine and pretended to plummet out of control until well out of sight behind a rocky jungle crag, then sped away at treetop level. Shortly after his clever escape, von Rosen's father died and the young man became Count Carl Gustav von Rosen.

When the Soviet Union invaded Finland in 1939, von Rosen again answered the call. He first raised money in Sweden to purchase two fighter planes and an old DC-2, which he converted into a bomber. The payload consisted of two 500-kilo bombs and four 100-kilo bombs. Von Rosen piloted his makeshift bomber for Finland throughout the punishingly cold Winter War. He probed deeply into Russian territory in nearly impossible weather to bomb the Karelian front and the railway at Murmansk. The war soon ended with a Russian victory. Privately bitter over the defeat of the brave Finns and angry at the brutal oppression introduced by the Soviets, von Rosen decided to return to Holland to seek a job at KLM, a commercial airline. The year was 1940.

On the way, he passed through Germany. It happened to be on the eve of Hitler's *blitzkrieg* into the Low Countries. The German air marshal Göring was delighted when von Rosen stopped off in Berlin for a visit. That evening, over brandy and cigars, Göring advised strongly against von Rosen's proceeding to Holland just then, although he refrained from giving a reason. Von Rosen didn't listen.

Four days after his return to Amsterdam, von Rosen awoke to find the sky filled with Luftwaffe aircraft. Donnier transports disgorged paratroopers into the cerulean sky. Stuka dive-bombers screamed in their vertical dives. The import of Göring's vague hints suddenly became painfully clear.

A battle raged around Schiphol Airport, and von Rosen enlisted the help of a Dutch radio operator to get a KLM DC-3 out of a hangar and away from the area of conflict. After they loaded the plane with important Dutch military and state papers, von Rosen and the chief pilot for KLM flew the DC-3 out to England, straight through a blinding curtain of German antiaircraft fire. Below them, Holland fell to the Nazis.

When they reached England, the British authorities were overjoyed to receive them—until, that is, they interviewed von Rosen, and he told them he had stayed with Göring.

When they overcame their astonishment, the British arrested von Rosen and took him to London. There he was intensely interrogated and given the usual roughing-up. Fortunately, a British official who had known him in Ethiopia learned what was happening and sorted matters out.

Von Rosen returned to Sweden by Finnish freighter, but he longed for adventure. By 1960, he was flying supplies into Léopoldville, Congo, in support of the United Nations contingent sent to bring an end to the secession of Katanga province under Moise Tsombe. His closest scrape with danger came when, as chief of Congo operations, von Rosen should have been at the controls of the aircraft that was to take United Nations Secretary General Dag Hammarskjöld to a meeting with Tsombe at Ndola, Northern Rhodesia. Seven miles short of the airfield at Ndola, the aircraft crashed under what the U.N. called mysterious circumstances. Everyone aboard was killed.

When the Katangan venture collapsed, von Rosen returned to Sweden. Then, in May 1967, Biafra split from Nigeria, and both sides began to prepare for war. By October, the situation had become critical.

Nigerian troops stormed through Biafran defenses and laid waste to the land, slaughtering women and children and blockading all ground sources for supplies. News of the atrocities grew more intense through the fall and winter. Spring, too, saw little hope for the Biafrans. Although the government employed hundreds of European mercenaries to train and lead their native troops, they could not make the least headway against the army of Nigeria.

Carl Gustav von Rosen had settled down to life as a senior pilot for Transair. After flying supplies for United Nations troops during the war in Congo, he had become disillusioned with these shoddy little foreign wars. He swore never again to become involved in the internecine squabbles of the emerging African states. Yet, as the year wore on, von Rosen could not prevent the growing anger that boiled within him at news of the slaughter and starvation in Biafra, or his outrage over the contrivances of the unethical gunrunners who profited from all this human misery. In early August 1968, von Rosen found his cause.

Early one morning in August, an unusual deputation arrived in the offices of Transair. They introduced themselves as representatives of a German branch of Caritas, an international Catholic relief organization. Over coffee, they negotiated to charter a cargo aircraft to fly food and medicine to the beseiged Biafrans. The Transair director, familiar with his employee's past African experiences, summoned Carl Gustav von Rosen.

Although he was reluctant at first, von Rosen's private agonies over the inhuman conditions endured by the Biafrans swayed him. Transair provided Caritas with a DC-7 piloted by von Rosen. Shortly prior to takeoff, one of the Germans came to him. "File a flight plan for Lisbon. We will take on the supplies there."

"And from there?" von Rosen asked.

A bleak smile creased the German's face. "You will be told when it is necessary for you to know."

On the final leg, von Rosen flew a huge cargo of relief supplies to the Portuguese island of São Tomé. There he learned that the Nigerian antiaircraft defenses had been reinforced to the point that even the most daring gunrunners would not risk flying into Biafra. In fact, no supply planes had flown there from São Tomé in nearly a week. The Caritas officials pleaded with von Rosen to carry his cargo all the way in.

"We have come so far, Herr von Rosen. Please understand, the people of Biafra are starving. They are dying in misery. There is no medicine. The sick and the wounded are left to their unbearable pain. We are not flying in guns and ammunition. The only soldiers we aid are the wounded. We can only . . . pray that you will accept the challenge."

Von Rosen, whose handpicked crew had participated in the Congo operation, could not resist the temptation.

The Transair crew received little help from the São Tomé blockade-running pilots, who resented the sudden presence of upstart, amateur competitors who would dare to challenge the Nigerian defenses for nothing more than their paltry Transair wages.

"It was in their commercial interest that we did not fly," von Rosen explained later, "and at least one description of a landing strip was totally false. If we had followed that, we would have ended up in catastrophe."

To make their situation more hazardous, the corrupt gunrunners refused to give von Rosen the code word needed for night landings. Unfamiliar with the terrain, the Transair crew would have to go in during daylight, making them vulnerable not only to ground fire but also to the swarm of Nigerian MiGs that would be scrambled when they were discovered. But von Rosen had no choice. So, on the morning of August 13, 1968, the DC-7 took off from São Tomé. Fully loaded with precious medical supplies and cartons of nonperishable food, the converted airliner ignored the usual takeoff pattern, climbing out to an altitude of only thirty feet off the lapping waves of the ocean. Their destination: Uli, Biafra. Von Rosen and his co-pilot, Pauli, fought the controls and trim wheel, seeking a happy attitude that would let the aircraft partly fly itself. They had a roughly seven-hundred-mile one-way trip ahead. Pauli later recalled the strained nature of their in-flight conversation:

"We've been promised a refueling at Uli."

Von Rosen cut a glance to his right. " 'Promised' *is the operative word, Pauli. With all the Biafrans are short of, or out of, who says they have aviation fuel?"*

"We're running on minimis as it is. If we have to fly back without topping off, we'll be gulping fumes when we turn final at São Tomé."

"Right now let's concentrate on keeping below the Nigerian radar horizon. And pray we don't encounter any of their patrol boats."

Their sporadic conversation from that point drifted to Sweden and home. *Pauli had a family. His wife did not know why he had volunteered for this mission. For that matter, he didn't, either. The crew chief/engineer brought them coffee and sandwiches. The DC-7 droned on. Silver shafts flared from the Plexiglas windshield as sunlight ricocheted from the choppy surface of the South Atlantic. Finally, the aircraft cleared the low jungle coast, and the undulating wave tops gave way to the verdant canopy of rain forest.*

"We did it," echoed in the headphones clamped to the ears of von Rosen. *The crew knew they had evaded the Nigerian defenses.*

Traversing the jungle took less time than von Rosen had expected. They were almost on top of their destination before the pilot realized it. Suddenly the threshold of the small Uli runway flashed large in the windshield. Thinking fast, von Rosen abruptly hauled up on the yoke to reveal to defenders that the incoming aircraft was a DC-7 cargo plane, not a bomber. After a critical three seconds or so, when the Biafran troops did not open fire, von Rosen decided to land. He made another turn around the pattern and lined up.

When the wheels of the DC-7 struck smoke from the runway, a decrepit jeep and two aged Indian motorcycles broke cover and raced for the active runway. Von Rosen applied breaks and feathered the props. The bikes and the jeep formed a "follow me" column and led the way to a taxi strip. Before the last propeller stopped turning, soldiers and civilian men, women, and children streamed onto the landing field and converged on the ramp.

Cheers rose when the wide cargo door opened. Von Rosen watched while hardened Biafran troopers broke into tears when they saw the bounty of relief supplies aboard the DC-7. Unloading began at once. Silently, von Rosen and his crew watched it all. None of them remained unmoved. Finally, von Rosen spoke.

"I'm going to stay here with our German friend and supervise the distribution of the supplies. Pauli, take the airplane back for another load. Use the same route we did coming in. It seems the Nigerians do not have any soldiers or heavy weapons through there."

The crew did as ordered, and when they left, they had the proper landing codes. Upon their return, unscathed, they brought a second load of medical supplies and bags of rice, meal, and beans. From then on, von Rosen and other crews flew dozens of missions through the new corridor plotted by the Transair mercenary. They could do so without fear of being shot down by those they came to aid, or being intercepted by Nigerian gunfire or MiG jets.

Although von Rosen had broken the Nigerian blockade, he soon realized that it was only a temporary, and inadequate, solution to Biafra's suffering. Over the days and nights of the supply missions, he developed a fantastic project—one that far surpassed the mere transportation of foodstuffs and medical supplies. It was the fate of the starving Biafran children, which he had witnessed firsthand, that jelled his venturing.

"I soon realized," the idealistic Swede would later observe, "that every priest, every doctor, every black and white man in Biafra was praying for arms and ammunition before food, because the idea of feeding children only to have them massacred later by cannon fire from Saladin armored cars or MiGs doesn't make sense." His plan, von Rosen explained, "was not to add fuel to the war but to keep the sophisticated war machine that the Nigerians had at their command away from the little children."

Before he would make such a precipitous move, von Rosen had to make certain there was no other way. He flew to Ethiopia to discuss it with his old friend and benefactor, Emperor Haile Selassie. Then he journeyed to New York in an attempt to see U.N. Secretary General U Thant. That effort proved fruitless.

Count von Rosen made a dizzying spin around the world in a doomed effort to rally support for humanitarian aid for Biafra on a broad-based, wholesale scale. Returning to the ravaged country shortly before Christmas in 1968, he came back to even worse news than that which he had taken on his quest.

The Nigerians had recently moved into positions from which they could even further restrict the flow of weapons to Biafra—and wipe out the airstrip at Uli as well. There was no time to waste. Quickly, he shared the basics of his plan with the disparing Biafran officials and hurried off to Sweden.

He made directly for Malmö. Von Rosen's son, Eric, worked at the Malmö Flygindustri, an aircraft manufacturing firm that was a subsidiary of the huge Swedish industrial combine, Saab. Several years before, Eric had prevailed upon his father to teach him to fly. The aircraft that provided flight instructions was a small, two-seater, propeller-driven light airplane produced by the company as a sport plane. It was designated the MFI-9B. Its maneuverability had impressed von Rosen, as had sketches he had seen of a military version, and he called it to mind when contriving his plan for Biafra.

The craft had an unusually strong wing structure that would provide anchors for hard points to carry rocket pods. Further, it could not be easily hit by antiaircraft fire or detected by radar. Even armed, the MFI-9B was nimble as a falcon and able to perform at extremely low altitudes. In a word, it was ideal for what von Rosen had in mind.

With the aid of a little diplomatic wizardry, the Tanzanian Embassy in Stockholm placed an order for 5 MFI-9Bs, ostensibly for a newly organized flying school in their country. Significant but apparently not noticed by the Swedish government, Tanzania was one of only a few African states that recognized Biafra. The funds to pay for the "flight school" aircraft, $51,600 in all, came from an unremarkable firm in

Paris. In fact, it was a front for the Biafran government. From Malmö, the planes were flown to an airfield outside Paris, where the MFI pilots were surprised to find themselves in a high-security military zone. To their astonishment, French air force armament experts showed up, took measurements of the wings, and then supervised the installation of two rocket pods, each capable of being loaded with six French 76mm rockets. That accomplished, the aircraft were dismantled, crated, and loaded aboard a pair of Super Constellations. The Swedish pilots, all except Per Hazelius, returned to their company at this point. When Hazelius boarded one of the Connies, he fully expected to land in Dar es Salaam. When the cargo plane finally touched down, it was on the opposite side of Africa, in Libreville, Gabon. Count von Rosen was there to greet him.

Hazelius recognized two other Swedish pilots and a pair of ground crewmen who accompanied von Rosen. One pilot was Martin Lang, a thirty-one-year-old flying instructor. The other, Gunnar Haglund, was a pilot for a Swedish steel company. The technical support were Torsten Nilsson and Bengt Weithz, a retired Swedish air force pilot and an engineer familiar with the MFI-9B, respectively. In the spirit of von Rosen, these mercenaries served out of true idealism; they did not accept one cent more than their normal salaries. With them were two Biafran pilots, Willie Bruce and Augustus Opke. Opke, who was only twenty-seven, was chief of the Biafran air force.

Everyone turned to with a will, and the five MFI-9Bs were unloaded, uncrated, and quickly assembled. After a checkout ride around the pattern, the aircraft were flown east to a secret airfield outside Libreville. There, the pre-fitted rocket pods were mounted and armed. The ground crew worked industriously to paint out the Swedish markings and registration numbers, then daubed on splashes of camouflage. Their efforts had taken only a few days. Proud of the evolved MFI-9Bs, von Rosen gave them the whimsical name of ''Minicoins,'' a play on words that revolved around their insignificant price and the fact that they were so ideally suited for mini-counterinsurgency ops. Later, von Rosen offered Hazelius the opportunity to remain with the group, but he chose to return to his job in Sweden.

For their first raid, von Rosen selected Port Harcourt, where the Nigerians had a radar base for guiding their fighters. Also based there were several MiGs and Ilyushin bombers. Von Rosen decided to attack at high noon on May 22, 1969. He later explained the daylight attack this way: "We wanted to get them when they were sleepy after their lunch."

Von Rosen himself briefed the pilots and would lead the initial raid. When the historic squadron scrambled, von Rosen wore a rumpled old flight jacket and a yellow baseball cap to contain his thinning gray hair; he was, after all, fifty-nine years old.

Gracefully, the five Minicoins completed their climb-out, jockeyed into squadron formation, and turned left to a heading of 310 degrees. Flat, in-line engines droning they headed northwest across Gabon, toward the Bight of Biafra, a deep inlet of the South Atlantic that divided Gabon from Nigeria. Thick jungle canopy gave way to cultivated fields and small villages. They skirted Libreville and went feet-wet a few miles north of the city. At once, they dropped low, less than 100 feet above the water, to avoid Nigerian radar.

It was an insufferably hot day, the sky pale blue, only a few tiny puffs of white wool dancing over the sparkling waters of the bight. In the lead, Count von Rosen sat behind the jagged silver lightning of his single-bladed, variable-pitch prop as it picked up the sunlight from behind. The Minicoin handled beautifully. The pilots hardly noticed the increased drag from the rocket pods. Even with that and their low altitude, there would be little effect on the fuel reserves because of the economical little engines. A sudden, unseen thermal dropped the lead aircraft 20 feet. With deft fingers, von Rosen adjusted the trim tab and felt the slight lift of the tail as the aircraft levelled itself. It would be a short flight, less than three hundred miles.

Sooner than expected, the misty haze that denoted landfall appeared on the horizon. Static crackled from the headphones clamped to the ears of von Rosen. "I have some oil tankers off the port wing, Captain."

"Damn it!" *von Rosen's wingman later recalled thinking,* "he's so eager to make a kill, he's broken radio silence. He's also let the Nigerians know we're here."

Resigned to their discovery, von Rosen took the squadron down even lower. The pilots lined up on their targets by guess and blew into Port Harcourt at barely above treetop level. Unheard over the engines, air-raid sirens wailed, and the pilots saw soldiers rushing about in an effort to cover the airport's runway with leaves. An instant later, they spotted a stomach-knotting sight.

Antiaircraft guns pointed in their direction, and an eye-blink later they opened up on the Minicoins. Bright flashes, which quickly became black puffs, dotted the sky around them. Still in the lead, von Rosen reacted to a loud blast directly below his aircraft, and the little MFI-9B nearly flipped over on him. Ironically, the shell came from a Swedish-made Bofors antiaircraft gun. Von Rosen keyed his mike.

"Take out that antiaircraft battery."

Intense light rode the head of thin white trails of smoke as the rockets fired. Von Rosen kicked in left and right rudder. Quickly, it was proved that his aim and that of his fellow raiders was good. The Bofors guns fell silent. Raising the nose of his Minicoin, von Rosen made a quick turn and screamed along the runway in a second pass. This time, only uncoordinated small-arms fire sought him. His finger closed on the firing switch, and two more rockets went berserk.

Von Rosen's Minicoin flashed past a moment before his rockets struck a pair of MiGs. The wings of one of the Soviet fighters snapped off and somersaulted through the smoke-filled air. Banking right, von Rosen led his hearty band on an attack of the Ilyushins. A small, cold smile creased the face of von Rosen as he watched two missiles strike an Ilyushin and engulf it in flame and smoke.

"One more pass," he commanded his squadron.

To the surprise of the pilots, none of the small-arms or machine-gun fire had come anywhere near the Minicoins. Von Rosen's aircraft shuddered as the last two rockets flashed from their tubes. From the corner of one eye, he saw the trails of the other eight missiles.

"Break off. We will return to base," he ordered.

The return to the secret base was uneventful. Immediately, the raiders had their rocket pods reloaded, and they took off again. This time the target was Benin, where they wiped out the Ilyushin belonging to an infamous Nigerian pilot who called himself "Genocide" and gloried in attacking hospitals, women, and children. Along with it, the strike force accounted for a second Ilyushin known as "the Intruder," which had also harried the airfield at Uli. Again, the newly born Biafran air force escaped any casualties. In three days, they would attack Enugu.

"They knew we were coming and had moved every available gun to the airport," von Rosen reported afterward. For all the Nigerian preparations, the raiders skipped through the ground fire and hit two bombers. Further, von Rosen recounted, "A MiG taxied out to take off after us . . . but was shot up as he tried to lift off."

Predictably, world reaction was mixed. Nigeria protested vehemently to Stockholm the moment they had established von Rosen's identity. The Swedish government conducted an investigation. It did not get far. Those involved soon proved that the United States did not hold an exclusive patent on stonewalling. Malmö Flygindustri expressed shock and surprise. Transair knew only that von Rosen was vacationing. Count von Rosen was, for the present, unavailable. None of them could provide any concrete evidence. Summoned to Stockholm to answer questions, von Rosen convinced the Swedish government that he had not been involved in the actual purchase and shipment of the aircraft and had not violated any specific law. While he did this, his brave little squadron continued to wreak havoc on the Nigerians.

His mission at an end, von Rosen settled down in Sweden to resume what he could of his life. Before long, word spread that he had returned to Biafra to lead his Minicoin squadron in more raids. But the fate of Biafra had already been sealed. Losses began to mount among the Minicoin pilots and, with that, the respite bought for the Biafran people by von Rosen dwindled. In January 1970, six months after the advent of von Rosen's Minicoin squadron, the Nigerian army trampled the last resistance, and Biafra ceased to exist as a free nation.

But what of Count von Rosen? In 1974, he was once more in Ethiopia, flying relief supplies and food to starving people in areas that had been hit by famine. Then, in 1977, after a border war got under way with Somalia, the governor of Harar province asked to be flown with some relief officials to the town of Gode, which had reported being under attack by Somali soldiers. Von Rosen agreed to take him and made the flight and landing without any problem. During that night, the Somalis began to shell the town with artillery. Some of those in the villa where the governor's party had settled for the night decided to make their escape. Others, including the governor and von Rosen, remained. Not long after the last few deserted, Somalis stormed the villa. Witnesses outside reported bursts of machine-gun fire.

Before dawn, the Ethiopian army retook the compound. Inside, they discovered the bullet-riddled body of Count von Rosen. The day was July 13, 1974, and Count Carl Gustav von Rosen was five months from his sixty-fifth birthday. The knight-errant had reached the end of his quest.

The Crusade against Castro

Alpha 66

by Mark Roberts

ALTHOUGH ITS ORGINS AND THE IDENTITY OF MANY OF ITS members are shrouded in mystery and lost in the mists of time, Alpha 66 created more grief and cost Fidel Castro's Cuba more in crippling expenses for surveillance and interdiction than any other anti-Castro militia operating from outside the island nation. Organized in 1961, Alpha 66 quickly attracted youthful freedom fighters and veteran opponents to the Castro regime. Among them were Geronimo Estevez, Eloy Gutiérrez Menoyo, Antonio Veciana, and a Coronel Guzman, an obvious alias affected by a former ranking officer in Castro's 26th of July Movement. There was also Enrique Cienfuegos, reputed to be brother of the man who had been Castro's pilot until the dictator's taste for Communism turned the portly flyer against him.

These latter two were only a small number of the former warriors who had fought for Castro and became disillusioned when Fidel openly embraced Marxism. The young came also, the sons of men slain by order of Castro. These volunteers were mostly simple policemen or soldiers, sailors, and flyers who had served in the armed forces of Fulgencio Batista y Zaldívar. *El Paridón*, the Firing Wall, made a good polarizer of those with a grudge against Fidel Castro. Although they acted out of patriotism, they were paid and thus qualify as soldiers of fortune. Anglo mercenaries came also—Americans, British, and South Africans for the most part, among them William Clay, a pilot of considerable experience. Some of these individuals were in the employ of the CIA. In fact, the CIA is believed to have equipped, financed, and supplied Alpha 66 and some six other major anti-Castro militias.

Although these mercenaries initially operated out of Puerto Rico, training soon began in not-so-secret bases in the Everglades and other Florida swamps that incorporated suitable dryland hummocks dotted with palmetto plants. Armed with sterile weapons (H&Ks, FN/FALs, MP-43 Schmeisser SMGs, 1911-A-1 Colt .45s, etc.—in later years, they would receive 7.62mm RPK LMGs and AK-47s), the eager Cuban expatriates learned personal marksmanship. Equipped with unusual steeds (Cigarette racers, converted PT boats, and other light patrol vessels) these knights-errant set off to the lists. Their first operations were training exercises, intended to familiarize the determined warriors with the heavy .50 caliber Browning machine guns, 82mm M-1937 Soviet mortars, 57mm recoilless rifles, and RPG-7 Soviet rocket launchers provided covertly by the CIA. One theory behind the inclusion of Soviet arms had it that the antirevolutionary guerrillas could easily resupply themselves from Cuban army munitions. Between nighttime excursions, they learned hand-to-hand techniques and the use of the knife and the garrote.

A Field Information Report of the CIA station chief in Puerto Rico, dated June 12, 1962, reveals the origins of both the organization and its name. As the illustration of the document indicates, a small group of Cuban professional technicians had "drawn up a plan which includes different and simultaneous guerrilla and commando actions, and sabotage, which has been called 'Operation Alpha 66.' According to the plans, *66 men of action* will be utilized. . . ."

Later, on December 4, 1962, the CIA circulated a most interesting two-page communiqué to the FBI, the State Department, and the intelligence branches of the U.S. armed forces. In it, they reveal that an agreement was made between Alpha 66 and the Segundo Frente Nacional del Escambray (Second

National Front of the Escambray, or SNFE) to engage in a series of commando raids against Cuba, beginning on or about December 6, 1962.

These operations were subsequently carried out with considerable success. Cuban patrol vessels were fired on and boarded, then sunk or taken to add to the fleet of Alpha 66. Acting in concert with the Second Front, Alpha 66 personnel participated in ambushes of Cuban army units, inflicting many casualties and even gaining some eager, willing recruits. These successes broadened the scope of the goals of the organization. Recruitment posters began to appear in the streets of Caracas and other Venezuelan cities. They urged patriotic young Cubans to examine the record of the Castro regime and then to examine their own consciences. The text pointed out that more than twenty thousand Cubans were living in Venezuela and that many more of them should be aiding the efforts of Alpha 66 in freeing Cuba from Castro's grasp. It also announced several successful actions agains Cuban and Russian forces, including:

on September 10 [1962] an attack at Caibarién, on October 9 Alpha 66 affected an exchange of Russians for a band of Cubans without incident, on December 4 they had attacked Castro troops at Playa de San Juan [San Juan Beach], and on March 18, 1963 they attacked the Russian troops occupying their fatherland and damaged Soviet shipping at Puerto de Isabela de Sagua.

The flyer ended with a promise of announcements of more actions and urged loyal Cubans to join their cause. A closer look at what happened at Puerto de Isabela de Sagua gives an idea of why the response of patriotic Cubans was so great.

". . . So—vi—et—skaya re—vo—lut—sia."

With brassy arrogance, the words of the International *blared out over the bay that enclosed Puerto de Isabela de Sagua, Cuba. A tropical mugginess that seemed oppressive to the Soviet sailors confined aboard the cargo vessels by duty or punishment bore down with invisible force. They longed for the cool, normal climate of the Vladivostok peninsula.*

But here they were, off-loading tons of supplies—military

equipment, mostly, along with the Communist ideal of a luxury car, the always-black, hard-sprung Volga. Some among the ranking petty officers knew that part of the cargo was caviar and champagne for Castro's closest clique. They would be taking on refined sugar, rum, and cigars, which would be distributed among the cronies of Comrade Khrushchev. The starboard watch drowsed, torpid in the tropical heat. Off to port of the three ships, the drone of muffled powerful engines contributed to the somnolent mood. Cuban music—drums, marimbas, and guitars—floated across the still waters of the bay. One Russian sailor yawned widely and swallowed air with a gulp. His eyelids drooped and, a moment later, snapped wide open as the hum of the boat motors roared to new, intense life.

Dark shapes raced toward the moored Soviet ships, white bones in their teeth, rooster-tail wakes behind them. Sudden orange-yellow light washed out the star-studded horizon and tinted the blue-green water beyond the fantail of one larger vessel.

Seconds later, a roaring shriek passed close over the weathered deck of the nearest Russian vessel. The projectile arced downward slightly and slammed into the side of the second craft. A dull boom sounded when the old 57mm recoilless rifle round failed to detonate. Moments later, another flash and bang announced a second shell in the air. It covered the decreasing space in moments, and an ear-splitting blast rewarded the fierce, determined men aboard the boat. Small flickers of muzzle flame winked from .50 caliber machine guns in tubs built into the waist of an old power boat with a hot new engine. Mortars coughed softly.

On the Soviet ships, sailors scurried wildly around the deck. A speaker system came to life and a voice cried stridently, "Mi pod prechetyii! (We are under attack!)"

Small-arms fire began to crackle from the decks of the Soviet ships. A louder rumble announced the arrival of a World War II–model PT boat, once converted for fishing but now decked out as a warship again. A tin fish launched from a tube on the port side in a hiss of compressed air. It flopped into the water and ran hot, straight, and true to the target. A dull flash, loud roar, and enormous concussion followed. Almost at once, although imperceptible to the agitated Russian sailors, the ship began to list. Suddenly, the small armada swung to a new heading and sped toward the dockyard and blocks of warehouses that lined the quay. Machine-gun fire and mortar discharges raked the buildings. Many had thatched roofs, and fires broke out immediately. Cuban soldiers spilled from a barracks area and began to engage the attackers.

Over the racket of battle, some of the Soviet sailors could hear a Cuban officer shouting imprecations at the raiders.
"Bastardos! Está Alpha Sesenta-seis!"

Swiftly as they had come, the band of anti-Castro patriots disappeared into the night. Behind them were damages that would amount to more than 7 million dollars. They also left a toll in dead, dying, and wounded Cubans and Soviets. Unknown to those they had attacked, Alpha 66 had incurred but a single man wounded.

More spectacular successes led to greater recruitment. By 1964, now joined with SFNE Directorio Revolucionario Estudiantil and Junta Revolucionario, better armed and equipped, with abundant veterans of previous raids, Alpha 66 began to have a telling effect on Castro's peace of mind. Raids against Communist Cuban and Soviet military units increased in number and potency.

Alpha 66 continued to operate throughout the 1960s, bringing grief to the Castro regime and causing literally millions of dollars in damage. At the height of their incursions, missions were conducted at least once a week. Combat-related wounds were frequent, and there are a number of recorded deaths, duly reported by the CIA. At least one unit in Venezuela and another in Puerto Rico are believed to still be active in anti-Castro operations, although a document search of CIA files reveals no references after December 3, 1964. In all candor, despite their heroic efforts, their overall effectiveness in bringing down the Castro regime cannot be rated as very high.

Buyer and Seller of Men

Jonathan Banks

by Mark Roberts

AT FIRST GLANCE, JONATHAN BANKS DOES NOT LOOK LIKE A fighting man, much less a mercenary. He stands only five feet, eight inches tall, with a lean, boyish body. His big, limpid brown eyes stare out of a narrow, angular face so lacking in pigment as to appear bloodless. With large, protruding ears and a long, straight nose, Banks has the look of a sly, devious, and somewhat malignant leprechaun. This willowy appearance is deceptive. For years, Banks has been a physical-conditioning fanatic and, it is rumored, still engages in regular workouts at a local gym.

Born in Great Britain in 1945, Banks grew up surrounded by rich military traditions. His father was an officer in the army medical corps, and John spent most of his early years in and around military installations, including the Royal Military Academy and the cluster of barracks at Aldershot. In 1962, at the age of seventeen, he joined the army. Upon completion of his basic training, Banks was posted to D Company, the elite Pathfinder unit of the Second Battalion of the Parachute Regiment.

John Banks proved to be a good soldier. After four years in D Company, Banks was transferred to Second Battalion's

Special Patrol Company, a crack unit that specialized in operations behind enemy lines. These consisted of deep penetration of enemy territory by small, fierce patrols. During his service with the Special Patrol Company, Banks saw action in several combat zones around the world, including Aden, Borneo, Cyprus, Malaya, and the Trucial States.

According to his own account, Banks was once shot in the stomach by a Communist insurgent's bullet. In Aden, he was shot in the back while carrying a wounded comrade to safety. Later, he was hit in the face by shrapnel from a Russian grenade. His experiences, together with some of the events he witnessed in Aden and Borneo, left him with a deep-rooted hatred of Communism. As a result of his various injuries, Banks was removed from active service. In 1968, he was posted to the Parachute Regiment Battle School as an unarmed combat instructor. His career in the army went downhill from there. He bought a Jaguar with a check that bounced. To add to his troubles, he was caught driving the Jag without insurance, while restricted from driving. Banks was sentenced to a year in prison by a civilian court, which resulted in an automatic discharge from the army.

Following his release from prison in 1971, Banks found that there was no demand for his specialized skills in civilian life. He was reduced to signing on at his local labor exchange. Manual labor only served to frustrate him. He actively sought some sort of more satisfying employment. According to him, he found it in the form of freelance mercenary soldiering.

In *Fire Power,* the authors observe that, ''Given the clandestine nature of most mercenary assignments it is practically impossible to prove or disprove many of John Banks' claims about himself. Only the CIA knows for sure what is fact and what is fiction in Banks' own account of his career.''

Banks claims that his introduction to the mercenary fraternity came through Watchguard, an organization run by Colonel David Stirling, a World War II hero best known for founding Britain's ''killer-elite'' commando group, the SAS (Special Air Service), which operates under the cover of Television International Enterprises, Ltd., at 22 Sloane Street, in London's fashionable Knightsbridge district. Watchguard served as both an employment agency for ex-SAS officers and an overseas security organization. In the latter function, Watchguard provided assassination-prone heads of state in Africa and the Middle East with teams of well-trained, experienced bodyguards.

In August of 1970, David Stirling accepted a contract for a project of a far different nature. The aged King Idris of Libya had recently been overthrown and exiled in the aftermath of a military coup led by a fanatical young officer, Colonel Mu'ammar al-Gadhafi. The contract offered to Watchguard came from Umaral al-Shalhi, a millionaire who supported King Idris and was himself an exile in Switzerland as a result of the coup.

Shalhi wanted Watchguard to organize and direct a counterrevolution to oust Gadhafi, and was willing to pay 4 million dollars to finance the operation. Stirling took to it at once.

Stirling proposed a plan that called for a group of mercenaries who would mount a surprise attack on Libya's main prison, known infamously as "the Hilton," in the port of Tripoli. Hundreds of loyal supporters of King Idris languished within its walls; once liberated and armed, they would strike at the heart of Gadhafi's regime. Simultaneous to this would be a synchronized uprising throughout Libya by other supporters of the deposed king.

Umaral al-Shalhi liked the plan and gave immediate acceptance. A transfer of funds was arranged. At once, the call for soldiers of fortune went out, spread by word of mouth among ex-soldiers.

Reluctant to involve himself in anything that might embarrass the British government, Stirling arranged for the majority of the twenty-five mercs chosen for the "Hilton Assignment" to be recruited among the French by Leon, a French ex-paratrooper who had fought at Dien Bien Phu and in Algeria. John Banks claims to be one of the few Britons chosen to take part in the assignment—he was appointed radio operator on the mission. When four of the soldiers of fortune sailed to Ploce in Yugoslavia, things began to go wrong.

Neither the mercs nor their recruiters were aware that the plot against Gadhafi had been compromised by British Intelligence (MI-6), who comped the details to the CIA. Still favorably inclined toward the charismatic young Gadhafi, the

Agency conveniently overlooked that he was a dictator and instead centered upon his intense faithfulness to Islam and his fanatical opposition to Communism. Concerned that any shift in power in Libya might work to Russia's advantage, the CIA asked the Italian secret service, the SID (Servizio Informazione Difensa), to step in and terminate the operation before it began.

Moving with alacrity, the Italians raided the ship that bore the mercs, their weapons, and their ammunition. The reward for the mercs' dedication was a stay in an Italian jail. With the cover blown, the Hilton Assignment rapidly disintegrated. Score one more for totalitarianism.

Now safe to consolidate his power, Colonel Gadhafi moved rapidly to appropriate a large portion of his country's vast oil revenue and use the immense supply of cash to shore up febrile fellow dictators, such as Idi Amin in Uganda, and provide financial support to terrorist groups throughout the world. Libya became a schoolhouse and training ground for terrorists, eventually adding Islamic Jihad and Hammas to its list of those receiving its largess.

Returned to England, John Banks found himself without a satisfying job. A reprise of his association with the labor board did not appeal to him. Encouraged by the example of Watchguard, he decided to set up his own company, which he named Agency Bodyguards. It was to become the first of his many attempts to break into the well-paying security and personal protection business.

At first, Banks enjoyed considerable success. He employed ex-soldiers to serve as bodyguards to famous show business and sporting personalities. A real coup was the contract he obtained to handle the security at one of London's premier gambling houses, the Victoria Sporting Club. One of the assignments was to detect dishonest croupiers.

Once again, trouble stalked Banks when he attempted to export his bodyguard business overseas. He dispatched a duo of ex-paratrooper friends to Tel Aviv to guard wealthy Jewish businessmen from terrorists' threats to kidnap them or their families. A short while after settling in, the two bodyguards, Derek ''Brummie'' Barker and Paddy McKay, devised an unfortunate sideline. They began to conduct cross-border "snatch" operations against Arabs in Jordan and Lebanon.

Ever vigilant, the Mossad Alayah Beth, Israeli intelligence, soon became aware of their freelance operations. They were not amused. Barker and McKay were arrested for their provocative activities. After a chill-out period in jail and intensive interrogation, the two men were allowed to return to England.

Needless to say, this incident cooled relations between Banks and the Israelis. It also cost Agency Bodyguards a lucrative contract to provide El Al airline with sky marshals to protect their planes in flight. All was not well on the home front, either. Some of the gambling interests Banks supplied had become dissatisfied with the quality of security. Rumors ran rampant about carloads of thugs sent out to find Banks and teach him a painful lesson. Once more, blind luck stepped in. The man who had sent the enforcers after Banks died suddenly of a coronary, and the search was suspended. Banks dissolved Agency Bodyguards soon afterward.

Unemployed again, John Banks decided upon a change of venue. He made application to join the United States Army. After passing his medical check and an entrance examination, Banks was conditionally accepted and assigned to join the Fifth Special Forces Group, stationed at Baden-Baden in West Germany.

Shortly before leaving for Germany, however, Banks claims that he was instructed to report to the American Embassy in Grosvenor Square, London. A U.S. Army colonel attached to the embassy regretfully informed him that his application to join the army had been vetoed because his brother Roger—a former Katangese mercenary—was believed to be running guns to the Vietcong in the Mekong Delta. Although entry into the army was now closed to him, another branch of the American government was interested in making use of Banks's many and varied talents.

That branch was the Central Intelligence Agency. Banks claims to have subsequently worked on a number of missions for the CIA, most of them involving the smuggling of VIP refugees out of East Germany to the West.

Following his service with the CIA, Banks became involved as a soldier of fortune in Vietnam, fighting against the North Vietnamese through infiltrations for the purpose of demolition, sabotage, kidnapping and assassination. He next surfaced in Iraq, training and leading Kurdish separatists against the government of Saddam Hussein. He claims to have found the Kurdish campaign far more onerous even than the jungles and mountains of Vietnam. After several close encounters with death, Banks returned to England and became involved with T.A.E. (Middle East) Ltd., a company that ferried trucks and cargo to the Middle East. Although lucrative, he found this employment boring, and he began to cast about for something more fulfilling.

Banks's experience told him that there had to be hundreds, even thousands, of ex–service men equally dissatisfied with a colorless civilian existence. Why not, he reasoned, take advantage of this large labor pool, the cream of the British army? If it were properly organized, he could create a company, or a "personnel service," that tapped into their expertise at intelligence gathering; ambush and harassment of insurgents; sabotage, assassination, and demolition; and border surveillance. Further, they could provide liaison with, training, and control of friendly guerrilla forces operating against the common enemy.

Banks immediately began to recruit his army by the same method Dave Tomkins, the head of T.A.E., Ltd., once used to secure drivers for a truck delivery service. To do this, Banks rang up two national newspapers, the *Daily Mirror* and the *Daily Mail*, and placed advertisements in their classified columns. They were cryptic and terse.

Ex-commandos, paratroopers, SAS troopers wanted for interesting work abroad. Ring Camberly 33456.

Immediate response was enormous. In fact, it totally overwhelmed Banks's ability to process inquires and applications. Thus began his first enterprise as a seller of men.

During the ensuing years, Banks remained active in the shadow world of counterterrorist operations and the active recruiting and training of mercenaries. His early failures were joined by later ones, including a contract to supply mercs for an anti-Amin faction in Uganda. Most emblematic of his penchant for picking the wrong side was his agreeing to become one of several suppliers of mercenaries to the National Front for the Liberation of Angola (FNLA), who sought to free their country from the control of the Marxist government and its Communist allies, the occupying Cuban troops. Like far too many such adventures, actual conditions on the ground proved far different from the terms of the contract. The men Banks provided met the same fate as the others: defeat, capture, and death—sometimes by firing squads following kangaroo courts.

Civilian Irregular Defense Group

Montagnard Mercenaries in Vietnam, 1961–1974

by Mark Roberts

LITTLE HAS BEEN WRITTEN ABOUT THE VIETNAMESE mountain-dwelling soldiers of fortune who served with distinction beside their larger allies in Fifth Special Forces. The Civilian Irregular Defense Group (CIDG) was the brainchild of the CIA, designed to recruit the fierce mountain tribesmen collectively and indifferently called "Montagnards" by the French during the colonial period. The name stuck to such diverse tribal groups as the Hre and the Bru.

All of the mountain folk resided in small, isolated villages, where they lived in traditional ways. Each community had its own laws, an elected headman, a council of elders, and doctors. To their way of seeing things, they had no need nor desire to involve their lives with the governments of North or South Vietnam. Indeed, the Montagnards had always been equally antipathetic to Saigon and Hanoi. When the Vietcong (VC) came on the scene, the extreme measures they employed served only to cement the enmity between the politically motivated lowlanders and the mountain tribesmen. Where intimidation failed, the VC used brutality and murder.

Many villages cooperated with their unwelcome Vietcong guests out of fear for the lives of the women and children. Yet

119

the Hre in particular had a long tradition as fierce warriors. Armed only with knives and crossbows, they offered unyielding opposition to the VC whenever possible. When American forces entered the conflict, this resistance took on a different form. Our Central Intelligence Agency had been covertly involved in Vietnam even before the fall of the French. Between 1954 and 1961, they greatly increased the scope of their actions, including the insertion of army Special Forces personnel. In 1961, CIA field officers and Special Forces troopers in MACV-SOG (Military Assistance Command Vietnam Special Operations Group) began to visit the mountain villages. Their initial intention was to recruit a civilian militia that would serve as a blocking force to prevent the infiltration of Communist agents and troops from Laos and Cambodia. They would also operate as an interdiction element to interrupt the flow of supplies along the mountain portions of the Ho Chi Minh trail. The Agency soon found their efforts more rewarding than expected.

The Montagnards liked the Americans, who brought them food, medical supplies, and tools. They considered the Americans "happy people" who laughed and smiled a lot. When the headmen were asked if the young men would join in the fight against the Vietcong and the North Vietnamese, young and old alike readily agreed. The fact that the Americans offered them good pay—more money each month than most of the Hre could claim as their own in a year—certainly aided the recruiting process. The promise of a new way of life, which would put them on an equal or perhaps superior footing to the flatlanders, also attracted many among the tribesmen. When the Americans left the villages, they provided the headmen with the location of one of several training camps for volunteers to seek out.

They came. Singly, in pairs, and in small groups of three or four, young men from the Bru and the Hre, as well as some older family men, ghosted down out of their mountains to camps such as the one at Lang Vei, near the Laotian border. Traditionally, the Hre and the Bru maintained separate camps. At Lang Vei, they received marksmanship training, were introduced to uniforms, were taught to march as a unit and do some dismounted drill, and learned to work as a team. Those who went through this basic course remarked later that this aspect impressed them the most.

"The Americans taught us to work as a team to find VC in the jungle and kill them," one Hre warrior recounted many years later in an interview in San Francisco.

Basically, the CIDG strikers had been hired on a contractual basis to serve as a screening, patrol, and camp defense force. They received extra pay for captured VC guns. The reason: the Vietcong could easily replace a man, but weapons were much more difficult. Their harsh life in the mountain jungle gave the strikers an appreciation of this logistical fact; nearly everything was hard to come by for them and their families. Taking a VC gun and making more money also appealed to their sense of humor, which even the seriousness of their employment could not entirely suppress.

Throughout the duration of the CIDG, there was little love lost between the Montagnards and the South Vietnamese government troops. The Army of the Republic of Vietnam (ARVN) soldiers held the mountain dwellers in contempt. They considered the tribesmen to be savages. The Montagnards saw their detractors as pseudo-sophisticated and somewhat effete. Despite the friction, the joint operations flourished. Over several years, the mixed camp at Lang Vei grew in size and its occupants in competence.

Their AO (area of operation) increased to encompass both sides of the river that forms the border between Laos and Vietnam. The CIDG also conducted patrol operations in the vicinity of Khe Sanh. Veteran strikers report that the U.S. Marines at Khe Sanh were not friendly toward the tribesmen. Eventually they returned to Lang Vei, which had become a literal thorn in the side of the area VC commanders.

In an effort to dispense with this irritant, the Communist leaders sent spies into the Bru and Laotian camps on a daily basis. Ethnic Vietnamese for the most part, they discounted the prowess of the Montagnards, seeking only every detail about the Americans. The number of spies increased to the point that the CIDG strikers became convinced that the VC were close at hand and that an attack on the base was imminent. When it came, it proved to be like no other in the experience of the Montagnards.

A column of armor, PT-76 amphibious light tanks, breached the Bru camp first, approaching along the road from the south. These were manned not by VC, but by North Vietnamese Army (NVA) regulars. The Communist soldiers opened the firefight with a salvo of cannon fire. Casualties were inordinately high among the Bru and their Special Forces advisors from the outset. According to witnesses, the CIDG strikers and the Green Berets held their own and did a fair share of killing while the NVA and their VC allies deployed through the camp and advanced on the main base at Lang Vei. Alerted by the initial engagement, the strikers on guard duty opened fire on the advancing tanks with mortars. Most rounds missed the mobile targets. The unit commander sent men forward to engage the tanks with rockets.

These, too, missed or failed to disable the light armor. Muzzle flashes came from everywhere. The ground shook from the rumble of treads and the repeated blast of the HEAP (High Explosive Anti-Personnel) rounds. The main guns of the tanks blasted into the pitch-black night, guided by bright halogen lights atop the turrets. Communist soldiers, VC and NVA, ran through the base yelling and shooting. Suddenly, flares burst above the beleaguered camp. They starkly illuminated the tanks. Young sergeants from the Special Forces troops went among the strikers. They told them to hold their positions, and the CIDG mercenaries held. They trusted the Americans to know what was best. After all, the Americans had the radios and would know what to do.

By now, hundreds of men were wounded, dead, or dying. The sounds of battle were deafening and numbing. There were many screams and calls for help from men on both sides. Through it all, the Communist troops kept up a constant ululation and shouted imprecations to shore up their courage. It became apparent to the strikers that another purpose of the clamor was to make them break and run. For a long, costly time, the Montagnard soldiers-for-hire held fast.

More firepower was unleashed on the camp. It gradually became evident that the enemy had struck with overwhelming forces. There were far too many Communist troops out there. No matter how well the strikers had been trained, how bravely they fought, they simply could not kill them all. From the controlled force and direction of their efforts, it became obvious that the Communists wanted to capture the Americans alive and kill the government (ARVN) troops. The NVA and VC had passed up several opportunities to annihilate the CIDG units. The Americans in the radio room (bunker) faced a fight-or-die option and resisted ferociously. One Special Forces sergeant died while directly engaging a tank. The enemy later took his body when they withdrew. When the CIDG mercenaries saw the vastly superior numbers of the enemy, they escaped from the doomed compound after some three hours under continuous attack. The fighting continued for nearly four hours and ended in disaster for the Americans.

There was little resentment among the Special Forces troopers for the desertion of the soldiers-for-hire of CIDG. In fact, their overall loyalty and courage had contributed to more than a few outstanding successes against the VC and NVA—so much so that a number of A Team commanders gave letters of recommendation to individuals and groups of Montagnards, outlining their services and recommending that they be permitted to enter the United States where they might live as free men. Many took advantage of that opportunity.

American Soldiers
of Fortune

Like many earlier soldiers of fortune, American mercenaries tend to be individuals—or, rather, "Individuals," with a capital *I*. In modern times, American mercenaries have almost always been eccentric, highly visible, and most American in their attitudes . . . not to mention often very, well, *mercenary* in the finest tradition of capitalism. They also are often inspired by an ideal, be it stopping Communism, Fascism, or the Kaiser.

American fliers were among the first real mercenaries of the twentieth century. Two men, Dean Ivan Lamb and Phil Rader, actually fought for both sides in the Mexican Civil War of 1913–15, the first in a Curtiss biplane and the second in a Christopher. Each of these aircraft resembled more a powered hang glider than a modern aircraft, and flying them at less than 100 miles per hour and fifty yards over rifle-armed enemy forces took a special breed of mercenary. These men became famous for dropping bombs by hand and scouting low over enemy lines, and they were regularly featured in the American newspapers. Air-to-air combat was limited to the occasional pistol shot.

One of the most famous groups of mercenaries in this century were the Lafayette Escadrille. Founded by six Americans in 1916, the group was named for the French Marquis de Lafayette, who assisted the young United States during the Revolutionary War. This was a volunteer air squadron serving the French in World War I on the Alsatian front. They were good pilots and, more importantly, very colorful men. They were, in a word, good press and were an incredible propaganda tool that helped tear the States from isolationism and into the war. Less well-known were the Kosciuszko Squadron that served with Poland against the Russian invasions that followed World War I and the Russian Revolution.

Colorful men who flew or fought with a peculiarly American style became common after World War I and could be found all over the world. Hubert Julian, the Black Eagle, flew for the Ethiopians in their battle against Italy in the late 1920s and early 1930s. This black pilot was eventually dismissed by Haile Selassie's generals, an action he blamed on their "jealousy." Hundreds of Americans fought in the Spanish civil war. Among these were such notables as Ernest Hemingway and the pilots of the Escuadrilla España.

By the late 1930s, many American "barnstormers" were occasionally finding paychecks as mercenary pilots in almost every corner of the world. One of the most popular comic strips of that decade was *Captain Easy, Soldier of Fortune*. Captain Easy was a spy for the Chinese air force in 1933, just after Manchuria fell to the Japanese in that long-lasting prelude to World War II. Scorchy Smith was another comic strip pilot, though he spent his time "scorching" Knuckles Maddox while flying for the Mexican government in the mid-1930s.

The comic strip pilots' exploits were themselves eclipsed by the real-life adventures and heroism of the Flying Tigers, American pilots who fought for China years before Pearl Harbor and whose exploits are detailed in the section beyond. But even as we read about their heroism, it serves to remember that they were true mercenaries, paid by the Japanese plane destroyed.

Revolution over China

Claire Chennault and the Flying Tigers, 1937–1942

by Mark Roberts

Claire Lee Chennault was one of those superheated men on horseback whose courage, violent energies and unswerving opinions gain them a place in history as either madmen or geniuses.

STERLING SEAGRAVES, *FLIGHT/SOLDIERS OF FORTUNE*

CLAIRE CHENNAULT WAS BORN IN COMMERCE, TEXAS, IN 1890 and raised in the backwoods of northeastern Louisiana. From an early age, Claire was fascinated by human flight.

When the United States entered World War I, he wanted to become an army pilot. Given his age of twenty-six, the powers that be considered him too old for flight training. Commissioned in the infantry, he completed his training and was stationed at Camp Travis in San Antonio, Texas. Kelly Field lay nearby, and Chennault soon talked the flight instructors into giving him flying lessons during off-duty hours.

His efforts won him an assignment as supply officer in the Forty-sixth Aero Squadron, then based at Roosevelt Field, Long Island. His hopes of service overseas were dashed, however, because the war was drawing to a close. Rather than going to a combat theater, he was sent to help suppress a violent strike of angry black construction troops at Langley Field, Virginia. When the war ended in November, Chennault found himself on his way back to Kelly Field to accept assignment to flight school.

Once he had won his wings and his assignment as a fighter pilot, his genius became apparent, particularly his exceptional skill at aerobatics. Chennault literally wrung out the Curtiss Jenny he had been assigned to fly. Inside and outside loops became his constant companions. He is credited with perfecting the Immelmann turn, which consists of a steep vertical climb, a ninety-degree turn at the top when the aircraft nears stall speed, and a reverse of direction in horizontal flight. He later mastered the complicated and dangerous Lumpchavok ("headache" in Polish). This maneuver involves allowing the aircraft to actually stall out at the top of a vertical climb, and to skid tail-first before nosing over and performing a sort of rocking-chair motion prior to resuming level, horizontal flight.

He also displayed an outstanding flair as an aerial tactician. One of his innovations was to "plant the germ" of an early warning system, which in its infancy consisted of sending a man to the top of a water tower to watch for approaching "enemy" aircraft during a series of war games. He would perfect this technique later in Asia.

Inevitably, Chennault's radical actions and ideas got him into trouble with the hidebound brass in the army air corps. These generals and colonels believed that the development of swift, heavily armed bombers had made fighter aircraft obsolete in wartime. The bomber, they maintained, was invincible. Chennault disagreed and made no secret of his beliefs. He also published them in a monograph that earned the ire of his superior officers the moment it was circulated. Among those he alienated was Lieutenant Colonel Henry H. "Hap" Arnold, who would become commander of the army air corps. "Who is this damned fellow Chennault?" Arnold is said to have asked bitingly.

Such rejection and, to Chennault, blind ignorance left the pilot embittered. It also ended his usefulness as a flight instructor. For a number of years, beginning in 1933, Chennault languished in the new air corps precision flying team. It proved to be arduous service. By the spring of 1937, Chennault suffered from exhaustion, chronic bronchitis, and low blood pressure. Grounded by the air corps, he decided to look for a civilian job. He found a source through an old friend and ex-air corps pilot, Roy Holbrook.

Holbrook had earlier gone to China as an aviation advisor to the government, which faced ever-increasing pressure from the Japanese. By the time Holbrook contacted Chennault, the Japanese Imperial Army had advanced through Mongolia and taken Manchuria in their fast-flowing tide of conquest in Asia. Their "Asian Co-Prosperity League" had claimed the lives of thousands of innocent women and children, and brought about the infamous Rape of Nanking.

Previously, Chennault had arranged for his two flying-team wingmen, William MacDonald and John Williamson, to get jobs with Holbrook. Since then, through letters from them, Chennault had heard details of the crisis in China spared the public by the media of the day. As it turned out, Holbrook was looking for Chennault, and he made Chennault an offer he could not refuse. Chennault would be paid one thousand dollars per month, plus expenses, to work for the Chinese government. His job would be to equip, train, and advise an air force of Chinese and foreign volunteers (mercenaries) to resist further invasion of Chinese territory by the Japanese. More importantly, he would be free to carry out the mission any way he saw fit. Chennault accepted at once and quickly found himself on his way, by ship, to Kobe, Japan. He was not unmindful of the irony of his first destination in Asia.

Once in China, Chennault spent three years working with the nation's fledgling air force. Compelled to accept the services of mercenaries from all around the world, he found them to be exactly what he expected. He soon discovered that most of the international pilots who reported to Hankow, as he put it, "subsisted almost entirely on high-octane beverages." There were, however, exceptions, among them George Weigel and Jim Allison, a lean, lanky Texan.

During that time, the "germ" he had planted earlier sprouted. He established his "early warning" system and worked to perfect it. In spite of an early failure, in which the Japanese caught a squadron of eighteen Vultee V-11 bombers on the ground and destroyed 80 percent of them, the warning system soon proved extremely effective.

Through this system called "Jing Bow"—the American's version of a Chinese word that meant "to be alert"—Chinese throughout the country began to report enemy aircraft sightings by radio, and even by telephone and telegraph. When these alerts came into a central plotting station, Chennault would immediately put his too-few fliers into the air.

It soon became apparent that much more help was needed if China was to survive the invasion of the Japanese. By 1940, only the United States was in a position to provide that aid. In October of that year, the Chinese sent Chennault to the United States to acquire both planes and pilots.

It was not an easy proposition, as Chennault soon found out, given President Franklin D. Roosevelt's public posture that America must stay out of foreign wars. Placed under the guidance of Madame Chiang's clever brother, T. V. Soong, Chennault met powerful connections in the capital. Further aid came from Thomas G. Corcoran, one of Roosevelt's closest aides.

From Corcoran, Chennault learned that President Roosevelt was privately quite bellicose and already predisposed to come to the aid of China—provided, of course, that a means could be found to do so with utmost discretion and without creating a political uproar. Everything seemed to be going well for China's cause until Soong informed Secretary of the Treasury Henry Morgenthau that China desired as many as five hundred aircraft. In the end, Chennault and Soong eked out a mere one hundred Curtiss P-40 fighters, known as Warhawks.

Now equipped with aircraft, if not yet delivered and assembled, the Chinese needed American combat pilots to fly them in China. Here, Chennault ran up against his old antagonist, Hap Arnold, who refused to allow Chennault to round up volunteers from among the armed services. "I cannot," he said, "deplete my own ranks by encouraging my men to leave for service in China." Admiral John Towers, chief of naval aviation, held the same position.

Then the president, perhaps alarmed over what seemed the inevitability of a Japanese victory in China, intervened on Chennault's behalf and overruled both senior officers. To Roosevelt, the time was ripe to create a mercenary unit to defend what God had abandoned. On April 15, 1941, the president issued an executive order permitting military personnel to resign, sign contracts with CAMCO (Central Aircraft Manufacturing Company, designed as a cover for receiving the aircraft and assembling them), and go with Chennault to China to fight the Japanese. After one year, they could return to their former positions in the American armed forces.

Known officially as the American Volunteer Group, or AVG, the volunteers consisted of a more serious, almost strait-laced variety of flyers than those in the International Squadron, the name given to the Chinese/mercenary squadron currently operating against the Japanese. To a man, they subscribed to the discipline and mores of the U.S. military services. The pilots were variously identified on their passports and travel documents as tourists, entertainers, students, salesmen, and bankers. Some entered China as missionaries. But missionaries they were not, and none less so than Gregory Boyington.

If ever a "black sheep" entered the fold of the AVG, it was Gregory Boyington. Born in South Dakota, one-quarter Sioux Indian, he could best be described as the consumate misfit, a renegade among the conformists. He also happened to be one of Chennault's best pilots. He quickly proved to be no man to cross swords with in a barroom or a dogfight. To sum it up, Greg Boyington was one of those star-crossed, bellicose quixotes fated for enduring fame. It did not, however, seem so when he was first contacted by Chennault's recruiter.

As a twenty-eight-year-old Marine Corps first lieutenant with six years of flying experience, Greg Boyington had been relegated to a dead-end duty assignment as a flight instructor at Pensacola Naval Air Station. He was constantly irritated by the strictures of discipline and found himself forced to provide Corps headquarters with monthly reports on his plans to pay off his ex-wife and his creditors. When the AVG recruiter arrived, Boyington saw his longed-for opportuinty.

Later he wrote of the encounter: "I didn't tell him that he was hiring an officer who had a fatal gap between his income and accounts payable. Nor did I tell him that I was a whiz at a cocktail party."

In light of his past, Boyington was mildly amused to be

carrying a passport that described him as a missionary. When he arrived in San Francisco to join other recruits, he quickly surmised that he would not fit in well with this surprisingly conventional clutch of pilots. Even before boarding the Dutch freighter for Rangoon, he had concluded that some of them were not there for the money.

After Boyington and some roistering soulmates had laid waste to a surprising number of bars in Batavia and Singapore, the recruits arrived in Rangoon. Boyington immediately decreed a safe-landfall celebration. It was held at the Silver Grill, the only nightspot in the staid British colony, and quickly became nearly as liquid as the voyage across the Pacific. Plagued by hangovers, the hearty band set off by train for the RAF air base at Toungoo, 166 miles to the north. There, Chennault had arranged for training facilities.

Training proved more perilous than rigorous. By December, three pilots had been killed in accidents, and others had opted out because of the incredibly primitive existence in the sweltering jungle and the stultifying living accommodations. Even so, the AVG steadily acquired a cohesivness that would meld the individualistic pilots into an effective fighting force. Chennault divided them into three squadrons, dubbed "Panda Bears," "Adams-and-Eves," and "Hell's Angels." (The latter is no relation to the motorcycle club of the same name, organized after the war.) The AGV was well on its way to a stunning immortality that none of its members could yet visualize.

When a disagreement arose as to which aircraft would be flown by the AVG, an incident occurred that welded the unit into a solidly committed whole. What happened was that some AVG pilots believed the RAF Brewster Buffalo fighters to be better planes than the P-40s acquired from the U.S. government. Chennault decided to find out for himself which airplane was better suited to the type of combat he envisioned. To carry out the contest, Chennault selected Eric Shilling—who had chosen the fanciful shark face as his AVG insignia—to fly the P-40. Opposite him, in the Brewster, would be an RAF squadron leader who had flown in the Battle of Britain the year before.

Their mock combat was over almost before it began. In swift order, Shilling bested the Buffalo in three out of three passes high in the azure globe of the sky over Toungoo. Chennault decided to keep his P-40s, and the overjoyed pilots, to a man, adopted the grinning shark's teeth and gimlet eye symbol for the cowling of their aircraft.

Eric Shilling was to contribute to another trademark of the Flying Tigers. On the initial ferrying flight to Kunming, Shilling's Curtiss CW-21's engine began to backfire. After exchanging fuel for higher-octane gasoline in Lashio, it started to backfire again. Soon it was running rough and sputtering. The high mountains below offered little hope of a safe landing strip, and the crude, mimeographed maps held even less promise. Shilling knew he had to abandon any hope of escorting the formation to Kunming. Frantically, he searched for a landing site. With the engine just short of its last gasp, he spotted a minute patch of wooded, level ground a short way below a mountain peak. Shilling feathered his ailing engine and mushed into the stand of saplings at 100 miles per hour. He sheared down several trees before losing both wings and the tail of the Curtiss. Groggy and disoriented, Shilling crawled from the wreckage and stumbled to the lower edge of the field. Gathering his resources, he ran down the steep mountain slope. In the morning, he slaked his thirst and watched in trepidation while a large group of armed Chinese peasants approached. One of them yelled at him in Chinese. He answered in English. Shilling was taken into custody and held prisoner for two days. Although not brutal, his treatment was far from kind. They carried him to a village lower in the mountains. There they contacted a radio operator who was part of Chennault's Jing Bow air-raid warning system.

In an effort to prevent a repeat of the troubles caused by the language barrier, Chennault directed the AVG to develop a back patch with the Nationalist flag and Chinese characters explaining who the pilot was and what he was doing in China, and offering a reward for helping him. An original of these leather flying jackets, bearing the famous "I am an American flier" patch, brings a small fortune from collectors today.

On December 20, 1941, shortly after the Flying Tigers settled in at Kunming, the sirens of Chennault's Jing Bow early warning system set the air ashiver over the airfield. Reports had come in of aircraft approaching from the direction of Hanoi, three hundred miles southeast of the city. At once, Chennault scrambled two of his squadrons. Most of the Panda Bears headed southeast, while the Adams-and-Eves and the remaining Pandas hung back as a rear guard and reserve.

Overconfident from a year of steadily bombing Kunming without opposition, the Japanese expected nothing different on this day. Imagine their surprise when, thirty miles southeast of the city, they ran into a flight of fighter aircraft, their noses painted with widely grinning sharks' mouths, machine guns blazing from above fierce painted eyes. Utilizing the superior diving speed of the P-40s, the American pilots slashed down on the formation of Mitsubishi Ki-21 twin-engine bombers. Red-orange streams of tracers arced toward the targets and struck home.

Wheeling and jinking through the pale blue sky, the war birds struck again and again at the helpless, unescorted bombers. The reserve squadron came up to join the fray. More half-inch slugs ripped into Japanese metal and flesh. Before long, nine Mitsubishis followed one another down long columns of black smoke to crash and burn, leaving one severely damaged Ki-21 to limp home to Hanoi, figurative tail between its legs. Even it did not escape pursuit. Edward F. Rector followed until his P-40 ran out of gas and he was forced to crash-land. His aircraft became the sole casualty of the battle.

The brief battle proved so brilliant and effective a baptism by fire that the enthusiastic and grateful Chinese immediately declared the daring American flyers *Fei Hou* . . . Flying Tigers. Thus was born the soon-world-famous Flying Tigers.

Greg Boyingon played only a small part in the portentous events of December 20. As he told the author during an interview in 1986, a year before his death: "I was itchin' for a fight and gettin' none. After their terrible screwup on the twentieth, the Japs decided not to hit Kunming again for a while. Rangoon was another game.

"Jap ground troops had kicked hell out of the British and then wiped them out at the Sittang River. They were now approaching Rangoon, so Chiang Kai-shek [Generalissimo Chiang Kai-shek, premier of China and commander in chief of the army] ordered Chennault to keep up constant, daily air attacks over the city. The fighting for Rangoon went on for seventy-five days. We were told the Japs put twenty-five thousand troops in the field. From the air, we could believe it. Of course, it put tremendous strain on the Tigers. What the hell, we were a small flying force, committed to protecting a huge city." A brief smile brightened the large, Sioux bulldog face before Boyington went on. "That gave me what I was waiting for. Chennault moved the Adams-and-Eves down to Mingaladon airfield, outside Rangoon, to give the Panda Bear guys a little R and R. So, at ten hundred on the morning of 26 January, our mostly unblooded squadron was scrambled to mix it up with some fifty Ki-27 Nip fighters. What we didn't know was that the enemy had come up with some special tactics to deal with the AVG, which their propaganda broadcasts called 'insolent.' "

So far, the Tigers' advantage had been threefold: the P-40's superior diving speed, armor around the cockpit, and a self-sealing fuel tank. Together, they made it possible for plane and pilot to survive most hits that would down another aircraft. In the beginning, these elements had badly shaken the Japanese pilots and their superiors, who considered the American tactics unorthodox.

Raised in an ages-old culture that taught that all things Japanese were inherently superior and the wisdom of one's betters always infallible, the Japanese could not account for the setbacks experienced at the hands of the *gaijin*, or "white barbarians." This is understandable in retrospect: they had yet to experience the Battles of Midway Island, the Coral Sea, Iwo Jima, Saipan, and Guadalcanal, and the lessons of Hiroshima and Nagasaki. Nevertheless, they adapted quickly. It now became the turn of the Tigers to experience surprise.

Boyington continued his account: "The Japs changed. Their new tactics called for the bomber escorts to open their formations as we dived on them, letting our P-40s pass through without makin' a score on a single one. Then, when we were climbin' back toward the Jap planes, their own fighter cover would pounce on us. What they'd do was flip over and pull up into tight loops—what pilots call a split-ess—and bring down scaldin' pee on our broken formation.

"My flight included a pilot named Louis Hoffman. At forty-three, he was the oldest pilot in AVG. Soon after we climbed to altitude and started our pass on the Japs, we found ourselves caught by the new tactics. I could see how it might turn out, and I didn't like it one damned bit.

"Sure enough, everything I was worried about came to pass. We'd no sooner dived through their broke[n] formation than the Japs hauled up into split-esses and opened up on us. Smoke puffed from their guns, and tracers came hunting us. Before I knew it, Hoffman's P-40 started to skid through the air. It looked like nothin' more than a fish floppin' out of water on the bank. Next thing, Hoffman's P-40 did a wingover and spun out of control. Last I saw was it augerin' into the ground." Even forty-six years later, Boyington had a thousand-mile stare, recalling the event. "I never saw Hoffman's parachute," he said, swallowing hard on an invisible knot.

"After that, I decided to get a little for Louie, so I picked a pair of Japs and closed in. Right before my eyes, before I could even blink, one of them pulled straight up and went into a loop. He came down right behind me, and his guns opened up at once. Tracers zipped past my cockpit, and I waited for the thump-thump of slugs hitting the fuselage while I tried to think of what the hell to do. Now, I'd always been able to outmaneuver any pilot in combat simulations, but this was one whole friggin' lot different. I kicked in left, then right rudder, and swung the stick side to side, but nothing helped. Even when I went into a violent series of aerobatics, I couldn't shake him. When it came to me that all I had left was my better diving speed, I got it on right away. I put the nose down and broke off contact by dropping a thousand feet in a couple of seconds. Then I got the hell out of there before I could get hurt."

"I don't imagine you hung it up for the day."

"Oh, hell no. On my next pass, I started a thousand feet above this Jap. I lined up quickly, and my tracers began to gobble up his Ki-27. Then, just like that—" Boyington snapped two fingers, "—the sucker executed a swift turn, and I found myself on the receiving end again." An expression of chagrin broke the deep lines in his leathery pilot's face. "Once more I was forced to dive to get away. It went that way for the whole squadron all through the raid. We managed to knock down a few, but nothing like at Kunming. I returned to Mingaladon after the fight and taxied up to the flight line. One of our squadron members—Robert Prescott, I think it was—thought that I'd bought the farm. When he saw my tail markings, he ran up and jumped on the wing. I cut the ignition switch and rolled back the canopy. He greeted me enthusiastically. I felt sick. All I could think to say was, 'We didn't do so hot, did we, podner?' "

From there on, the Tigers would have to fight for every victory. And fight they did. The AVG pilots soon proved that they could devise new tactics of their own. Rather than attempting to maneuver with the Japanese, the Tigers adopted a practice of scattering them by means of repeated dives that were, in fact, feints designed to separate individual enemy pilots from their comrades and then cut them to pieces, one by one. In Boyington's second aerial combat, this strategem worked exceedingly well. The squadron tagged a total of sixteen, with Greg Boyington accounting for two of them. Before the end of spring 1942, he would increase this tally to six. The fluid unorthodoxy that the Tigers brought to aerial warfare continued to confound the pilots of the Rising Sun, who couldn't adapt to the spontaneity of the unconventional outfit.

The same unorthodoxy on the ground had caused trouble when the volunteers first arrived in Rangoon. The sedate colonial British had been appalled by the boisterous American mercenaries, their drinking parties at the Silver Grill, and their habit of strolling about the city in khaki shorts with languid Burmese maidens, sipping bourbon or pulling on warm beers. But after the Battle of Rangoon, local hostility was transformed into grateful tolerance and finally wholehearted enthusiasm for the American roughnecks.

The British were so appreciative, in fact, that Prime Minister Winston Churchill, praising both the Flying Tigers and the RAF pilots who fought alongside them, stated, ''The magnificent victories they have won over the paddy fields of Burma may well prove comparable in character, if not in scale, with those won over the orchards and hop fields of Kent in the Battle of Britain.''

Shortly after Rangoon fell, the American presence in Asia began to be felt. By late spring of 1942, the Tigers had grown tired and dejected. The infusion of the American military into

China and Burma had not brought the anticipated increase in supplies and equipment. To the contrary, it appeared that the Yanks jealously guarded their material goods and would only grudgingly provide the AVG pilots an engine part or even an ignition glow-plug or battery. Supplies, they were informed, were for the express use of the United States Army Air Forces. In fact, Lieutenant General Joseph W. Stilwell, the senior U.S. military officer in the area, had paid a visit to Kunming in early March and had wangled an agreement out of Chennault to eventually integrate the AVG into the army air forces. With the arrival of regular air officers to take over operations in China, the independence of the Tigers slowly faded away. Along with it went their unique ability to conduct combat operations in their usual innovative manner.

Greg Boyington was likely the most prominent casualty of this transition. One day, when his squadron was scrambled to meet a Japanese attack at Loiwing, his engine cut out and died during takeoff. He crash-landed a short distance beyond the runway. The impact rammed him forward, and he injured his knees against the instrument panel. During the weeks of recovery that followed, and what passed for occupational therapy in those days, he began to chafe at his inactivity. Eventually, his entire state of affairs weighed heavily upon him. His mental state brought him to a momentous decision.

"I didn't like China, and I sure as hell didn't want to die there. I figured it would be a good idea to move on before we got absorbed by the army [air forces]. With six enemy kills to my credit, I figured I'd get a warm welcome back in the Corps. So I tendered my resignation and returned to the States. I had no trouble getting back in the Corps," Boyington continued, offering a wry smile. "But I had a hell of a time getting a flying assignment—at least at first. Then I pulled a few strings, called in some markers, and got back my wings."

Boyington was shipped to the Pacific theater and eventually commanded VMS-24, his infamous Black Sheep Squadron. He went on to confound his critics by reaching the rank of lieutenant colonel before the end of the war and winning the Congressional Medal of Honor.

For the remainder of the Flying Tigers, they endured a brief and unpleasant transition into the hands of the army air forces.

Claire Chennault was reinstated in the army air forces as a brigadier general, though his men remained civilian mercenaries. As such, he was obliged to obey orders from General Stilwell. Most onerous among these were orders to provide low-level support missions for the Chinese troops of Generalissimo Chiang, despite the fact that this made the Tigers' P-40s vulnerable to ground fire and, with the sun behind them, to attack by Japanese aircraft. Worse were equally dangerous low-altitude reconnaissance flights. The final blow came when the Tigers were ordered to escort a flight of slow, lumbering, low-flying RAF Blenheim bombers. The pilots staged a protest that came just short of mutiny.

At last, on July 4, 1942, it was announced that the entire unit would cease its civilian role and be amalgamated into the army air forces, under the command of Brigadier General Clayton Bissel, who had been one of Chennault's detractors since the early 1930s. What particularly galled was that Bissel outranked Chennault by a single day. The appearance of a new commander, and an arrogant one at that, proved the final straw. The Tigers, who were fiercely loyal to Chennault, refused to join up. When Bissel learned of this, he ordered Chennault to bring the pilots together for a "policy" confrontation. Seated in silence, the Tigers listened to all the arguments and, when polled individually, gave the same answer. "No."

Bissel replied with a threat. If they did not sign up, they would be inducted into service anyway—most likely as privates, if he had his way. After an angry Bissel stormed out, Chennault addressed his loyal pilots. His appeal was personal and to the point, concluding with: "All that counts is getting the Japanese out of China and winning this war. That's our job; that's our sacred duty."

It was of no use. The men were tired of fighting and risking their lives for a foreign land, and, most of all, they had no use for Bissel and his officiousness. Most chose to resign; only five joined up. Thus, on the Fourth of July, 1942, the American Volunteer Group, arguably the finest unit of mercenary pilots ever created, ceased to exist.

Larger Than Life

Captain James B. "Earthquake" McGovern

by Mark Roberts

THE MOST COLORFUL OF ALL OF CLAIRE CHENNAULT'S CIVIL
Air Transport (CAT) pilots, Captain James B. McGovern, was
known throughout Asia as "Earthquake McGoon." Earthquake McGoon was huge. He weighed three hundred pounds
and wore a full, fluffy beard. He ate peanuts incessantly. As
a result, he often returned from a mission with his cockpit
knee-deep in shells. He was noted for always landing tail-high.
The reason: with his great girth, he could not pull his control
stick past his knees.

McGovern was no stranger to the mercenary game. He had
flown for other fly-for-pay outfits in Asia prior to Chennault's
forming CAT in 1946. When Chennault began recruiting pilots, McGovern joined up at once, along with several other
Americans and the former RAF pilots George Davis and Dave
Lampard, who used among their fellow mercenaries the mon-
ickers "King George" and "the Duke of Windsor." Before
long, CAT had its ranks swelled by other old hands. One of
them was Eric Shilling, an original member of the Flying Tigers. He had quit in 1942 and returned to the States. He later
returned to the Orient to fly for China National Aviation Corporation. In 1947, when he and a dozen other former Tigers

got fired, Shilling headed for CAT and General Chennault. He soon became chief pilot and, later, chief of operations. Earthquake McGoon got along well with him, being also much given to mixing routine flying duties and corporate responsibilities with intermittent bouts of swashbuckling adventure.

Gradually, Mao and his Communist army drove the Nationalists from city to city by unrelenting military pressure. Earthquake McGoon got involved in a wild touch-and-go rescue involving five CAT pilots at Weihsien. McGoon had flown two of them, Alvin L. Burridge and John R. Plank, in to retrieve company records. While there, the two pilots were cut off by Communist troops. They took refuge in a walled school yard and contacted CAT for deliverance. With Chennault out of the country at the time, the rescue operation was mounted by Whiting Willauer. He sent Richard B. Kruske to the beleaguered school yard in a two-seater Stinson L-5 aircraft. From that point, the mission began more to resemble a comedy of errors than a professional venture.

Kruske took Burridge aboard, only to crash into a wall on takeoff. The next day, Willauer dispatched Edwin L. Trout in another L-5. He broke his prop on landing. Now CAT had four pilots stranded behind Communist lines. McGoon showed up the next day in his C-47 and parachuted a new prop. Kruske and Burridge repaired Trout's L-5 and flew out. That left two men.

Next came Robert Rousselot, who took in another L-5, followed by Marshall Staynor flying a Piper Cub. Obviously, this was a *big* school yard. Staynor and Trout made good their escape in the Piper and flew to Tsingtao. Unfortunately, Rousselot smashed into a wall in the L-5. Staynor took the Cub in again—and broke the prop on landing. Enter McGoon, who dutifully flew over and dropped yet another prop. This time he added several cases of empty beer bottles that whistled like bombs as they fell and struck panic among the Communist troops, who dived wildly for cover. Plank gave it a whirl this time and got out alone in the Piper Cub, which left Staynor and Rousselot behind. In true musical-chairs fashion, Kruske came back in the Piper and took out Staynor, which left Rousselot alone.

By this time, the Communists had overcome their fright and

began to close the ring around the school. Time was running thin for the CAT pilot on the ground. During the night, Willauer ordered several cargo planes to harass the Communists. They flew over and dropped small bombs on the besiegers. Shortly after dawn, Kruske returned in an L-5, followed by Staynor in the Cub. Rousselot was a considerably larger man then either of the other two. Staynor and Kruske fitted themselves into the Stinson and flew out, which left the heavier Rousselot to get off in the Cub.

Everyone held their breath while Rousselot slowly lifted off the overweight Cub and climbed into the sky. Following behind, in his C-47, McGoon threw out a few more empty beer bottles to pelt down on the heads of the Chinese Communists, sending them into another panic.

For all their heroic efforts, the pilots of CAT and the Nationalist Chinese cause were doomed to failure. In 1949, when the remaining Nationalists were compelled to flee the mainland, CAT went along. On December 4, 1949, CAT C-46 XT-812 departed from Kai Tak, Hong Kong, at 5:05 P.M. on an unscheduled direct flight to Kunming, Yunnan Province, China. The crew consisted of Captain Earthquake McGoon, copilot M. L. Lay, and flight operator S. F. Chang. The only other occupants were Mrs. James Liu and her infant daughter. Mrs. Liu was the Russian-born wife of James Liu, an employee of CATC. The reason for the flight was that British immigration officials in Hong Kong refused to allow entry to Mrs. Liu and ordered her flown to Kunming instead on the first available airplane.

Misfortune once again stalked Earthquake McGoon. It was later theorized that failure of his radio compass made it impossible for him to find Kunming. After a prolonged search, he turned south in hope of finding a landing spot in safe territory. At 2:01 A.M., McGoon informed another CAT pilot by voice radio that he had only forty gallons of fuel left and intended to land on a sandbar in a riverbed. That was the last communication from him.

Initially it was believed that the plane had landed in French Indochina (Vietnam) or possibly in Thailand. An intensive search was laid on. Searchers included elements of the French air force and the Chinese and Thai air forces, as well as CAT aircraft. No sign of the downed plane was discovered, nor was word received either directly or indirectly as to the passengers' whereabouts or condition.

Then, on December 29, a CAT search plane piloted by Captains Dutch Brognersma and Bob Snoddy sighted the lost aircraft on a sandbar in a riverbed at latitude 22° 20', longitude 110° 26', approximately twenty-three miles southeast of Yulin, in Kwangai Province, China. Brognersma flew dangerously low and definitively identified both the CAT insignia and the plane number, and also observed that the plane had suffered very little damage in landing.

On January 6, 1950, Claire Chennault addressed an appeal to the United States State Department to negotiate on behalf of McGovern with the Communist Chinese government. In it, Chennault related that "On the same day (29 Dec.), we received information from a reliable source that the crew and passengers were safe and being well-treated, but were being held incommunicado at Yulin. Later it was reported that they were transferred to Jung-hsien, a town about forty miles northeast of Yulin and that they were being held pending receipt of instructions from Peiping.

"On January 5, we received information that Captain McGovern and possibly the entire party had been transferred to Nanning, and were presumably en route to a railway head at Liuchow.

"Civil Air Transport has employed all possible means within its power to locate and secure the release of Captain McGovern and party. The latest information received indicates that he is probably en route to Peiping by rail.

"We request that the State Department be notified of the detention of Captain McGovern and request that you effect his release at the earliest possible moment."

McGoon regained his freedom on May 31, 1950, the day he reached Hong Kong after being detained in Communist China for six months. In an account written by Anna Chennault for *CAT BULLETIN*, she recounts his reunion with the CAT pilots:

"When I got home on the afternoon of May 31, I found my husband chatting with a number of guests in the sitting room. Among them was a heavy-bearded man whom I could not recognize for the moment, but I was quite sure I had known him before.

"His big build, bearded-face and a pair of Kwangsi cloth-shoes on his feet impressed me that he was a missionary. 'Anna,' asked my husband while I was still guessing to myself who that gentleman was, 'can you recognize this gentleman?' Then everyone broke out in great laughter. 'He is our released pilot, Captain McGovern, who has just come back,' my husband told me.''

Then, in 1950, Chennault sold CAT outright to the Central Intelligence Agency. They grouped it under a blind front of the holding company known as the Pacific Corporation. Always the consummate soldier, Chennault never revealed that CAT was anything but a private airline hauling freight and passengers around Asia. By 1953, the Agency was committed to aiding the French in Indochina. In addition to ground advisers, the CIA employed CAT to deliver airdrops of supplies to the beleaguered French in such isolated bases as the one at Dien Bien Phu.

Because of the Korean War, which concluded in 1953, few people in the United States were aware of the fanatical warfare in French Indochina. After almost a century of French colonial domination, the Vietnamese had sought their independence. Unfortunately, the major military arm prosecuting the liberation was the Communist-dominated Vietminh. In late 1953 and early 1954, the showdown between the Vietminh and the French army was about to take center stage. It would happen in a broad upland valley, edged on two sides by steep hills. There, the last stand of the soldiers of the French Foreign Legion would come at a fortified base known as Dien Bien Phu.

At the time, the United States was not prepared to support the French openly. A compromise was arranged by which Civilian Air Transport Service (CATS), now a part of the CIA's cover operation, Pacific Corporation, would be sent in under contract to provide covert military assistance by means of parachuting supplies to the besieged fort. For its part in the scheme, the U.S. Air Force provided C-119 cargo aircraft, known as Flying Boxcars. These were to be flown by twenty-four CATS pilots whose uniforms consisted of shorts and aloha shirts.

For the pilots, this was not voluntary service. They had been told by CATS management that they would fly or lose their jobs. Among them were Richard Kruske, Eric Shilling, and Earthquake McGoon.

"These airdrops are 'specially dangerous, because the Vietminh completely surround Dien Bien Phu."

Earthquake McGoon would recall Eric Shilling's initial briefing as the huge pilot easily handled the yoke of the C-119 he guided over the verdant, three-tier jungle canopy of eastern Vietnam.

"Their guns are positioned on these ridges that overlook the French outpost from two sides. We've got to fly in daylight, because at night the AA fire screws your night vision, and it bugs the crews. That makes us sitting ducks. I don't like it, and you won't, either. But you've literally got to run a gauntlet to get in the slot and drop the supplies where the French can get them."

Easy for Shilling to say. McGoon saw it differently one afternoon in early May, 1957. He was flying with five other C-119s and checking their positions, using the prominent, liquid navigational aid: the Mekong River. McGoon dipped the starboard wing and turned slightly right to correct his approach. The bright red wind sock that the Foreign Legionnaires always elevated on a tall pole to give the pilots an idea of wind currents over the drop zone waved fitfully in the far distance. Recently, McGoon had suggested an idea that impressed him as a way to reduce the risk of flying into Dien Bien Phu.

"Maybe if those Frogs didn't put up the wind sock until the last second, like after we turned for the approach, those little brown buggers down there wouldn't be layin' for us."

As though in confirmation of his theory, small puffs of black appeared ahead of the aircraft. Suddenly, the Vietminh began a continuous, murderous barrage of deadly fire. Hundreds of rounds of 37mm projectiles streamed toward the C-119s, accompanied by a veritable gush of 12.7mm machine-gun bullets. The metal fuselage of McGoon's Flying Boxcar crackled and spanged from the impacts. Always the same old thing.

Yet the hundreds of fusillades had not deprived McGoon of

*his generous streak or his sense of humor. As he had done on
many flights, McGoon had brought along cartons of cigarettes,
which he purchased with his own funds, and several bundles
of unpaid bills. The former he would pitch out to the legionnaires; he would gift the enemy with the latter. Inexorably, all
six C-119s droned through the thick veil of Vietminh fire.
Abruptly, there was a bright flash to port, followed by a loud,
sharp report, and the screech of rending metal filled the cockpit of McGoon's C-119. Beside him, the copilot keyed the radio set on the squadron net.*

"We've got a direct hit. Where the hell are the fighters?"

*Battling the suddenly uncooperative controls, McGoon was
seen to risk a quick look out the left window. The first round
had blown off the leading edge of the port wing. Strips of
shredded aluminum skin vibrated wildly in the slipstream. A
loud explosion from behind drew McGoon's attention rear-
ward.*

*"We've got one bitch kitty of a hole in the starboard tail
boom. Jeez, it's shakin' the hell outta the elevator," he reported to ground control. "We're gonna abort."*

*Desperately, McGoon fought to maintain control of his
wounded aircraft as it steadily lost altitude. Thick wisps of
smoke streamed into the cargo space. Working together,
McGoon and his copilot yanked back on the yokes in a maddening effort to avoid auguring in as they barely cleared the
mountaintops. Seconds counted in their frantic attempt to
reach the base at Haiphong.*

"Earthquake, this is Redbird. Can you make it?"

*"Roger that," Earthquake returned loud and clear, his
voice masking his deep concern. "Piece of cake."*

*Yet the damaged aircraft continued to lose altitude. In sec-
onds that seemed to drag like hours to those watching, the C-
119 skimmed along only inches above the treetops. "Looks
like this is it, son," came the final words of Earthquake
McGoon over the squadron net.*

*In a flash, the Flying Boxcar slipped below the canopy and
disappeared. The left wingtip gouged into a hillside, and the
C-119 did a slow cartwheel and blew apart in a huge, orange
mushroom. Sadly, it was short of a small riverside landing
strip by only a few dozen yards.*

Two days later, on May 7, 1954, the French surrendered.

A EULOGY FOR EARTHQUAKE MCGOON

by Felix Smith, longtime associate and fellow pilot
(first published in the *Cat Bulletin*)

It is fitting that a few words of tribute be paid James McGovern by his fellow pilots and perhaps doing Mac the injustice of waxing sentimental, for the greatest thing about the fabulous Earthquake McGoon was not his adventurous exploits or uproarious jokes, but his acts of kindness, from which he so skillfully severed the maudlin traits.

When Gingle left his sickbed on Christmas day to fight his body into the back bar of his cafe and pay homage to his friends, McGovern swooped up Gingle's cane, and with malicious glee, used it as a billiard stick on the barroom table, sending the inner sanctum into fits of laughter, Mac seeming least mindful of all that he was transforming the symbol of Gingle's misery into a prop for merriment.

Mac joshed about playing hookey and defying schoolteachers with the comradeship of an equal when talking to an orphan lad we pilots know, and none but the shrewdest observers realized that Mac was painlessly driving home lessons on the value of school and study far more effectively than all of our serious preachings to the boy.

And when passers-by in Hong Kong saw Mac waving wildly to an unfortunate looking Chinese, casually ignoring the stares of the curious, few knew that Mac was conversing in a sort of bastard sign language with an old friend whose tongue had been torn from his mouth by the enemy during the war because he would not betray his friends in Hongkong. These two were discussing the results of the second fitting of the fine Chinese suit Mac had ordered for his friend at one of Hongkong's finest tailors. When the weird conversation ended, Mac surreptitiously passed his friend a huge wad of money in a manner that escaped notice.

The last thing anyone could say about McGovern was

that he was a pious do-gooder. But countless acts such as these, untainted with sentimentality or subtle bids for recognition, are the clues to his greatness.

Mac showed that he was in tune to the human part that lies so deeply buried in most of us in a unique way that lent dignity to our somewhat shady human race.

Mac occasionally visited our families when on leave and my father spoke, not of Mac's fabulous tales, uproarious clowning, or even of his awe-inspiring size, but said, with the infinite wisdom of an old man the simple words, "Your friend McGovern is a man."

THE BALLAD OF EARTHQUAKE MCGOON

by Al Kind

From Hong Kong to Shanghai to far-off Tibet
This legend is growing with time
Of the behemoth creature who flies in the sky
Who knows neither reason or rhyme
His three hundred pounds shake the earth
    when he walks
Yet he soars with the grace of a loon
The legend makes claim that this beast from the East
Is known as Earthquake McGoon.

While still a mere lad in his tenderest years
He seemed a precocious young boy
Who knew naught of vices like women and beer
To his parson a true pride and joy
But tales of "The East" and the streetcars that ran
In an easterly-westerly way
Sowed dreams of wild oats in our young hero's head
He vowed that he'd go there to stay.

But it looked like the doom of Earthquake McGoon
And we swore he would never come back
When he dead-sticked his plane onto Liuchow one day
His future looked truly quite black
They threw him in jail and granted no bail

They took both the shoes off his feet
Yet he stomped on the floor and beat on the door
For whiskey and something to eat.

In fear of their lives or because of the din
From the behemoth creature within
His captors relented and gave him a bottle
Of rice wind diluted with gin
But they still couldn't feed this ponderous hulk
Whose temper grew worse by the day
And quaking with fear they finally released him
After six months and a day.

So believe what I say, friend, and lend me an ear
To prove to yourself if you must
That the legend of Earthquake, the stomach and beard
Is true as a Venus's bust
Go down into Kowloon in Gingle's back room
And there, staring you in the face
Is this behemoth creature, his hand on his prop
With a smile on his lecherous face.

Soldier, Jurist, Patriot

David "Mickey" Marcus (1902–1948)

by Mark Roberts

ON THE AFTERNOON OF MAY 14, 1948, WITH THE BRITISH scheduled to withdraw from Palestine in frustration the next day, the independent state of Israel was proclaimed. It was immediately invaded by the armed forces of Egypt, Iraq, Lebanon, Syria, and Transjordan.

The minute new state, whose enemies occupied territories one hundred times as large, with a stunning population edge of nearly sixty to one, now found itself fighting for its life. Yet fight it did—and exceedingly well. The brief war was a classic: the people of a nation with few reserves and little territory fell back and used thoughtfully calculated offensive engagements to maintain an exceptional defense.

When Egyptian troops poured into the Negev, spearheaded by tanks and armored cars and followed by heavy artillery, "Michael Stone," an American advisor, told the Israeli high command, "You'll say we haven't the forces to attack. I say we have. Even with light units, we can raid the enemy's military centers before he's had time to get organized—stop him from placing his guns and preparing his armor."

David Ben-Gurion, the first elected prime minister of Israel as well as commander of the army, listened. He dispatched an

Israeli unit outfitted with newly received machine guns and radio-equipped jeeps to the Negev. He sent "Stone" with them in a supervisory position, with an Israeli officer in formal command. The results proved to be spectacular. But who exactly was this Michael Stone?

Michael Stone was the *nom de guerre* of Colonel David "Mickey" Marcus, an American Jew, a graduate of the U.S. Military Academy at West Point, a veteran of the European Theater in World War II, a former jurist—at thirty-four, Marcus was the youngest judge on the New York bench in 1936— a highly successful lawyer, and first deputy commissioner of correction during the administration of Fiorello La Guardia in New York City. A man of many hats, Marcus was well suited for his mission as a soldier of fortune to Israel.

When the combined Arab offensive collapsed and degenerated into a siege of Jerusalem, Mickey Marcus was the toast of the Ben-Gurion government and its military leaders. On May 28, 1948, Ben-Gurion rewarded Stone by making him the commander of the Jerusalem Front.

This historic moment—Mickey Marcus achieving the rank of brigadier general and command of the Israeli Army—was not without a touch of irony. He was an American soldier of fortune, and the enemy he would be fighting was led by another soldier of fortune, Major General John Bagot Glubb, a Briton who became a pasha and was better known as "General Glubb Pasha." This was a confrontation definitely not made in heaven. Their conflict of skills and wills would affect the future of an entire new nation.

Jerusalem had been occupied in the first days of the invasion. Now the Arab allies remaining within the city found themselves surrounded on three sides by the Israeli army. Key to driving the enemy forces from the city was the old Roman-built Latrun Road. Defending it, and denying access to the city, were the Egyptian and Syrian armies. Armor and artillery ranked nearly hub to hub along the commanding heights that overlooked the Latrun. The elite Syrian divisions had been whipped into a *jihad* fervor. Eager to avenge the insult of defeats handed to them earlier by the upstart Jew general Stone, they looked forward to further engagements with their enemy.

Some among the combined Arab armies thought of fleeing the ring of determined Jews—in particular, the Egyptians. When the order came from Ben-Gurion to break the occupation and free Jerusalem, the task fell to the Har-El Brigade, one of those commanded by Stone.

Pitch black. Only a faint silver glow of stars illuminated the old Latrun Road that dated back to the Roman occupation. The only lights along Highway 1, the Latrun, came from the repair facility tents of the Egyptian and combined Arab armies. The Israelis drove without lights, ideal for what Mickey Marcus had in mind. As General "Stone," he had already led Israeli troops in lightning strikes against the invaders, leaving the Lebanese and Syrians in particular disorder. This time it would be different. The small column of three Land Rovers— military surplus left behind by the departed British—seven trucks, and two American jeeps were tasked with breaking through the Syrian armor at Laterun and effecting the relief of Jerusalem.

Quite an assignment. But then, Ben-Gurion had a lot of faith in his General Stone. Mickey's grip tightened on the Sten gun in his lap as the lead Land Rover rounded a bend. They were well inside the enemy corridor now. Less than five miles separated them from their objective. So far, none of the machine-gun positions located on previous days appeared to be aware of their presence. Too bad that would not last beyond the next fifteen minutes.

Not a man in that small task force feared combat. Their recent experiences in the war with the Arabs had evaporated their fear. They were scared, of course. A sane man would not lack that hollow, queasy sensation that preceded combat. Hell, there was ample reason to be scared. At any moment now, a 12.7mm slug, manufactured in the Soviet Union, could smash through a man's chest and end his life.

Their commander mused on how oddly the lines had been drawn in the Middle East after the last shot was fired in Berlin. The Soviets had embraced the Arab world as brothers. Or was it that they saw the Arab states as ready customers for the literal tons of military surplus left by the end of the war? His own country had been one of the first to recognize the fledgling state of Israel, but it did not follow that American political recognition brought with it an outpouring of military aid. More's the pity, Stone acknowledged. He could have used a few of Patton's tanks right then. All of that Egyptian armor out there, those T-34s provided by the Russians . . . better not to dwell on that.

What Stone commanded was a spearhead. The task of the 155 men was to penetrate the weak point at the delicate juncture of the Egyptian and Syrian forces. The relief force would follow. He had also rehearsed the relieving element and given a final briefing, mostly a pep talk. More and more of the Israeli command were beginning to believe in his concept of striking hard and fast and in unexpected places. But not all of the rank and file agreed. At least this lot was highly motivated. For another ten minutes, the vehicles ground along the Latrun.

Abruptly, the blackness before them exploded into a ball of intense white, which quickly faded to the yellow-orange of gunfire.

Thumb-thick, half-inch bullets cracked through the air around them as a Soviet-made Syrian DshK-38 machine gun chugged out its slow-crawl cyclic rate of 550 rounds per minute. The fifty-round link belt was rapidly depleted as the ill-trained soldiers manning the weapon did the natural thing and fired above them in the darkness. For that, the Israeli soldiers were sincerely grateful. They heard shouted Arabic, the tone one of confusion. The machine gun opened up again.

"Take that out!" Stone shouted over one shoulder.

In the American jeep behind Stone's Land Rover, a long tongue of flame roared from the back of a 57mm recoilless rifle—the product of German military technology and American military aid—and a shell screamed through the night. A bright flash-bang that jarred the teeth of every Israeli silenced the 12.7mm machine gun. Behind the lead element, acting according to the attack plan, the trucks went off the road and accelerated forward. Heaving grenades and firing American and British automatic weapons, the Israeli soldiers smashed through the disorganized Syrian forces, some of whom mistakenly turned their weapons on their Egyptian allies. Stone slapped his driver on the shoulder.

"Hit it!"

Engine whining, the Land Rover leaped forward and soon

raced past the smoldering remains of the Russian machine gun. Israeli troops streamed through the Latrun heights. Using grenades generously, they drove the demoralized Syrians from their entrenchments and sent them racing toward Damascus. Smoke rose from damaged equipment. The fighting dwindled as the Arab forces ran. In a matter of hours, it was over. The road to Jerusalem lay ahead, uncontested.

Unfortunately, the story of Mickey Marcus did not end in joy and triumph. Instead, it concluded in tragedy. On the night of June 10, 1948, in the village of Abu Ghosh, a party was held to celebrate the negotiated truce that was to go into effect at 10:00 A.M. the next day.

Marcus retired to his room shortly after midnight. Finding himself restless and unable to sleep, he slipped on shorts and boots and silently eased his way out of the building. A sentry who knew him saw him and waved him on.

Later, at 3:35 A.M., after a relief soldier took over the guard post, the new sentry heard the sound of trampling in the bush. He peered through the dim light and saw a figure moving about. He called a challenge in Hebrew and received an indistinct answer.

The soldier acted properly, aware that he was guarding a military headquarters, and fired a warning shot in the air.

Without hesitation, the figure continued to advance. One hand was held upward, the guard could not tell whether in greeting or holding a grenade. He fired once again.

By the time the sentry, accompanied by the sergeant of the guard and several officers, reached him, Mickey Marcus lay dead with an Israeli bullet in his heart. He turned out to be the last Israeli fatality prior to the truce.

The Unknown Mercs

Allen Pope and the Freedom Fighters of Asia

by Mark Roberts

IT ALL STARTED OUT AS ANOTHER ROUTINE AIR-INCURSION mission. The venerable B-26 lifted effortlessly off the runway on Celebes island, waggled wings and completed its turnout. Then things went rapidly downhill from there.

Not a cloud marred the dazzling blue, tropical sea. The cornflower sky matched the ocean's color so perfectly that no horizon was discernible. The twin engines of the veteran B-26 created a steady vibration familiar to the pilot, Allen Lawrence Pope. He flew uncomfortably low to avoid radar. For all he could tell, he was alone in the air. Ahead, he spotted a halo of mist and the thin line of white beaches, on Amboina Island, that pointed to his target.

Beyond, the dark green mass of the island's jungle, so dense as to appear black, loomed against the sea. Tension built in Pope's gut. Once more he consulted his map.

"No problem finding the target," he had been told.

He abandoned his reverie as Amboina Island's rim flashed by under his aircraft. At once, he began a steep climb. Head swiveling, he sought his goal. There! At eleven o'clock he saw a raw gash in the jungle. Hauling back on the yoke, Pope climbed higher, aligning his aircraft for the first pass.

Engines roaring and the slipstream howling, the B-26 swooped down toward the target. Allen Pope took a deep breath and thumbed the firing button on the yoke. The entire airframe shuddered as the eight forward-firing .50 caliber machine guns in the nose opened up. [The aircraft Pope flew had been modified earlier to carry eight guns in the nose rather than the usual two.] *The red-orange glow of tracers guided the way.*

A deadly hail of half-inch-diameter slugs slashed into the parked aircraft and the buildings housing the Indonesian army garrison at one end of the airfield. The troops were there to guard the airstrip against rebel incursions. Fires broke out as incendiary rounds shredded the thatched roofs. Another burst ripped into some fifty-five-gallon fuel drums and ignited them. Abruptly, Pope wheeled the aircraft and climbed precipitously. Below the belly of the B-26, the Indonesian soldiers scrambled to antiaircraft mounts.

Ground fire began to grow as Pope leveled out, headed into his approach, and dived again. Blazing fire poured into the target. A fuel truck exploded in an orange ball of flame. Black smoke tinged the edges. A curtain of bright yellow-and-black pom-poms danced in the air in front of him. Allen Pope completed his run and climbed again. He banked right while he made mental note of the sound of small-arms fire that had struck the fuselage.

After a third pass, through a curtain of AA fire, his machine guns empty, Pope banked and headed out over the calm ocean. His destination was the same secret rebel base on the far-off island of Celebes from which he had flown earlier in the morning. Before he could get out of range, however, the Indonesians opened up again with the antiaircraft guns.

Small, white puffs of AA fire capered around the converted bomber. A violent shudder transmitted itself through the airframe and up the yoke, jarring Pope to his shoulders. Suddenly, the plane's right wing burst into flame. The B-26 faltered and shuddered violently. In seeming slow motion, it began to lose altitude, then plunged toward the sea.

In the vacant sky, a speck appeared as a man fell clear of the doomed aircraft. A parachute blossomed . . . and former

U.S. Air Force pilot Allen Lawrence Pope descended slowly toward a coral reef.

His leg broken by the fall, Pope was captured by the Indonesian forces. After his capture, an Indonesian tribunal sentenced him to die by firing squad. Eventually the sentence was commuted, and the revolution failed. Following his capture in the spring of 1958, the U.S. ambassador to Indonesia was instructed to state that the condemned pilot was a mere "private American citizen involved as a paid soldier of fortune." Allen Pope was to languish in an Indonesian prison for four years until relations with the United States improved. By then, John F. Kennedy had become president of the United States.

Allen Lawrence Pope was born around 1928. Little is known of his childhood and youth until he dropped out of the University of Florida to try his luck as a Texas ranch hand. Apparently he found that not exciting enough. He volunteered for the Korean War, took his flight training, and flew fifty-five night combat missions. Following the truce and the Panmunjom peace talks, Pope left the air force to return to Texas. He took a job as an airline pilot and was married. Routine soon began to chafe at him. His marriage ended in divorce, and the airline job was boring. Pope headed back to Asia, this time as a contract pilot for CAT. Long before Air America reached notoriety in Vietnam, the CIA coopted CAT, which had become a reservoir for all the romantics, swashbucklers, and misfits in modern flying circles. That included Allen Pope. He was typical of most American mercenaries of the time, who tended to be pilots sought-after by clients for their professional skills. Not long after joining CAT, following the French surrender and withdrawal from Indochina, Pope and a few of his close friends went to Indonesia to participate in the secret CIA operation to dislodge President Sukarno.

Unquestionably a dictator, "President" Sukarno had exhibited increasingly leftist leanings over the past few years. He had expelled foreign diplomats and formed a close alliance with the People's Republic of China. He suppressed all of his people's freedoms, closed newspapers and imprisoned the editors, silenced all opposition ruthlessly, and sought to expand his fledgling empire to neighboring nations like Malaysia. He was believed also to have designs on the Philippines. In that, he ran at direct cross-purposes with American policy. The administration of President Eisenhower authorized covert operations to aid the small but determined bands of rebels who sought to overthrow Sukarno. Their main strength lay on the island of Celebes. Former government ministers and ranking officers of the army had joined forces with discontented civilians and organized, with CIA help, an impressive rebel army. Pope and his fellow pilots were to train Indonesian pilots and provide the rebels with an air force. They turned out to be temporary combat pilots.

After his release from prison, Pope had had enough of Asia. He changed hats again, replacing his thirty-mission crush chapeau for a spook's beret. For a number of years, Pope worked for the CIA under less trying circumstances in Latin America.

The Cuban Second Front

William Morgan and the Directorio Revolucionario

by Mark Roberts

MANY PEOPLE THROUGHOUT THE WORLD BELIEVE THAT FIDEL Castro won the Cuban civil war/revolution single-handedly. We are sure Fidel Castro believes this. But it simply is not so. In truth, Castro's 26th of July Movement was only one of several revolutionary organizations to which Cubans of every class and occupation gave their efforts, and even their lives. A number of mercenaries also played highly important leadership roles in the revolution. One of them was an American named William Alexander Morgan.

Morgan was born April 18, 1928, in Cleveland, Ohio. His early life does not reflect his later accomplishments. He fell in with the wrong group and frequently ran away from home. At fifteen, he ran away from school and never returned. In March of 1946, he was apprehended by the San Antonio police. A month later, the Toledo cops nabbed him. They suspected him of armed robbery but did not book him. At eighteen, he enlisted in the army and, after basic and AIT, was assigned to serve with the occupation forces in Japan.

In November 1947, Morgan was arrested for being AWOL. He was sentenced in an Article 13 to three months at hard labor and forfeiture of pay for that period. But his "gone bad" past had not yet deserted him. While in the stockade in Kyoto, Japan, Morgan attacked and overpowered a guard, took his pistol and uniform, and escaped. He was soon recaptured and subjected to court-martial. Found guilty on charges of escape and armed robbery, he was sentenced to a dishonorable discharge, forfeit of all pay and allowances, and confinement at hard labor for five years.

Morgan did his time, and for a few years his life blended into the misty background of America in the 1950s. Then, in November of 1956, a major uprising in the eastern city of Santiago, Cuba, focused world attention on the open insurrections against the dictatorial rule of Fuglencio Batista y Zaldivar. The incident in Santiago galvanized the opposition into civil war. Morgan showed up in Cuba shortly thereafter. One of the major organized groups opposing Batista was the Directorio Revolucionario (DR), the militant arm of the Federation of University Students. Morgan made contact with the DR, which was led by Eloy Gutiérrez Menoyo, in the Escambray Mountains, which bisect central Cuba.

He was tentatively accepted and brought to the rebels' base camp. There he got a cool reception. Roger Redondo, one of the original members of Directorio Revolucionario, later recounted Morgan's arrival.

"Lazaro Artola was with a great big American, all red, fat . . . he had no shirt on. Artola said the American was an adventurer. He said, 'I brought him up to see how long he'll last. Because he's so fat, I don't think he'll last too long. He probably works for the CIA or the FBI.' "

Menoyo instituted an intensive three-day program of physical training to condition his men and the new recruits. Morgan joined in with a will. During the long runs up and down the mountains, he struggled over the steep inclines along with the rest of the twenty-nine men in the unit. He lost weight rapidly and built up his strength.

From the beginning, his military experience showed; after all, he had his training from the U.S. Army to rely upon. He taught the troops discipline, for which Menoyo was silently grateful. After ten days, the guerrilla unit moved deeper into the mountains and there encountered and ambushed a five-man Cuban army patrol. The result was a disaster for Batista's army and provided Morgan's first combat experience.

Exhilarated over their easy success, the fledgling revolutionaries marched back and forth through the mountains for thirteen days. Their odyssey took them over two hundred miles of trails and primitive roads. They constantly exchanged shots with a larger, pursuing force of Batista soldiers.

Morgan began to learn Spanish by the tried-and-true method of vocabulary building. *"¿Como se dice esta en Español?* (How do you say this in Spanish?)"* became his most exercised phrase. The new year came with Morgan learning Spanish rapidly.

In February 1957, the DR guerrilla band believed themselves secure enough in their mountain bastion to write a manifesto that set forth their military strategy and political goals. Issued on February 24, the document called for simultaneous urban and rural guerrilla warfare toward the goal of a restoration of democracy and a social revolution.

Their declaration had an immediate effect on the oppressed people of Cuba. Revolutionary zeal burgeoned throughout the island nation. The stalwart band in the Escambray Mountains benefitted also. Their ranks began to expand with raw recruits and experienced urban fighters.

With their numbers increased, incidents with the army grew in number. They engaged the army in hit-and-run battles in such places as Fomento, Guinia de Miranda, Hanabanilla, Pedrero, and Saltillo. In each incident, the standard rules of guerrilla warfare were strictly observed.

Never did the Second Front of the Escambray Mountains, or Segundo Fuente de las Escambray, as they called themselves, engage in pitched battle. They would strike and fall back, drawing incautious soldiers after them into an ambush. Then the DR troops would withdraw again. This strategy totally confounded the rigid, doctrinaire tactics of the army.

In frustration, the army redefined their objectives. Warfare in the Escambray mountains had always been brutal and vicious. By now, Morgan had a leadership role, leading a "guerrilla," which consisted of five to twelve men. Whenever informers were discovered by his men, they would be executed at once, and on them would be hung a sign that bore a single word: "Morgan." At all times, the revolutionaries concentrated on Batista's army and secret police. The army and police, on the other hand, turned their attention to terrorizing the populace.

Big mistake. This only served to exacerbate the flames of outrage among the people, who rushed to join the rebel cause by the hundreds. Fanned by the cruelty of Batista's minions, the flames of revolution became a wildfire. As a result, the army grew more frustrated and repressive in its program to suppress this popular insurrection. Menoyo and Morgan were quick to take advantage, as the following account reveals:

Near midday in late April 1957, an eighty-seven-man Batista patrol entered a small village in the Escambray Mountains. Crisply barked commands rang through the scattering of mud brick houses from the lips of the officer and noncoms in charge.

"Bring them out! Bring everyone out here."

Unknown to any of the army marauders, Bill Morgan and a seventeen-man commando unit watched from hiding near the village. Only the tight discipline they had learned kept the men silent and unmoving while they observed the systematic pillaging of the small community. Soon the villagers had been herded into a tight group, under guard of cold-eyed thugs in uniform. "Their terror can almost be tasted," Morgan thought to himself.

"¡Oye! Aqui esta rón," called one soldier.

Eagerly, the soldiers grabbed wicker-sheathed bottles of rum and began drinking greedily while they pursued their work. Piles of belongings began to mount in front of the houses. The ravaging of the villagers grew more and more difficult for the outnumbered guerrillas to witness.

"You. Come here," the captain in command demanded of the mayor.

Hesitantly, the middle-aged official approached. Within seconds, the mayor found the burly officer bent over him, face jammed up close to his own.

"The American," the captain snapped. "Where is Morgan?"

The Mayor shrugged. "I do not know, Señor Capitán."

At the officer's signal, a soldier butt-stroked the mayor in the gut. Doubled over, coughing and wheezing, vomit running from his lips, the village leader made feeble gestures of disclaimer.

"I swear it. I do not know. He could be anywhere."

Immediately the soldier butt-stroked him in the kidneys, and he sprawled on the ground, his face inches from the boots of the captain.

"Tell me what I want to know."

Through tear-dimmed eyes, the mayor tried to focus on the captain. Gasping, he fought for air with which to speak. "How can I tell you what I do not know?"

"Kill him," commanded the officer.

Laughing, the soldier shot the mayor in the back of the head. Lips curled in a smirk, he gave the captain a slovenly salute and turned away to accept a bottle of rum. As though given a command, soldiers began to drag people from the huddle of misery and beat them.

Screams rose from in front of a hut to one side as a sergeant supervised the torture of a young village man. The corporal and soldier who conducted the torment seemed to enjoy their work.

"You know they are out there somewhere," the sergeant screamed about the guerrilla band, who were only a few hundred feet away. "Tell us where."

More torture went on as the people, having no information to impart, remained silent and the soldiers' anger raged higher. When they had nearly exhausted their supply of victims to torment, several soldiers turned to a new source.

From one of the last huts at the end of the single street, a huge, burly, black sergeant dragged a tottering old man of seventy years. Unaware that he was the village idiot, although that would not have mattered given the mood of the soldiers, the sergeant turned his fury on the old man.

Ignorant of all that happened around him, the retarded man responded to the shouted questions of the sergeant in his simple and direct way. "Why don't you go look for them in the mountains?"

That broke the last strand of control. "Hold him tightly," the sergeant demanded of two soldiers.

Quickly they accomplished that task. The sergeant advanced on the pinioned old man, brandishing a sheath knife. While the soldiers held their victim helpless, the sergeant methodically cut off the old man's lips.

His piteous screams easily reached the ears of the hidden rebels. Unable to do anything, they watched while a noose was strung around the neck of the bleeding, screeching old man. The loose end was attached to a truck bumper. Laughing, the soldiers jumped into the vehicle, under the benign supervision of the sergeant, and raced down the street, dragging their hapless victim behind.

When the spectacle ceased to amuse him, the captain made a gesture, and the sergeant formed up the men. Weaving drunkenly, the patrol marched out of town.

William Morgan gave quiet instructions to his men. The guerrillas faded into the undergrowth and quickly outdistanced the patrol. Morgan hastily laid out an ambush.

At the propitious moment, the rebels struck. "Fuego!" Morgan shouted.

Bullets cracked and moaned through the air, thick as hailstones in a thunderstorm. A soldier screamed and went down, gut-shot.

"Over there," Morgan's sergeant shouted.

Two short bursts toppled a pair of Batista troopers. Fueled by the outrage they had witnessed, the guerrillas fought with a cold fury beyond courage. In a flash, the soldiers' nerve broke, and they began to flee. The guerrillas streamed along the flanks, blasting at the demoralized, drunken troops.

Suddenly the truck that had dragged the poor old man burst into flames. With grim determination, the rebels ignored it and continued the slaughter. Numbers abruptly became meaningless. Powder smoke, dust, and a thin haze of blood droplets clouded the air. For more than twenty minutes, the engagement continued while the soldiers streamed along the narrow mountain track. Slowly, the guerrillas begin to notice a slackening of return fire.

"Cease firing," Morgan commanded.

After the last shot sounded, the guerrillas came out of the underbrush. The air reeked of acrid powder smoke, the sickly sweet odor of blood, and the inevitable stench of human offal from men who had befouled themselves in death.

"Search for wounded," Morgan commanded, then looked around with grim satisfaction.

The patrol had been virtually annihilated. He made a quick body count and determined that only sixteen out of the eighty-seven who raided the village had escaped with their lives.

"Over here, Jefe," called one of the rebels.

Morgan joined the man and found that among the corpses and the wounded, the large, black sergeant has been discovered alive and taken captive.

"What do we do with him?" they asked Morgan.

Morgan stared grimly at the quailing noncom. "Give him a lesson he won't forget."

Most of the guerrillas on that operation were armed with shotguns, so their lesson soon became quite grisly as they took turns on the torturer. After a few minutes, when the rebels departed the area, the sergeant's body remained behind, riddled with holes.

Morgan was to later recount that for up to eight miles along the trail, "nothing but blood, guts, and buzzards were left" after their prolonged engagement with Batista's troops. It would not be the last time.

Yet when victory came, and Fidel, flanked by Raul Castro and Che Guevara, marched proudly into Havana to wildly cheering crowds, the heroes of the Escambray were pointedly absent from the ranks of the victors. Gutiérrez Menoyo and Bill Morgan quickly became disenchanted with Castro as the alleged liberator moved swiftly to consolidate power and establish himself as a Communist dictator in the style of Joseph Stalin.

Bloody reprisals began against university professors, and student organizations that had fought against Batista's repressive government became targets. Soon the firing wall (*El Paredón*) became the standard tool of Castro's newly created Department of State Security (DSG). Shortly thereafter, Castro made his bold announcement before the United Nations General Assembly that he was and had always been a Communist.

Today's Legionnaire

Djibouti, 1973

by Mark Roberts

FROM THE BEGINNING, WILLIAM BROOKS OF THE UNITED States found the French Foreign Legion vastly different than anything he had imagined. Nowhere did he see the romantic aura of the movies of his youth. *Beau Gest* simply did not exist. Even getting enlisted was difficult, and contrary to everything he had heard. On January 23, 1972, a Sunday, he presented himself at Fort de Nogent, Paris, France.

The guard at the gate challenged him in German and demanded to know what Brooks wanted. Brooks did not speak French, and his German was far from perfect. When he replied to the guard in broken German that he wanted to volunteer, he was taken inside to the sergeant of the guard and told to wait in a small room. The duty sergeant telephoned the OD, and, a few minutes later, a senior noncom who wore the rank of adjutant (master sergeant) entered the room and told Brooks to empty his pockets. Immediately, the adjutant took everything Brooks owned, including his passport, and stuffed the objects into an envelope.

Still ignorant of what was going on, Brooks followed the man across a courtyard and up the stairs, past a door that gave into a sullied squad bay. The whole place was filthy, looking more like one of the housing projects in the Bronx than a military barracks—but the food was hot, and it tasted good. Brooks ended his first day lying on a cot, with a full belly and a television for company.

It was a simple task to sign the enlistment contract the next day. He had been given an alias—mandatory for the first three years in the Legion—and signed up for the minimum of five years. Then he was issued a badly worn—one could honestly say worn-out—World War II uniform, a musette, a beret, and ten francs. Not until that Friday, January 28, did Brooks and a group of some fifty other volunteers set out by train for Aubagne, a small community east of Marseilles, where the general headquarters of the Legion was located. They were supervised by a single NCO.

Shock followed shock for William Brooks. When the complement of engaged volunteers reached Aubagne, they were marched to a separate barracks, one fenced off by a high, wire-mesh fence. It looked to Brooks like nothing more than a concentration camp or prison—he soon learned it actually was. An adjutant addressed them.

"You will remain here for the next three weeks. During that time, you will be given physical and mental tests. Your clothing allowance will be issued. And . . ." His eyes narrowed, and the twist of his mouth made his words sound more ominous than Brooks cared to think about. "You will be screened by the Security Bureau." He concluded his comments with an ironic note. "If, at any time during these three weeks, anyone wishes to drop out, you will be escorted to the train station and given a ticket to anywhere in France you wish to go. There will be no penalties, and your record with the Legion will not exist."

With that, the men were left more or less on their own. Boredom quickly set in. Although Brooks kept to himself most of the time, he managed to find some friends. Peters, an offensive-tackle-sized Finnish seaman, wanted to try living on land. Matic, the Slav, had only gone as far as eighth grade in school but was a self-taught intellectual who had a working knowledge of ten languages, including old and new Greek. With them were Brunin, the Irish farm boy and Queen's Irish Guard, whose love and knowledge of the Confederate army of the American Civil War endeared him to Brooks; Penson, the group's translator and French expatriate; Moeller, the son of a World War II German paratrooper; Keller, the French-hating ex-Bundeswehr Panzer driver; and the Turk, an Istanbul pickpocket. These eight were seldom separated during their years of service.

Surprises continued to descend on Brooks. The least welcome of these were the unexaggerated rumors of grueling interrogations of applicants by the Security Bureau. Actually, there were good reasons for the bureau's close questioning of the aspiring legionnaires. They wanted—in fact, needed—to know exactly who each one was, where he came from, and why he wanted to join the Legion. In most cases, they could develop this information easily, provided the volunteer had a passport. That accomplished, it left only the *why*. When an interrogator finally believed the man he examined, the recruit would have his "envelope of secrets" safely filed away. He would then receive his Legion identity card made out in the name of his chosen alias and would be shipped off to Corsica for training.

It all sounded easy to William Brooks, although he learned that problems do arise when a person with no valid form of identification attempts to enlist in the Legion. Then the interrogation becomes exhaustive, continuing until the Security Bureau interrogator believes the story. Such volunteers arouse great suspicion and require in-depth investigation, often through police agencies such as Interpol or a check of the Bundes List, a compilation of criminals wanted by the German police and sent monthly to the Legion. As a result, major criminals rarely enter the Legion.

Following his own bout of intensive interrogation, Brooks was ordered to sign a document. Of course, it was written in French, and he had not the slightest idea what it was that he signed, but he did affix his signature. He soon learned that his comrades had been accepted as well. Accordingly, late on the evening of Friday of the last week, the new legionnaires boarded a ferry in the harbor of Marseilles and headed for Calvi, a citadel located on the western coast of Corsica, headquarters of the Second Legion Parachute Regiment.

On board, Brooks quickly learned about the multiclass passage accommodations on European vessels. The men were delivered to sixth-class compartments in the cargo hold. They were issued lawn chairs and directed to sit elbow-to-elbow. Conditions rapidly grew from bad to ghastly when some three hundred Arabs, with their livestock and belongings, moved in. With a mournful hoot, the ferry pulled out of its slip. After two hours of unusually rough seas, every wretched soul in sixth class suffered from *mal de mer*. A rash of vomiting spread rapidly through the hold. Before long, the steel deck plates were awash with vomit and urine.

Bedraggled by their experience, the men staggered off the ferry the next morning. Without respite, they were loaded into trucks and set en route to Bonifacio, a small tourist spot on the southern tip of Corsica. Ten hours later, they arrived.

Everything in Bonifacio was filthy. Brooks came to learn that to be common in the Legion. The barracks, mess halls, and latrines were pigsties. The French, however, saw nothing out of the ordinary. Worse, the men were allowed to shower only twice a week for five minutes. Sheets were changed only twice in four months. Even more appalling to Brooks was the medical treatment—or lack of it—tendered to the legionnaires. The slightest cut on one's face or hand swelled overnight into a festering wound. Blood poisoning and hideous skin sores abounded. The medical personnel at the infirmary were unable to offer any treatment or prevention. Penicillin was forbidden because it "cost too much." This was hardly the Foreign Legion envisioned by Brooks before joining up. It was not, he concluded, the ideal service for a soldier of fortune.

Equally astonishing were the conditions they underwent in training. The French Foreign Legion was a world unto itself, in which orders were never questioned. Beginning the second day in camp, heavy emphasis was placed on physical conditioning. Forced marches were the norm. The Legion's great emphasis on marksmanship turned out to be firing practice two days a week for thirteen weeks. Like penicillin, rifle ammunition "cost too much." There was no bayonet training or night maneuvers. Through it all, the men were compelled to use rifles that should have been cut up for scrap metal. The barrels were pitted; the cleaning methods, crude. The Legion provided neither bore cleaner nor rifle oil. If one had any oil at all, it was usually 10W30 motor oil or 90 weight gearbox oil.

Although time was also devoted to the manual of arms and dismounted drill, the Legion proved remarkably devoid of imagination. The manual of arms consisted of only five commands: Attention, Right Shoulder Arms, Order Arms, Present Arms, and Rest. Marching commands were even less enlightened, consisting of: Forward March, Right/Left Turn, and Halt. That was all. To add insult to injury, there was no effort made toward precision. Keeping an entire platoon in step was considered a major accomplishment. Brooks endured it with gritted teeth.

Eventully, the training in Bonifacio ended. The legionnaires were marched overland 100 kilometers to the Legion encampment at the town of Corte. Most were sent to specialty school, including Brooks. For him, the Legion had chosen communications training. Instruction was given in French, which Brooks still did not understand, and he soon found that he had no ear for Morse code, failing to pass the requisite 480 letters a minute. Brooks requested of the commandant that he be transferred to the Republic of Djibouti.

His request was approved, and on January 9, 1973, Brooks left Corsica for the transient company at Aubagne. There, orders were cut for Djibouti. Brooks was issued hot-weather gear, given the required shots, and provided with a poorly fitted, wool civilian suit. The latter was to preclude difficulties if the plane should have to go down in some country unfriendly to France. On February 13, 1973, Brooks reached Djibouti Airport. He was quickly transported to Camp Gabode, some two kilometers distant, on the outskirts of the city of Djibouti. Brooks found himself assigned to the historic Thirteenth Demi-Brigade of the Legion, whose predecessors had been the heroes of France in World War II. Clad in kepi, neck scarf, camouflage jacket, and khaki shorts, Brooks cut quite a figure. This, at last, was the *real* Legion.

In March of 1974, orders were cut sending Brooks to Corporals' School. His assignment was to be trained as a team leader for a machine-gun team. It turned out to be nothing more than a grueling eight-week test of the students' endurance. The regulations were petty, being of the "Catch 22" variety, and the exercises bore little resemblance to command of troops in combat.

If filthy conditions, rampant disease, and virulent infections can be said to harden a man for battle, Brooks certainly received his share of hardening. He ended the training with a severe case of blood poisoning in one finger—on the point of gangrene—a throbbing tooth cavity, various infections, and a severe case of diarrhea. He returned to his unit, which was then stationed at Holl-Holl, near the Sudan border. After the formality of his "presentation" to everyone in the chain of command to report on his progress through the school, his ailments were treated at the infirmary at Gabode. After ten days, he returned to Holl-Holl in time for the solemn (by Legion standards) celebration of Camerone.

April 30, the anniversary of the Battle of Camerone, marks the start of the Legion's year. The troops are assembled in dress uniform in a hollow square formation on the parade ground. A ritual recitation of the battle is read by an officer. Drums roll, and the trumpeters sound the solemn notes of "Le Boudin." The drums continue in cadence with the trumpets while a procession parades to a table that represents the Monument to the Dead in the First RE (Regimende Étrangère). There they place a representation of the artificial hand of Captain Danjou, from where it presides over the ceremony that follows. After the legionnaires are paraded to music provided by the Legion band, they are dismissed.

During the afternoon, a carnival atmosphere prevails, centered around painstakingly prepared displays. Wine and beer flow freely while officers, NCOs, enlisted men, and former legionnaires mix freely without the usual restraints of rank. There are meetings, reunions, and open expressions of friendship, which reinforce the links of comradeship that are so critical to the *esprit* of the Legion.

Early the next day, Brooks received his corporal's stripes and was given command of a machine-gun team. The small tactical unit consisted of the team leader (himself), the gunner, the assistant gunner, and a grenadier-*voltigieur*—a rifleman equipped with a grenade launcher. Time flew by, and, late that summer, Brooks found himself engaged in a combat situation for the first time.

Late on a chill desert night, shrill blasts on a whistle pealed through the barracks. Several voices called out "Alert! Alert!" in French. William Brooks heard the commotion, which jerked him from sleep in a growing dread. For reasons of its own, the Legion got one up in the middle of the night only if it was for real.

Suddenly the duty sergeant ran through the barracks, shouting the accompaniment to the alert, "Aux armes!"

Utter confusion reigned among the aisles of bunks. Men cursed and stumbled about; the yelling became cacophonous.

"Respond to the alert! Long camouflage tunic and beret!"

"Hey, where are you?"

"Where are you?"

"Assembly in five minutes."

Through it all, order and conditioning prevailed. Gradually the teams began to assemble, despite the screaming and running about. Within ten minutes, Brooks stood in front of the ammunition bunker, waiting for his gun crew. With nothing else to do at the moment, Brooks followed the prime dictum of the legionnaire: "Whenever you get the chance to rest, take it." He had barely leaned back against the sandbags protecting the ammo bunker when he caught hell from Adjutant Cara, his perennial nemesis. In the midst of Cara's tirade, Brooks dashed off to round up his missing team.

Just as he assembled them and drew their ammunition issue, the command came to board trucks. "This is for real," Brooks realized. "Lauf! (Run!)" he shouted in German. They barely managed to find a place on the last truck.

"Roll call!" came the command after the company had assembled. [The Legion loves to call roll.]

When the roll call ended, team leaders received maps that they spread on truck hoods. Lanterns provided illumination. "Somalian forces have crossed the frontier border at Ghuister," announced the captain. "Our mission is to establish a defensive position. Our company is to defend the water hole, the access road located at . . . ," he gave the coordinates, "and the fort . . . Machine-gun sections one and two will . . . Machine-gun section three [Brooks's] will cover the road." The remaining assignments concluded the captain's orders. "Board the trucks. We leave at once."

"Vive la Légion!" *shouted the men. Eagerly they boarded the trucks, which wheeled out the gate at high speed, surrounded by billows of dust.*

Two hours of misery followed before the company reached the staging area outside Ghuister. They had been there three times before, Brooks thought morosely, all of them false alarms.

Six days went by in irritation, thirst, and dehydration before the legionnaires discovered that they had not come out there in vain. By then, the section Brooks commanded had been positioned some two hundred meters from the Somalia border and around eight hundred meters from the fort. They were overlooking the road, which ran along a dry riverbed, or oued. *The platoon leader, or* chef de section, *was Adjutant Cara. On the eve of that fateful sixth night, Cara summoned Brooks and another section leader, Batkin.*

His eyes alight with self-assumed cleverness, he announced his plan. "Tonight, les bounjouls *are going to attack in force, and the Legion will not be caught sleeping. Batkin, you are to move your* équipe *to within fifty meters of the frontier, but farther off to the left of the* oued *than you presently are. You will then turn to the right and have the* oued *to your front. That way, the Legion position will be like an L"*

"Mon Adjutant," Brooks spoke up, *"that will leave the base shorter than the arm."*

"Shut up!" screamed Cara. "You will take your machine-gun team to this hilltop, a hundred meters to the rear of Batkin's team. There, place your machine gun in battery and establish a point for your grenadier. Sergeant Minini is to place himself somewhere between both of your teams." Cara rubbed his hands in self-congratulation and satisfaction. "When the Somalis pass the border marker, we legionnaires will have them in an L ambush."

"How original," mumbled Brooks.

"Like it or not, Bride," Cara screamed, "you'll stay on that hill until hell freezes over. Get out of my sight!"

Brooks drew himself up sharply and saluted with crisp smartness. "Oui, mon Adjutant," he replied, straight-faced. Turning on his heel, he marched out of the tent.

After being joined by Sergeant Minini, the team loaded up

a case of .50 caliber ammunition ordered along by Cara, their machine gun, grenades, and other supplies and headed for the hill. Brooks organized their position so that the team could fire from the top of the hill during the day and from the base at night. He also purposely moved his men thirty meters closer to the frontier so that they wouldn't be shooting into the backs of their comrades.

By the time that was accomplished, darkness was rapidly descending. The legionnaires began to look for secure places to sleep, preferably somewhere free of scorpions and tarantulas. Brooks designated two men to stay by the machine gun on guard duty.

"You'll be replaced in two hours," he assured them.

Before the relief time came, the sound of vehicles impinged on the deep slumber of William Brooks.

"They're coming up the oued," *whispered one of the sentries.*

"To arms, to arms!"

Despite all of the alchoholism and slovenliness that assailed the legionnaires, the entire section got into place within one minute. As the men geared up for battle, Brooks looked on in amazement while Cara strode out into the middle of the dry riverbed. He raised the large, white walking stick that he carried and drove the base into the ground.

"If they pass this point, shoot!" he ordered.

Brooks could not fathom this seemingly mad act. He jumped up and worked his way to the foxhole of Sergeant Minini. "What the hell is he doing?" he asked after he slithered into the dugout.

*Minini shrugged. "*Le cafard *(the bug)—he's crazy and looking for flies."*

Under the illumination of a clear moon, Brooks had full command of the scene. He saw a patrol of Somalian regulars in Russian trucks creeping along the road in the wash. The Zil trucks groaned in low gear. Unlike the French, Brooks soon discovered, the Somalis made use of their blackout lights at night. The silver orb's near-day brightness allowed Brooks to make out the Somalis' distinct camouflage pattern.

Abruptly, the lead truck came to a halt. An officer dismounted and walked toward Cara. Two of the regulars climbed from the rear of the truck and spread out on either side of the vehicle. Cara and the Somali began a heated discussion. Ridiculous, Brooks considered, since neither one could understand the other. After several garbled exchanges, the Somali officer angrily slapped a riding crop against the outside of one thigh, turned, and stomped back to the truck, which drove away.

To the astonishment of Brooks, Cara remained in the middle of the oued. *The adjutant drew his pistol and began to walk back and forth nervously. A moment later, Adjutant Wilson, Second Section leader, came at a run.*

"Look, we're emplaced along the opposite side of the oued. *What are you going to do out here?"*

With Brooks looking on in amazement, Cara answered calmly, "I am going to stand in the middle of the oued.*"*

Wilson gave him a look that he would usually direct to a crazy man, then turned and trotted back toward his men.

Brooks climbed from the hole Minini occupied and crossed to where his team waited. He found his gunner, Bandera, cursing in Spanish and burning nervous energy by caressing the feed cover of the heavy machine gun. "Minini says Cara has been taken by le cafard,*" Brooks told him.*

"Shit, we could all say that," came Bandera's reply as Brooks eased himself down behind a large rock.

Before he could draw a relaxing breath, the sky lit up and the shooting war began in earnest. With soft pops, parachute flares ignited, while the muted thumps of dozens of mines detonating filled the air. Machine guns began to fire on both sides. Red and blue tracers swapped positions, to ricochet off small boulders and fat rocks. Rising, Brooks spotted the central resistance point over in Second Section. Loud, sharp krangs! *indicated that someone was throwing grenades. Their own team's gun opened with a ground-thumping roar.*

"Stop it; cease firing!" Brooks shouted to the gunner.

Bandera went through a hundred rounds before Brooks could silence the gun. "What the hell are you shooting at?" he bellowed over the tumult.

"Somalis!" Bandera yelped.

"Where?"

He got no answer. Instead, Bandera burned off two more

long bursts into the oued *before reloading. Brooks cut his gaze to the dry riverbed. He blinked when he saw Cara standing in the midst of it, at the center of the road, pistol in hand, cracking away at shadows.*

Confusion reigned. Brooks was quickly learning the old adage that the best-laid plans go into the toilet the instant the enemy is engaged. He had not the least idea what was happening. To him, it seemed that no one knew where to find the Somalis.

Abruptly, it ended. Parachute flares still floated laggardly toward the ground. In the silence, their distinctive fizzing could be heard clearly. A few seconds passed with no one speaking. Then the night's quiet ripped apart in a inundation of curses and epithets. In Arabic, French, German, Italian, Somalian, and Spanish, the most unspeakably vile, profane oaths erupted between the Somalis and the Legion. William Brooks stared in astonishment while for five minutes the rocks echoed with scores of imprecations that excoriated the desert, the Legion, the Somalis, France, Arabs, niggers, Jesus Christ, the Virgin Mary, the Lord God Jehovah, and everyone's mother.

"Shut up, all of you," Cara commanded after another half minute. "Bride, what can you see?"

"Rien, mon Adjutant." *In truth, he did see nothing.*

"Minini, you and Bride run across the frontier and see what's up. Come back in five minutes."

Not until they reached a strip of the oued *that was the Second Section's area of responsibility did they discover a body, sprawled among the rocks. A careful look-around revealed another a few meters away.*

Minini studied the corpses. "Must have come back on foot. Maybe some more will show up."

Brooks pursed his lips. "I doubt it. They only make a habit of doing this every month or so."

Brooks picked up an East German MP-44 assault rifle from among the rocks, and they walked back down the oued. *Rounding the bend in the riverbed, they came upon five dark, shadowy figures.*

"Halt!" came a low command in French.

"It's a patrol from Second Section," Brooks correctly identified the challenger.

"What did you find out there?"

Brooks addressed his peer, who led the patrol. *"The So-malis came back on foot in approximately platoon strength. There are two of them dead beyond this bend. The rest are a good two kilometers inside their border."* He knew that the Legion could not follow.

Adjutant Wilson and Captain Kaye were standing with Cara when the two NCOs returned. *"Two Somalis dead, two hun-dred meters down the* oued,*"* Minini reported, saluting. *"Sec-ond Section has a patrol out."*

"Thank you, Sergeant," Captain Kaye responded.

"Minini, pull your équipe choc *back to where you were this afternoon,"* Cara ordered. *"Leave Bride on the hill."*

Brooks saluted and remained silent. He turned and walked away to join his team. Dragging from the letdown of his adrenaline high, he failed even to get angry over the rip-off of the MP-44 by a covetous Cara. He found their position recamouflaged and Bandera linking together ammo belts. The young gunner was obviously agitated.

"How many did I get, Corporal Bride? Come on and tell me. I know I got the lot, Bride; they were on foot, must have been ten or fifteen."

Cara shouted from the oued *for everyone to shut their mouths. Dimly noted, Brooks heard him threaten eight days' extra duty. Feeling even worse, Brooks headed for his foxhole.*

"Come on, Corporal Bride, tell me how many I got," Ban-dera persisted.

Sighing, Brooks stopped and turned to face the gunner. *"You killed six, Bandera, and scared the rest away. You saved the company from being overrun. You can go and see for yourself in the morning."*

Grinning like a ninny, Bandera puffed out his chest. *"Maybe they'll come back. I'm gonna stand guard all night, Corporal Bride. I'm gonna sit right here behind my piece."*

"You do that, Bandera. I'm gonna go to sleep." Groggy, Brooks stumbled over lesser rocks until he reached his hole. Not bothering to remove his gear, he lay down on his back and leaned his weapon against a small boulder. Cupping his hands behind his neck, he gazed up into the dark bowl of the

desert sky. "So this is combat?" he thought. Stifling a yawn, he rolled over and went to sleep.

Conditions have improved somewhat from the time Brooks served with the Legion in the 1970s. Medical facilities have been modernized, with better and more readily provided treatment for all ailments. Basic hygiene is taught to all legionnaires. Married legionnaries are common now, and the French military establishment has provided married quarters. Granted, most of the married men are NCOs, usually holding the rank of *sergent-chef* or adjutant.

The mission of the Legion has changed considerably also. With the far-flung French Empire nonexistent, there are few wars for the Legion to be sent into. The Legion has been involved in securing peace in Guiana, and it returned to Somalia in 1983. With Corsica still French, and given the unrest and the proliferation of terrorism around the world, it is a good bet that the Legion will be needed for a good long time.

An American in Angola

George Bacon III (1946–1976)

by Mark Roberts

GEORGE BACON III WAS BORN AUGUST 4, 1946, IN BIDDE-ford, Maine, and spent his childhood in Longmeadow, Massachussets. Bacon's deep feelings for other people became evident early in his life. At one point in time, his younger sister wanted a tricycle. The family did not have one, nor the spare cash to buy one. With his own money, George purchased her a bike at a church bazaar. In a later incident, while visiting his grandmother in North Carolina, George found an abandoned puppy. He immediately adopted it and subsequently gave it to his sister. "He was always doing things like that," his mother observed later.

While attending Georgetown University, George Bacon developed his commitment to anti-Communism and to liberating the oppressed. His guidepost was a book written by Carroll Quigley, one of Bacon's professors: *Tragedy and Hope: A History of the World in Our Time.*

Bacon always enjoyed sports; swimming and deep-sea diving were among his favorites. A natural athlete, he tried hard and kept right on trying until the final whistle blew. That attitude, and an ability to remain calm in hazardous situations, would prove invaluable to him later in Vietnam and Laos.

After two years at Georgetown, Bacon abruptly joined the army. He found the attitudes of his professors and fellow students about America's past and its present course markedly at odds with his own. The army made a profound change in his life. At first bitterly disillusioned, to the point of actually considering desertion, he was eventually accepted for training in Special Forces.

In addition to the grueling training schedule undergone by candidates for Special Forces and the continuing exactitude of instructions and FTXs (field training exercises) expected of active Special Forces personnel, George Bacon decided that he would be most effective in Vietnam if he spoke the language. He began to study Vietnamese with a tutor in his spare time while still in training. By the time he reached Vietnam, he was fluent in the language and could speak Chinese with enough proficiency to communicate with the Nung mercenaries assigned to their unit. He later became an acknowledged authority on the Meo mountain tribesmen, whom he fought with in northern Laos. It is commonly accepted that the Meo dialect is the most difficult of all spoken languages, having never been standardized in any written or even alphabetical form.

By far, the language accomplishments of George Bacon were not his most outstanding achievements during his tours in Vietnam. One incident that came to light was reported by his father, who received an account in a letter in which George casually mentioned that a helicopter he was riding in had been shot down. One of the troops had been shot through the leg, and George recounted how he had bandaged it for him. He also related that, when the chopper went down behind enemy lines, the crew panicked. George told how he was able to "lay down enough firepower to keep the enemy at bay until another helicopter could land" and pick them up.

Bacon served in MACV-SOG—Studies and Observation Group. It conducted operations in North Vietnam, Laos, and Cambodia, which were carried out by Special Forces and native personnel; it had originally been called what it actually was, Special Operations Group, but the CIA adopted the euphemistic cover name to keep opponents ignorant of any escalation of U.S. involvement. A fellow soldier, who also served in that group, provided additional insight into Bacon's in-country experiences.

"I worked with George for three or four months in early 1969, and he was always in the thick of things. In February 1969, our team conducted a bomb damage assessment of what, up to that time, was the largest B-52 strike of the war—over one hundred B-52 sorties in twenty-four hours on the same target. The strike was directed against the headquarters of the North Vietnamese army's Twenty-seventh Regiment's base camp. The last bombs fell at 0730 hours, and we were inserted at 0830 hours. We stayed on the ground for less than six hours. Our team consisted of eight men—three Americans and five Vietnamese . . . We found numerous bunkers, and there were NVA all around us. We had blundered into a hornet's nest. Because of the large number of enemy in the area, the powers that be considered the raid to have been a success."

A second operation took them into the same area on a reconnaissance mission and prisoner snatch.

"We were inserted at 1100 hours. We had moved only one hundred meters away from the landing zone when we began taking heavy ground fire. Our point man took an AK round through the arm, and two other Vietnamese were wounded, though they could walk. George and I stayed behind and held off the enemy while the team leader and remainder of the team withdrew to the LZ and established a tight perimeter on the far side. It was hot and heavy as George and I detonated Claymores, threw grenades, and fired bursts—he from his CAR-15 and myself from a silenced Swedish K. We don't know how many we got, though I heard NVA screams after I tossed a white phosphorous grenade.

"During the firefight, I kept telling George to get out. He would not leave. We began arguing, as we were firing, about who should stay and who could leave. In the end, we compromised: both of us stayed. About fifteen minutes later, back at the perimeter of the LZ, I said, 'You ass! What are you trying to do? Be John Wayne?' He replied, 'Nope, just George Bacon.' "

When George returned to college that April, he wrote to his comrade and expressed his displeasure with the attitudes of his classmates. In the same letter, he stated that he was going to work for "Christians in Action," a popular code for the CIA. George attended Agency training in North Carolina, Florida, and Virginia. He wrote to his friend often but never said exactly what he was doing.

Bacon was recruited for the Agency through an old friend from Vietnam and was offered a job advising the Meo tribesmen in northern Laos. On a personal level, Bacon was not satisfied with the situation in Southeast Asia as reported in the newspapers or on television. When he accepted the offer, his father asked him the reason for interrupting his education a second time. Bacon replied that the university would always be there, but an opportunity with the CIA might not.

He went into the months of intensive Agency training with the same zeal with which he had embraced that of Special Forces. It soon paid dividends. Bacon was assigned to northern Laos as a case officer. His position was as the American counterpart to the Meo general Vang Pao. Over the months that followed, he roamed the Plain of Jars and Skyline Ridge with large combat units of the Meo in an effort to contain the North Vietnamese regular units, who were showing up in increasingly large numbers. Bacon was responsible for millions of dollars' worth of material and for hundreds of thousands of dollars in cash funds. During the course of his service with the Meo, he was promoted three times and awarded the Intelligence Star, the Agency's second-highest award, for the example of leadership he set among the Meo troops while under fire.

The citation that accompanied the medal stated:

Mr. George W. Bacon III is hereby awarded the Intelligence Star in recognition of his outstanding services performed under conditions of grave personal risk. While serving as an advisor to a large indigenous force in Southeast Asia, the key strategic military base to which he was assigned was subjected to a massive enemy attack. During the four-month siege, Mr. Bacon and his associates handled a myriad of organizational, logistical, and tactical problems experienced by the friendly forces. Despite heavy enemy bombardment, Mr. Bacon volunteered to remain on duty at the base pro-

viding moral and physical support, thus inspiring the indigenous defenders to withstand the attack. Mr. Bacon's courageous and professional performance was in keeping with the highest tradition of the Agency, reflecting great credit on him and the Federal service.

While serving as a case officer for the CIA, Bacon was placed in charge of Site 15, one of a string of support elements to the main CIA base at Long Tieng, located in a long, narrow valley reminiscent of Dien Bien Phu. It was there that he locked horns with some of the pilots of Air America. It boiled down to a simple point: Bacon was more aggressive then they were. The support site was manned by a battalion, sometimes two, of Thai mercenaries, and ringed by the enemy. It was therefore necessary for Bacon to send out his wounded and get out for meetings by air, and to get himself and all supplies back in the same way.

Unfortunately, the Pathet Lao had circled the firebase with 12.7mm antiaircraft machine guns. That made it quite unpleasant, if not downright dangerous, for the chopper pilots and their slow-moving birds. Bacon was constantly on their cases because he believed they should be more assertive in executing their missions. They should at least, he thought, show as much zeal as he did. The pilots did not agree.

The impasse was eventually resolved in Bacon's favor, although all Americans were pulled out of the Long Tieng Valley shortly thereafter.

After his return to the States, Bacon entered a literal roller coaster of existence. He completed his studies of political science at the University of Massachusetts, graduating *summa cum laude* in June 1974. Following that, he flirted briefly with Veterans and Volunteers for Vietnam (VVV), a recruiting center for personnel to return to Southeast Asia for the purpose of fighting the NVA in the twilight days of the Nguyen Van Thieu regime. There he met the head of the organization, Bart Bonner. Bonner and Bacon hit it off at once, and Bacon was chosen to organize the military aspect of the organization.

When the efforts of VVV terminated, Bacon attended the Commercial Diving Center at Wilmington, California, where he successfully completed an advance course in skin and scuba diving, air and mixed-gas diving, and underwater photography. After graduating first in his class, Bacon went to work for a diving firm in Louisiana. With this job experience, he flew to England in search of employment with one of the oil firms operating in the North Sea. When a job failed to materialize, Bacon found that a new place to fight Communism had reared its inviting head.

In December 1975, Bacon flew to South Africa. He planned to do a photojournalism piece on the situation in Angola. Cuban troops had recently moved in to help the leftist MPLA (Popular Movement for the Liberation of Angola) seize control of the country. The photojournalism project fell through, but that did not slow George Bacon.

He went to Lusaka, Zambia, where he offered his services to Dr. Jonas Savimbi's UNITA (National Union for the Total Independence of Angola). UNITA was one of several anti-Communist groups fighting the MPLA. Bacon was well received by Savimbi's lieutenants, yet when he met with Savimbi's number-two man, he was inexplicably rejected out of hand.

Bacon returned to the United States and in January (1976) met with a group of blacks who were supposedly recruiting for Angola and who were sponsored by the Congress for Racial Equality (CORE). It soon became evident to Bacon that nothing would come of this group. More ups and downs would follow.

Eventually, Bacon got to Kinshasa through the good offices of David Bufkin. Bart Bonner later recalled that he believed that if Bacon had been told the truth about the situation in Angola, he would not have gone. He expected to go there and find an active company of American volunteers. Instead, he found half a dozen men trying to stop a Cuban deluge. Regardless, Bacon leaped into the Angolan conflict in the way he knew best: as a fighting man.

He awoke early in the morning in the FNLA camp [National Front for the Liberation of Angola, a combative anti-Communist group] *with the feeling that the day would be crappy. As usual, no one else stirred yet. After a bitter cup of C-rat coffee* [Antique C rations, declared "surplus" by the U.S. military and sold on the open market] *he began his usual rounds of the RON* [Rest Over Night] *camp. Their mission was to mine two bridges. Bacon checked over the wooden cases of TNT blocks. By then, the mercenary known as "The Englishman" had awakened and groped for coffee with heavy-lidded eyes.*

"Bloody hell, George, I wish there was some decent tea out here."

George Bacon shrugged and nodded toward the C rats.

Within half an hour, the six Africans in the team had awakened and also broken their fast. The small unit set out at once for their objective. George still bore a sense of unease. Dappled sunlight danced through the jungle canopy. Bacon sighed in relief when they reached the two concrete bridges without incident. The level, unarched spans crossed a small gorge formed by a dry riverbed. He could not understand why he felt as nervous as a hooker in the Vatican.

Through the offices of The Englishman, Bacon told the African troopers to begin digging shallow trenches at each end of the first bridge. "I'll place the charges myself," he concluded.

While the Zairean mercenaries labored, the jungle animal sounds gradually returned to normal. Bacon appeared completely at ease. He had been in one jungle or another for most of his adult life, so the incessant buzz and dive-bombing of the myriad insects did not bother him very much, nor did the sickly sweet odor of the endless cycle of rot and rebirth of the jungle flora.

Bacon took a shovel and began to clean out the bottom of one trench. When the first bridge was in readiness, he took up a canvas bag and began to trail out fuse from the edges of the trenches to a secure spot where he estimated that none of the concrete or dirt would fall. Then he placed the charges and directed the African mercs to cover them and pack the earth tightly over the top. Abruptly, his heightened sense of hearing picked out an indistinct, man-made sound that came from the direction of Quimba Junction. His eyes swept the jungle to the north.

Gradually, the grind and the groan of an internal combustion engine could be heard. Immediately alert, Bacon had his weapon at the ready.

Ten seconds later, a Land Rover rounded a curve and came into view among the trees. Bacon eased off the trigger. After a moment, he recognized a former English paratrooper, Michael T. Sharpley, whom he had met two days earlier in Kinshasa. Sharpley had served with the Territorial Reserves and was a veteran of the Rhodesian army. A good man, Bacon judged. With Sharpley was another American, Gary Acker, an ex-Marine and Vietnam veteran. Another proven soldier. The Land Rover drew up close, and Sharpley dismounted, addressing the other occupants of the vehicle. "We'll take a break here for a spot of breakfast." To Bacon: "Rigging the bloody bridges, is it?"

Bacon nodded and reached for several blocks of TNT. "Right. The frigging Cubans are close to San Salvador. If they and the Angolans take the town, it's our job to see they don't go any farther."

"I wish you luck, Yank. Here, let me help you with that."

Working with Bacon, Sharpley helped set the charges in the first ditch at the end of the second bridge. Sweating although it was still early morning, they proceded to implant the others.

"Now we put in the detonators and cover up," Bacon indicated the obvious.

Sharpley scrutinized the lines of fuse trailing off the bridge and expressed his appreciation of Bacon's skill. "Good thinking to lay the fuses first. Everything nice and tidy, what?"

Bacon knelt and used a nonferrous metal awl to pierce the small waxed-paper diaphragm in the central block of TNT. "Yep," he agreed as he inserted a copper fuse cap into the explosive. "Learned that in Laos. Makes it quicker if you're pressed for time."

The moment they stepped away from the charge, the African mercs began to cover them with shovelsful of dirt. Sharpley appraised the progress on the second bridge. One fist on his hip over a holstered Browning Hi-Power, he spoke briskly. "Well, you've a bit to do yet. And we have a patrol to complete. The team we're relieving should be on the way back to Quimba. I'll send Acker with them. He has a radio, and you can keep in touch with us."

Bacon made a face of disgust. "Don't count on it. Those vacuum-tube jobs don't function all that well in this jungle."

He went on to express a pet peeve. "At home, I've got a transistor radio that fits in my pocket. Why can't we get modern, solid-state gear out here?"

"Because the Khafirs in FNLA don't have the money, old boy. One can pick up these old blowers for pence on the dollar. So that's what we have."

"When we have it," Bacon replied, thinking of his own lack of a radio.

Sharpley turned toward his Land Rover. "We're off, then. Good luck."

By ten o'clock in the morning, Bacon and his team completed the mining of the second bridge. He and the team sought a spot of convenient shade and ate a hurried, early lunch. The fare was C rations again. Bacon opened his and examined an olive green can. "Beans and Vienna Sausages."

"Hell, the closest these things ever got to Vienna was Hoboken, New Jersey," Bacon groused aloud.

After they had eaten, the young American made ready to detonate the charges. He paused at the distant sound of an approaching engine, this time coming from the south. In a short while, another Land Rover came into view. Riding shotgun was Gary Acker. He greeted Bacon in a state of agitation.

"These guys told us the Cubans are closing in on San Salvador. Sharpley said that if they haven't taken the town already, he'll come back this way. We're to wait for him."

"All right. Then I won't blow the bridges right now. Don't want to attract attention our way. Best send this patrol on to Quimba to report. The Englishman can go with them."

"Leaving us here alone?" Acker asked in concern.

Bacon's decision had come from experiences in Laos and Vietnam. "Sure. The fewer of us there are, the less chance of being seen. We'll keep my Land Rover so we don't have to walk out."

Within seconds, the patrol departed for Quimba Junction. The tingling sensation of something just not right intensified for George Bacon. Shortly after eleven, static crackled for attention on Acker's radio. He responded with alacrity.

Acker turned to Bacon with a troubled expression. "The relieved patrol has not yet reached Quimba. And Sharpley's team has not reported in on schedule. There's something wrong out there.''

Frowning, Bacon stood upright. "We'd better look for Sharpley.''

Acker gestured to the parked vehicle. "Are we taking the Land Rover?''

"Naw. No sense in advertising our presence. We'll walk.''

Observing excellent noise discipline, the two veteran soldiers set off down the narrow jungle track toward San Salvador. They fully expected to encounter Sharpley's patrol on its way back. It was around noon when the Cubans sprang an ambush with a suddenness that momentarily immobilized Bacon and Acker. Then they reacted with blinding speed.

Bacon dove for one side of the road, Acker for the other. Overhead, 7.62×39mm rounds cracked from the AK-47s in the hands of Fidel's finest. Acker heard a low groan and looked over to see that Bacon had taken a hit in the abdomen. While he watched, George Bacon took two more rounds, one in the chest. Acker returned fire, trying to suppress the fusillade coming from the Cubans. Bacon received two more wounds, both sufficient to be mortal, and sank to his knees. The Cubans broke cover.

Bacon fell onto one side. Acker laid down his FLN and raised his hands. A moment later, at approximately 12:04 P.M., February 14, 1976, George Washington Bacon III died in the stinking jungle of Angola.

Modern Mercs

A New World with New Mercenaries

The level of military training and quality of soldier that is available for purchase in the world today is incredible. Rather than just former Belgian army officers (some of whom were incredibly skilled) you can now find for hire a wide number of Spetsnatz (the Russian equivalent of navy SEALs) and pilots from all of Eastern Europe. You can hire hundreds of highly trained South African military personnel released from service at the end of apartheid. For security, you can now find state-trained KGB, GRU, and South African Internal Police force personnel, often with ten or twenty years of experience. Even former SEALs and similar highly skilled Americans are de facto mercenaries operating as security companies, providing protection for people and locations in every corner of the world and at all levels of risk.

The equipment, too, has changed. Where once a mercenary needed to be able to fire a weapon and know tactics, today the demand includes computer skills, aircraft repair skills, and similar high-technology abilities, though the need to shoot well certainly hasn't lessened in any way. This increased demand is reflected in the two Harriers actually owned and flown in Africa by one mercenary group formed from men who have left the South African military. Satellite communications and location devices have also changed the way mercenaries fight. Finally, the incredible amount of former Soviet and Eastern Bloc military hardware being sold openly on the world's black market has immeasurably escalated the demands on paid military personnel. Today, everyone is much better armed than even twenty years ago.

One other factor has made a massive difference. This is who the mercenaries are fighting for. As the cold war has passed and the need for mercenaries to maintain control of colonies has all but disappeared, a new group of employers has arisen. They are, not surprisingly, those with money. The two most prominent groups are not nations or revolutionaries, but corporations and cartels. When you have a fifty-million-dollar investment in the equipment alone at a well head or drilling sight, the mere threat of terrorist actions or simply bandits requires that the location be well protected. In many cases, the multinational corporations do not trust the local governments to provide the quality of protection they desire. Instead, they provide their own security—in effect, mercenary teams who protect rather than attack. These highly skilled mercenaries often earn well over $100,000 annually.

The other group with money is the dark side of the modern mercenary: a group of individuals and organizations that have massive wealth and hire large numbers of mercenaries, from specialists and pilots to simply rifle-armed guards. These are the drug cartels. While most mercenaries won't work for a group this destructive and untrustworthy, some do. In this last section, we examine the actions and personalities of the modern mercenary. It begins with mercenaries who, you may be surprised to discover, plied their trade in the eastern U.S., and it continues by examining the dark reality of mercenary life in the South American wars.

Coal Miners' Mercenaries

Appalachia, 1985

by Kevin Dockery

MERCENARIES ARE NOT JUST THOSE MEN WHO ARE RECRUITED to fight actions in lands foreign to their own. There are mercenaries who operate openly within the United States and other countries, acting as security specialists or consultants for both private individuals and corporations. Foreign employers of such men need to be on the State Department–approved list or the specialists may face criminal charges, if not worse on their return home.

A large number of corporations, mostly those involved in the defense industries, hire ex-military and otherwise qualified individuals to do military-oriented contact work overseas. And in some of these contracts, the risks can be fairly high, with the pay commensurate to those risks. But the men who work in these areas tend to be technicians more than trigger-pullers.

There are organizations in the United States and elsewhere who hire out their men with the expectation that their employees may easily see combat. Though a prospective employer intending to hire men to conduct a coup against some government would quickly find himself out on the street, employers from areas where terrorist or other activities are common could hire himself some very hard men capable of doing a difficult job.

In Great Britain, one of these companies is GSG Ltd., which has branch offices in Kathmandu, Nepal, Durban, South Africa, and Nairobi, Kenya. Through the GSG Ltd. offices, specialists in explosive ordnance disposal who can clear bombs and mines from combat areas, or security forces made up of retired Gurkhas from the British army, are both available. In South Africa, Executive Outcomes supplies specialized security forces for a high-risk environment. The men from Executive Outcomes come from diverse backgrounds such as the South African military, the German Bundeswehr, and even the Australian SAS. Specialists such as these can protect a farm or mine property, hunt down poachers, or reorganize a small country's military forces.

In the United States, such men are used for security work in much the same situations. During the mid-1980s, serious problems arose in the Appalachian Mountain areas of southern West Virginia and southeastern Kentucky. Negotiations on labor disputes between the United Mine Workers of America (UMWA) and the A.T. Massey Coal Company had failed, with violent results.

Who started this violence depends on who you ask. Both sides in the strike, the union and the mine owner, have their defenders and detractors. What is easily seen is that a simpler and more direct brand of justice is common to the citizens of the affected areas.

Violence has proven itself a common thread throughout the history of coal mining in the United States. Mine owners have shot strikers, such as during a strike in Colorado in 1914, when security forces opened fire on a crowd of miners, wounding twenty-five. The mine workers' union itself has a difficult history. As recently as 1970, UMWA reform presidential candidate Joe Yablonsky and his family were murdered. Orders for the murder were later traced to then–UMWA president W. A. "Tony" Boyle.

The background of the Appalachian Mountains also added to the volatility of the strike situation. Well-paying jobs are few and far between in some of the rural areas of Kentucky and West Virginia. And families feel threatened when their source of livelihood is taken away. Crossing a man by not dealing in what he would consider good faith will also cause a reaction. The culture of the area has a tradition of men taking a hands-on approach to solving their own problems. And with the background of clan feuds and other brutal actions, opinions about disputes can be spoken from the barrel of a gun.

Early in 1985, the equivalent of a guerrilla war broke out when mines under the A. T. Massey corporate umbrella hired temporary workers to keep the coal coming during a strike. Union members, seeing their primary weapon—the closing of the mines—threatened, resorted to more direct action.

It is difficult to say who fired the first shot, and it is not in the purview of this writing to make the attempt. But the striking workers and their sympathizers did benefit from a variety of paramilitary actions against the mines. Homes and cars of the mine executives and the replacement workers were shot up. Mine offices came under sporadic fire. Electrical supplies were cut off by demolition of the substations and suspension lines. Communications for the mines were cut off when telephone lines were brought down and radio transmission towers dynamited. Roads were blocked, and, when the replacement drivers tried to clear the blockage, their trucks were fired on.

Straightforward ambushes were also conducted against the mine owners' interests. A convoy of coal trucks was attacked on May 29, 1985. After the hail of automatic-weapons fire was over, the lead driver, Hayes West, lay dying where he had crawled to cover underneath his truck. The ambushers were never caught or publicly charged.

To combat actions like this, dozens of specialized security personnel were brought in by the mine owners. Some of these security men were professional mercenaries, ex-soldiers, and ex–police officers. And some of the men hired were little more than thugs. Sniping and countersniping experts who had fought in several wars were brought in. Physical security was boosted with barbed wire and concertinas, steel fencing, and reinforced barricades across the roads approaching the mines.

The sheer size of the mines' properties, their status as private property, the ruggedness of the terrain, and the limited manpower available prevented the local or state police agencies from being able to protect the mines directly. But the police did do their best to contain the worst of the violence.

The mine owners considered no expense for the security of their continued operations to be too great. Several armored locomotives were acquired to move the long coal trains while protecting the crews. Two military-style armored personnel carriers showed up at one of the mines to provide additional security. But the two carriers were kept under wraps most of the time as it was found that their appearance raised the likelihood of violence more than they calmed things down.

During the eighteen-month-long strike, many of the lower-quality security personnel of the mines created more violence than they prevented. But some of the security personnel brought in by the mine owners were top-quality men. One company, owned and directed by an ex–Secret Service agent, supplied mercenaries who had fought in Africa, the Middle East, and Central America to one of the mines. These men included ex–Special Forces officers who directed field operations with a professional hand.

Countersnipers had armored observations posts put up to their specifications to oversee a mine's property. Medical personnel with military experience and bomb-disposal experts were also brought on-site to curb the situation.

Eventually, the mine workers returned to work, the mines reopened fully, and the situation died down. But the background causes of the violence that erupted still exist. It would only take another strike or other such incident to set the regions on fire again.

The Cocaine Wars

Drug Mercs in the 1980s

by Kevin Dockery

THE 1980S SAW A NEW AVENUE OF EMPLOYMENT FOR MER-cenaries, as well as a new kind of mercenary. In Colombia, the cocaine lords had gathered together to form the Medellín Cartel, named after the city they were based in. The control of this cartel was such that they held power not only in the city of Medellín itself, but also in a large portion of the surrounding countryside. With illicit drug money flowing into their coffers, the cartel rose in wealth and power to a point that it was able to openly defy the elected government of the country.

Though many elements of both the Colombian police and the military were being directed by the wealthy cocaine cartel, the drug leaders needed even more manpower to extend their control and further secure their territory. One source of this manpower was a terrorist guerrilla organization operating in Colombia, the Movimiento 19 de Abril (19th of April Movement), also known as M-19.

Operating in the jungles and mountains of Colombia since 1970, M-19 was a ready source of trained and experienced men. Operations by M-19 to style themselves a popular peoples' army, able to overthrow the elected government of Colombia, had proven ineffective by the mid-1980s. Antiguerrilla actions by the Colombian military were becoming more successful, badly limiting the movements of the M-19 force. To try to force the military to cut back their operations, the terrorists performed an action that quickly won them the attention of both the world and the Medellín Cartel.

In a countering move against the government's actions, M-19 seized the Bogotá Palace of Justice on November 6, 1985. Almost five hundred hostages were taken in the seizure, including a number of high-ranking Colombian justice officials. In the counterattack by government troops, fifty hostages, including eleven Supreme Court judges, were killed. All of the M-19 terrorists were killed during the assault.

The stepped-up actions of the Colombian government against M-19 after the Palace of Justice seizure almost succeeded in destroying the organization. Losses for M-19 following the November 1985 attack included a number of top leaders captured or killed. To increase the organization's money flow and support structure, M-19 hired out as "protectors" to a number of major Colombian cocaine traffickers. Some of this "hiring" may have been the result of extortion on the part of the M-19 group and the drug traffickers.

Though not able to directly face heavy military force, M-19 was more than capable of protecting cocaine production and processing facilities. Experienced in moving undetected, the guerrillas were also able to escort the finished product into the northbound smuggling pipeline.

M-19 needed the funds available from the cartel to pay for the restoration of their Communist-oriented battle against the government of Colombia. The arms supplied by the cartel also went a long way to restoring the military power of the guerrillas. The Medellín Cartel simply needed the forces of the guerrillas to protect its own interests. Through this cooperation, the era of the terrorist/guerrilla as mercenary and the position of narco-terrorism was solidified in South America.

With its estimated two hundred to one thousand members, M-19 was not the first terrorist organization in Colombia to take advantage of the funds available from the drug trade. The Fuerzas Armadas Revolucionarias de Colombia (Revolutionary Armed Forces of Colombia, or FARC) was a slightly older and much larger organization than M-19. Established in 1966, the active membership of FARC was estimated to include four thousand to five thousand armed guerrillas by the 1980s. The size of the organization was due in no small part to the money of the drug trade.

In the early 1980s, FARC organized a protection racket for the Colombian cocaine producers. Payments to FARC saw to it that no damages befell cocaine production, storage, or growing facilities. The drug lords could see the advantages of the straightforward criminal enterprise FARC was proposing, and money was soon forthcoming. With the very lucrative cocaine trade as a base, FARC was able to grow into a larger organization and spread its influence from the rural areas into the major cities of Colombia.

In spite of its proposed dedication to the Communist-oriented guerrilla movement in Colombia, FARC moved to strengthen its situation with the Colombian cartels and the drug trade in general. Targets for FARC centered around any perceived threat to their drug-trade links. Besides providing protection to the cartels, FARC has also been suspected of providing manpower for the basic processing of coca leaves.

By the late 1980s, the Medellín Cartel had grown to the point that the leader of the organization, Pablo Escobar Gaviria, was able to offer to pay off the national debt of Colombia. In exchange for paying off the debt, Escobar simply wanted to be left alone to conduct his business. Rejection of his offer caused Escobar to "declare war" on the Colombian government, a threat not taken lightly due to his army of thousands of M-19 and FARC guerrillas.

Pablo Escobar had developed his own following among the people of the Medellín area that was much more successful than the actions of FARC and M-19 had been in winning over the peasant population. Building and maintaining a large housing development, almost a private suburb, Escobar allowed Medellín's poor to live on his estates rent-free. In addition to giving away housing and protection, Escobar also supplied his "tenants" with *bazuko,* a smokable and highly addictive mixture of raw cocaine base and tobacco. This generosity insured the loyalty of the now-addicted poor to the supplier of their homes and drugs, Pablo Escobar.

Cooperation between the drug barons and the guerrillas could be a very unstable situation. Generally, the political desires of the guerrillas were in direct opposition to the situations that allowed the drug cartels to operate so profitably. Alliances could change overnight, and former business partners would suddenly find themselves enemies. And this situation existed not just between the drug cartels and the terrorists; even the uncorrupted segments of the Colombian government found it occasionally necessary to forge links with allies they otherwise considered a dread foe.

By late 1987, the situation changed between at least some of the drug lords and their guerrilla allies. Jose Gonzalo Rodriguez "El Mejicano" Gacha, a senior member of the Medellín Cartel, saw that the FARC and M-19 forces were setting themselves up as major players in the local narcotics economy, to such a point that they could become rivals to the cartel itself. It was in Gacha's best interests to see that this situation ended before it could establish itself further, but he didn't have the manpower to do the job himself.

In a very unusual turn of events, Gacha joined forces with some elements of the Colombian military to develop a strike force to use against the guerrillas. Gacha would supply the men for the operation, in the form of a detachment of his own bodyguards, and the Colombian military would supply arms and instruction in weapons and tactics.

In effect, the Colombian military was working with the cartel's men in order to destroy a group that might become direct competition to the cartel's drug trade. This was an extreme example of "the enemy of my enemy is my friend." However, the Colombians did not wish to use their own forces to supply the training because it would greatly risk their relationship with, and aid received from, the United States, which was strongly against the drug trade in any form.

The use of American military advisers was completely out of the question, and even the use of qualified American mercenaries was considered too risky. If word got out in the U.S. that the Colombian government was working closely with the Medellín Cartel, quick action would soon follow in the U.S. Congress that would severely curtail any further U.S.-Colombian cooperation.

A decision was made to tap the British mercenary market for the needed military instructors. In the spring of 1988, a Colombian military intelligence colonel arrived in England to initiate the recruitment of the needed personnel. Since this was, at least on the surface, an officially sponsored Colombian government operation, well-qualified professional soldiers were not difficult to locate. David Tomkins, considered an excellent administrator as well as an experienced mercenary, was approached with the contract to put together and lead the training team.

Tomkins was well known to the various British agencies that keep an eye on their homegrown mercenaries. The fact that no members of the British intelligence services or military approached him about the Colombian contract probably guided Tomkins' decision to accept the job. It was long a rule among the more successful mercenaries not to work in the narcotics trade. Though the money might be excellent and the working conditions good, job security was even less stable than being on the losing side in a civil war. Along with that, the rest of the world tended to deal harshly with any captured mercenaries abandoned by their employers.

With what appeared to be a good, government-sponsored contract in his hands, Tomkins turned to recruiting the balance of his training team. Peter McAleese, a British former soldier with tours in the Special Air Service and British Parachute Regiment, as well as mercenary experience in Angola, was picked by Tomkins to command the operation in Colombia.

A number of mercenaries were contacted by Tomkins in June 1988 and asked if they would be willing to join "a company of men to kill Communist terrorists." That the operation was officially sanctioned and that Peter McAleese would be the commander, combined with the reported $5,000 (U.S.) per month pay for a three-month contract, was enough for most of the mercs to sign on.

Eight British and two Australian mercenaries finally made up the group under McAleese that would report to Colombia and conduct training. After a stand-by of several months, a sudden call in early August put the mercenaries in Paris with just a few days' notice. They were there to catch a plane to Bogotá, Colombia.

During a few days' layover in Bogotá, at least some of the mercenaries were again told that the operation was to fight Communist terrorists. Most of the mercs had fought this same enemy in Africa and elsewhere in the world, so the idea of fighting the same type of group in Colombia held no particular fears for them. That the operation was sanctioned by the Colombian government helped eliminate fears by the mercs that they would be sucked into the drug trade without knowing it. But it may be very possible that the Colombian government officials directing the op were in the pay of the Medellín Cartel or others. This fact was never made public. What was eventually known was that Gacha was bankrolling a majority of the operation.

Within a few days of their arrival in Bogotá, the mercs were driven to a river, where they boarded a boat that would take them to the primary training area. The training area was on an island, soon christened "Fantasy Island" by the impressed mercenaries.

Instead of the rough living conditions that mercenary teams often found themselves in, the training island was more along the lines of a professional vacation resort. A large house with a full support staff [maid service, cooks, etc.] along with a generous booze ration and a number of women brought in every Saturday gave the beginning of the operation a satisfactory feel to the surprised mercs.

A light training schedule to acclimatize the mercs to the high heat and humidity of the area was begun by McAleese prior to the first trainees' arriving. The mornings were begun at dawn with a run followed by refresher military training. The afternoons were spent avoiding the worst heat of the day with an additional hour of training toward the early part of the evening. Nights were mostly personal time.

A week or so after their arrival on the island, the first of the trainees arrived. Fairly well outfitted with equipment and personal weapons, including CAR-15 rifles and sidearms, the trainees may not have been the personal bodyguards of Gacha as was originally suggested. It is suspected that the Colombians were instead members of the paramilitary death squad called Muerte a Secuestradores (Death to Kidnappers, or MAS).

Founded in December 1981 by over two hundred of Colombia's top drug lords, MAS was intended to combat the kidnappings for ransom of the families of the drug kingpins by M-19 and possibly other terrorist groups. Rumors and announcements by the Medellín Cartel indicated that MAS had a war chest of over seven million dollars and a force of over two thousand men. Though these numbers sound excessive in regard to the men, the funding of MAS could easily have been met by the drug lords.

A rare public announcement by the Medellín Cartel stated that the "basic objective [of MAS] will be the public and immediate execution of all those involved in the kidnappings." It was the kidnapping of Marta Nieves Ochoa, the youngest sister of Jorge Luis "Fat Man" Ochoa Vasques of the cartel, that finally caused the drug lords to establish MAS in defense of their families.

In light of the reason for the training being given by the mercenaries—actions against M-19 and FARC—it is very likely that the trainees were either members of MAS or veterans from that organization. A number of reports concerning the Colombian personnel involved with this operation are in conflict with one another. But the suggestion that the men supplied by Gacha were involved with MAS seems to fit the facts as known.

Orders for the operation had come to the mercenaries through legitimate Colombian government channels, so the identity of the men to be trained had little importance. Soon after the first group of Colombians arrived, training began to turn them into a coordinated team. The instruction program for the Colombians was based on British and South African doctrines. The trainees responded well, as long as instructions were clear and complete. Orders had to be exact, as the students had little experience in operating as part of a military team, and whatever their previous employment, it appeared to have held little encouragement for individual action.

Even with the cooperation of the students, training did not run as smoothly as the mercenaries would have liked. Though Gacha was known to have put up a good deal of money for the operation's expenses, much of these funds never made it to a place where it could help the trainees. Instead, a large amount of the funds for the mission went into the pockets of some of the Colombian authorities in charge of supplies and support. Instead of the five tons of weapons and munitions requested by the mercenaries, only a small quantity of poor matériel showed up at irregular times. The Colombian government had reneged on their commitment to supply weapons from official stocks, if it had ever been intended from the beginning.

The few Uzis and AK-47s that arrived were insufficient to arm all eleven of the mercenaries. Though an M-60 machine gun was supplied, none of the needed belted ammunition ever arrived to allow its use. Even the small number of weapons that were supplied to the trainees were of poor quality. Most of the weapons were missing some portion of their sights, making training with them and their effective use difficult at best.

But the training mission continued in spite of the difficulties. Cooperation between the trainees and the merc team was satisfactory, and there was apparently little friction between the two groups. This situation continued on the island for the better part of a month before things changed. The number of men the mercenaries were working with had increased to around sixty trainees when orders came down from the government that disrupted the smoothly running program. Now the Colombian officials wanted the mercenaries to put a hold on the ultimate mission, the elimination of the terrorist guerrillas.

Apparently, the government was talking with the terrorists the mercenaries were intended to target with their Colombian troops. As the situation shifted, so did the mercenaries' situation. With the government becoming increasingly concerned that the whole mercenary operation might be found out, the merc team and their students had to move off the island to a substantially less comfortable camp.

In total, the mercs and their students were moved through three different camps. And with each change of location, the living conditions deteriorated. A diet of often poorly prepared lentils, fried bananas, and canned tuna resulted in a number of the mercenaries and students becoming ill from both disease and malnutrition.

As a final straw to the mercenaries' situation, information came to the men that Gacha might be about to remove his support for the operation and switch back to being on the same side as the terrorist guerrillas the mercenaries were intended to target. One of the basic rules for being a successful, or surviving, mercenary is knowing when to say "no." Along with this rule is one of equal importance: knowing when to say "That's enough."

Very early in November, Tomkins and McAleese decided that the situation had become too confused for them to remain. Gacha was on the verge of moving back to the side of the guerrillas, which would have put the mercenaries in the position of training forces that would be fighting the legitimate government of Colombia. Continuing training would result in the mercenaries' being on the wrong side of international law, which was not a situation they were willing to accept.

Leaving the trainees at their final camp, the merc team moved by boat and then vehicle to a small town where they holed up to assess their situation. There was a possibility that the mission against the guerrillas would still go on. That chance was a small one, but it was against the mercenaries' nature to abandon a twelve-week contract after only nine weeks had passed.

During the three days the mercenaries spent in the small town, they saw a news program that finalized their decision to get out of Colombia while they still could. Though none of the mercs were fluent in Spanish, they were able to make some sense out of a news program that appeared to connect "mercenaries" with another story, this one on executions in the electric chair. That was enough to put the mercs on a plane to Bogotá, where they quickly booked separate flights out of the country.

Direct Action in Cali

The Assault on Hacienda Napoles, 1989

by Kevin Dockery

THOUGH THE MERCENARIES HAD LEFT COLOMBIA UNDER less-than-ideal circumstances during the first week of November 1988, the team had apparently left a worthwhile impression on at least some of the government officials they had been working with. Although they had been training what was effectively a private army, the mercenaries had been doing so under the direction of the legitimate government of Colombia, and that had kept them from breaking any laws, Colombian or international.

In January 1989, Dave Tomkins was again approached by the same Colombian colonel who had contacted him for the training operation. This time, the contract offered by the colonel was for a much more serious operation, the assassination of Pablo Escobar himself. In addition to targeting Escobar, any other Medellín Cartel who were in the target area during the proposed strike would be fair game, including Jose Gacha, who was no longer working with the government.

That it was the same government officer who had approached him earlier held some significance for Tomkins. Since the target this time was the leadership of the Medellín Cartel, it was very doubtful that the operation was being guided by the drug lords. The apparent official sanction of at least part of the Colombian government was enough to convince Tomkins to accept the contract, and he immediately set to recruiting the necessary force.

Again, Tomkins turned to Peter McAleese to initiate the recruiting contacts and lead the team in the field. Some of the mercenaries for the new contract came from the same group that had run the training mission in Colombia only a few months before. Additional men, again British and South African, were brought on board to work with the team for the first time. In early February, the initial calls to the mercenary recruits went out from McAleese. Later in February, McAleese and two of the new recruits went on as an advance party to Colombia to set up the situation before the main force arrived.

The men McAleese had selected to make up the balance of the team were contacted by Tomkins in March. Tomkins arranged individual meetings with each of the potential recruits and gave them a basic outline of the intended mission. The fact that Tomkins and McAleese were putting the operation together was apparently enough for a majority of the mercenaries, and the team was quickly assembled. Each man accepted was given around three thousand dollars for expenses and to act as a retainer.

Five of the mercenaries met at Tomkins's home in Hampshire, England, on March 23 to leave for the mission in Colombia. After an evening in Tomkins's home, the group traveled to Heathrow Airport, where they caught a flight to Bogotá, Colombia. The long flight put the mercenaries in Colombia, five time zones earlier than England, on Friday, March 24.

After an overnight stay at the Hotel Bacata, the group took a short flight to Cali, several hundred miles southwest of Bogotá's location in central Colombia, Cali had been chosen as the temporary gathering point for the mercenaries for a number of reasons. Other major cities, such as Cartagena and Barranquilla, on the Caribbean coast of Colombia, were too public, and the mercenary team would not blend in well as tourists. Medellín was riddled with informers to the cartel and could not possibly have been used. Cali was the nearest large city to Medellín that could be considered safe, and it was also close to the actual training ground the mercenaries would be using to prepare for their mission.

McAleese and a Colombian government contact met the arriving mercenary team in Cali. "George," the government official, was reportedly an officer from Colombian Intelligence, a fact that the mercenaries took at face value. Gathered into transportation, the mercenaries were moved to an apartment block some distance away, where a number of apartments had been reserved for them. Soon, an additional three mercenaries arrived from South Africa, filling out the team to twelve men.

An additional Colombian official—"Mario," reportedly an infantry colonel in the Colombian army—worked with George to keep the mercenary team under wraps and unseen by the public. The team was intended to be in Cali for only a short while before moving out to a training base, but difficulties in the operational plan soon arose.

From the first day in Colombia, it was thought that helicopters would be a necessary part of the tentative plan to take out Pablo Escobar. Problems in locating and acquiring the necessary aircraft began almost immediately. Personal contacts the mercenary leaders had in England and, through those contacts, in the United States failed to come up with the wanted helicopters. One of the people the mercenaries contacted in England even went so far as to get in touch with the SAS barracks at Hereford. Though the SAS unit was not able to help in any way, it was very interesting that they were not surprised to hear about the operation. This should not be read as to imply that the British SAS were involved in any way with the assassination mission against Escobar. But it does help reinforce the story that the operation was sanctioned by the government of Colombia.

The individuals contacted in England did not hear from the mercs in Cali for several months and thought the team missing in action. What had actually taken place was almost as serious. The whole mercenary team remained in Cali for about a week. During this time, the men, in small groups of two or three, would eat dinner at the Hotel Continental just a few hundred meters from their apartments. The level of operational security demanded by the Colombians kept the mercs from enjoying much of their time in Cali, but at least one incident did take place.

One of the mercs visited a bar in Cali that was run by an Englishman. Having drunk more than was wise, the merc was loudly heard to say exactly who he was and what his reason was for being in Colombia in the first place. This was a very bad breach of security, and the majority of the merc team was soon taken out of Cali.

Cali is on the eastern side of the Cordillera Occidental mountain range. The *hacienda* the mercs were taken to was fifteen miles outside of Cali but about seven thousand feet higher up in the mountains. This made what the mercenaries called "the farm" much colder than it had been in the city. But security was much better at the farm, and the mercs were able to begin at least a light training program for their mission. McAleese and Tomkins separated from the team when they moved to the *hacienda*, remaining in Cali for an additional week. During this time, Tomkins and McAleese had a number of meetings with officials from Colombian Intelligence.

One member of the team had been very nervous while back in the city. He had thought that the merc team was coming under attack several times while still in the apartment block and had made that first weekend very tense for the mercs. Only a few weeks after moving out to the farm, that same mercenary left Colombia and was replaced on the team by an experienced ex-SAS man.

Now the team was divided into two training groups of five men each. Training was limited while at the farm, since the grounds could be seen from several other *haciendas* in the immediate area. But the team was still able to run a light training program to get used to working together in a coordinated way. Security of the area, issue of weapons, and establishing emergency rendezvous points in case the team was broken up by an outside attack were all conducted. A daily routine was established and followed;

0600   Physical training (exercise)
0700   Personal prep time
0800   Breakfast

0915	Training (with a fifteen-minute break during the time block)
1300	Lunch
1430	Sports-oriented physical training
1630	Meal
2000	Dinner

The time between the light 1630 meal (around teatime) and dinner was filled with planning sessions and free time for the men. The sports-oriented exercise increased the mercs' ability to work with one another well and added to the overall conditioning of the men. Without detailed information on the mission, and given the restrictions of the local area, this was about the most intense training program that could be conducted by the mercs at the time.

General training involved becoming familiar with the weapons available to the team, but was not able to include live firing at the farm. The weapons available included MAG-58 belt-fed machine guns, .50 caliber rifles, Uzis, M16A2s, and CAR-15s, as well as various grenades, pistols, and M72 LAW rockets. What the mercenaries considered specialist equipment was also available, and this included mines and rifle grenades along with a minimum of one H&K G3 rifle for launching the grenades. A good amount of explosives and detonators were also available in the supplies at the farm.

After about a week of training at the farm, Tomkins and McAleese arrived from Cali. It was now that the whole team learned who their primary target was, Pablo Escobar, and that they would attack him while he was home at his estate, the Hacienda Napoles near Medellín. Intelligence supplied to the mercenaries suggested that the attack would take place while a meeting was being held at the *hacienda,* a meeting that would be attended by other members of the Medellín Cartel, including Gacha and Jorge Ochoa.

Following common mercenary custom, the team held an election at this time to decide who the leaders would be. The men chosen would be in addition to McAleese, who would remain in overall command of the operation. The team broke up into three groups according to the operation plan. Alpha was the support group, which was led by one of the elected leaders and had two Colombians in it in addition to Tomkins and another mercenary. Bravo was one of the assault groups, with four mercenaries; Delta, the other assault group, was also made up of four mercenaries.

While the mercenaries were at the *hacienda*, an incident took place that caused a great deal of concern to the group. One of the Colombian officials, an intelligence officer, was shot and killed in Cali. The murdered man was not one of the primary Colombians working with the mercs but had been with them at least part of the time that they spent in Cali. The concern was that the team had been found out somehow and that the murdered man was just the beginning of trouble for the mercs. What turned out to have happened was that the man was simply recognized as a government official and considered a target of opportunity.

Combined with the fact that a number of journalists had been tortured and killed by the Medellín Cartel at around the same time, the death of the intelligence man graphically demonstrated what the mercs could expect in the way of mercy from the drug lords. The reason the journalists were forced to suffer prior to dying was that they had written a number of articles disrespectful of the cartel. If the torture/murder of three men for simply writing articles was considered a proper response by the cartel, any captured mercs on an assassination mission could expect very little in the way of understanding.

In spite of their concerns, it appeared that the mercenaries were still unknown to the cartel. It was time to move on to the active training portion of the operation. After a few more days in Cali, the team moved out to a training area in the southwest region of Colombia. The jungle training site was near the Pacific Ocean and in an area of Colombia with a very low population. Training with live ammunition, heavy weapons, and even explosives could be done without much chance of observation.

Escobar's estate is a huge area—seven thousand acres, almost eleven square miles—containing buildings, roads, airstrips, lakes, guard towers, even a private zoo. The large main house of the *hacienda* is near the Medellín/Magdalena Valley road with the whole estate about eighty miles east-southeast of Medellín, along the Magdalena River. On top of the main gate of the *hacienda* compound is mounted a plane, supposedly the first one used by Escobar to move narcotics. The concrete gate is part of an electrified fence surrounding the compound.

To the southeast of the main gate is a swimming pool, with open tennis courts farther east of the gate. Due south of the gate is the main house, which faces an open soccer field to the east. Farther south of the main house is the building holding the living quarters of the *hacienda*'s staff and large bodyguard force. Behind the north-facing personnel quarters is a series of three guard towers overlooking the grounds. Small rivers are on either side of the *hacienda,* some little distance away. At the far side of the eastern river is an airstrip. To the south of the house is very rough country, impassable for a quick escape except for men on foot.

For all of the natural and man-made fortifications of the *hacienda*, the major obstacle for the mercenaries' mission was the large bodyguard and servant force that Escobar maintained. The employees were loyal to Escobar but were not considered innocent bystanders to the mercenaries. The team would not go out of its way to kill civilians, but it wouldn't put itself at risk for their sake, either. What was a major risk for the mercs were the nearly 100 bodyguards on the estate.

The bodyguards had almost the strength of a military infantry company and were well armed, though primarily with light weapons. It was not known by the mercs whether the guard towers were armed with anything heavier than the personal weapons of the guards, but that situation could not be left to chance. What had to be done was a sudden strike with enough firepower and shock to overwhelm the *hacienda*'s forces before they could mount an effective defense.

Some of the same defenses that protected the house also worked to the mercenaries' benefit. The electrified fence would act to hold people inside the compound, just as it did to keep them out. The rough area to the south of the *hacienda* could be controlled by a few properly armed marksmen. And the main airstrip across the river could not be quickly reached for an escape. Through the gate and out onto the main road was the primary escape route for the compound, and it could be held by a sufficient blocking force.

Lack of heavy weapons or air support caused a number of assault plans to be considered and dropped. The plan finally decided on would require a combined effort from the mercenaries and a small unit from the Colombian military. It had been decided from the very earliest days in Cali that the mercs would need helicopters to pull off the operation with a good chance of success. Since the team had had problems getting the aircraft through their own sources, they finally turned over the demand for helicopters to their Colombian Intelligence contacts, and the needed material showed up at the jungle training compound.

Two birds arrived, a Hughes 500 (OH-6) apparently rented from a civilian source and piloted by a Colombian police lieutenant. The second, and larger, bird showed up from the United States after being delayed for several days in Mexico. That helicopter, a Bell 204, was delivered suddenly by a pilot who landed the bird, shut off the engines, and immediately ran to a waiting boat. The boat had been sent by the Colombians and had been waiting to pull the chopper pilot out and down river without giving any of the mercenaries a chance to speak to him. The pilot's total time at the training compound was something like two minutes on the ground.

Though the mercs were surprised at the speed of the delivery pilot's exit, they were pleased with the helicopters. Both birds were soon painted in official Colombian colors and with government markings. Any unmarked aircraft near Medellín would be quickly reported to the cartel by any one of the many police and other personnel under the cartel's control. Unmarked aircraft would put the entire area on alert; even civilian-marked craft could be considered as being from a rival organization and dealt with violently. Only officially marked aircraft had any chance of approaching to within striking distance of a relaxed *hacienda*. Though the aircraft could not come from government sources for security reasons, the mercs figured they were on official business anyway and why not mark the helicopters accordingly.

Now with air transport, resupply of the camp was made much easier and faster. Prior to the helicopters' arrival, everything needed by the mercenaries was brought in by boat, a slow method that could be seen by the few people living near the water. Now the plan could be finalized and the details worked out in training.

The Colombians would supply a fifteen-man military force to block off the main road from Escobar's *hacienda* during the mercenaries' attack. Four men would be in the OH-6, along with the Colombian police pilot: McAleese and Tomkins, from support group Alpha, with two Colombian officers, Mario and Omar, assisting.

The OH-6 would reach the target area from the south and initiate the assault with explosives and automatic-weapons fire. Tomkins and McAleese would fire on the guard towers with 7.62mm machine guns from the doors of the OH-6. Tomkins would also drop explosive satchel charges along the west side of the main house, blasting in the windows and at least stunning, if not killing outright, anyone inside. The bombing run alone could be sufficient to complete the mission and kill Escobar, but it would take forces on the ground to confirm the target.

As the OH-6 would begin its assault, the Bell 204 would land on the soccer field, dropping off the balance of the support group and the two assault teams. The support group would move out to a line of trees between the main house and the field, set up their weapons, and take the house under fire with rifle grenades and LAW rockets, starting from the north end. Both of the assault groups, Bravo and Delta, would move around to the north of the swimming pool and approach the north wing of the house from the direction of the main gate. While the different groups were getting into position, the Bell would lift off and add its firepower to that of the OH-6, which would be firing on the bodyguard and servant quarters, pinning down anyone trying to reach the main house.

As the assault groups prepared to enter the north wing of the house, the support group would immediately switch its fire to the central portion of the building. The assault group would move into the house, each team covering the other as they moved in. The assault teams would go through the entire house, room to room, killing all occupants of the building. When the assault groups were ready to enter the central section, the support group's fire would immediately switch to the south wing of the house.

The same procedure would be followed as the central portion of the house was cleared. As soon as the assault teams were ready to clear the rooms of the southern wing of the house, the support group's fire would be moved to the bodyguards and servants quarters, several hundred yards south of the main house.

When the main house was cleared and all occupants killed or incapacitated, the two assault groups would turn their attention to the bodyguard and servant quarters to the south. Room-to-room techniques would again be used on the bodyguards' quarters while the support unit would direct its fire throughout the compound on any targets of opportunity that might come up. This last action would finally secure the main buildings of the Hacienda Napoles.

During the mercenaries' actions on-site, a fifteen-man unit from the Colombian military would have secured the road leading to the main gates of the *hacienda*. Far enough back from the site of the raid, the Colombian soldiers would be able to prevent any escape from the compound while still maintaining the pretense that they were not directly involved.

As soon as both buildings were cleared and secured, the mercs would put out guards to watch over the compound. Then the remainder of the merc force would move back through the buildings, concentrating on spotting any survivors from the assault, any documents or intelligence materials of the cartel's activities, and that item so dear to a mercenary— valuables and loot.

If time was available, the mercs had permission to open Escobar's safe and help themselves to any valuables they found inside. Any particularly valuable intelligence documents would be expected to be in the safe, but what interested the mercenaries most were the rumors of up to several million dollars in cash also being in the safe. One of the few concerns for discipline during the operation centered on the contents of the safe. The temptation of such a large amount of cash could cause the team to pause in its primary mission, the elimination of Escobar. Getting the mercenaries to break off contact and reboard the helicopters in the case of an emergency could also prove a difficult order to enforce, especially if the compound was secured and the mercs thought they were being cheated out of their chance for loot.

The few possible discipline problems aside, the operation looked to have every chance of success. The total time on the ground at the target was estimated to be only about fifteen minutes, including searching and opening the safe. The speed of the operation, combined with the shock of the explosions and firepower of the team, gave a good edge to the mercenaries. Also, the mercs were a well-trained, coordinated military unit, used to being under fire and still moving forward with the mission. This, too, would give the mercenaries a good chance of completely overwhelming the *hacienda*'s bodyguard force before they could mount an effective defense.

Much of the mercenaries' training prior to the operation centered on the coordination of the teams and the application of the necessary firepower. The switching from wing to wing and building to building of the support unit's fire made live-fire practice an absolute necessity. The internal layout of the buildings at the *hacienda* were made available to the mercenaries, and they incorporated this information in their training. Sheets and poles were used to erect mock-ups of the rooms at the *hacienda* to practice house-clearing techniques.

Timing and coordination between the two assault units, support unit, and helicopters came together during the training with only one major incident. One of the mercenaries was injured by the back blast from one of the M72 series LAW rockets during a live-fire exercise. Whether the merc didn't move fast enough or the firer launched his rocket too early was not made clear after the accident. The injured mercenary was able to continue with the operation, and the men had it made very clear to them that timing had to be exact to keep such an incident from happening again.

On June 4 information came to the mercenaries that Escobar and other members of the cartel were on-site at the hacienda, and the mission was go. Within thirty minutes, the mercs were loaded into the helicopters and on their way to the target. The Bell 204 was in the lead of the flight while the OH-6, flown by another Colombian police pilot, brought up the rear.

Dense clouds over a mountain range caused some problems for the two helicopters, which separated as they both found different holes through the cloud layer. The OH-6 was last seen several hundred feet below the Bell and flying in the opposite direction. Only five minutes later, the Bell was about ten minutes' flying time from the target, and a landing was made to refuel the bird before the op. The OH-6 was nowhere to be seen.

After about ten minutes had gone by, still no word was heard from the missing OH-6 with the three Colombians and two mercenaries on board. The Bell went back up to search for the missing helicopter. Less than half an hour into the search, the crashed OH-6 was seen near the peak of one of the mountains with someone standing near the bird and waving a red cloth. Only the one person was visible to the searchers, and radio contact with the downed bird could not be established. About six kilometers from the crash site was a clear area where the Bell could set down and put out some of the mercenaries as a search team.

After a very short time of easy travel, the mercenaries were slowed down by the heavy jungle. By nightfall, the team was still a kilometer from the downed OH-6, and contact still couldn't be made. Near a field of crops was a small hut that the mercenaries were able to reach before darkness fully settled in. Three Colombian farmers were inside the hut, more than a little startled to see the gringo mercenaries, armed and wearing Colombian camouflage uniforms. While a decision was being made about spending the night in the hut and continuing on in the morning, a radio call came in from the Bell telling the mercenaries that they had to return immediately.

After arriving at the hut, one of the mercenaries had wanted to kill the three farmers, since they could identify the team to the drug lords. The leader of that merc team would not allow the civilians to be killed, and it was later proved to be a very good decision. In spite of a decided lack of communication, the mercs convinced the three farmers to lead them through the jungle back to the other helicopter. In four hours of travel, the mercs were able to get back to the Bell, something they would not have been able to do at all except for the guides.

The only problem found at the Bell was that the pilot had been worried about the mercenaries on the search team. The mission was still considered secret, and the pilot may have been concerned about his future in Colombia if additional mercenaries under his care went missing. A small nearby farmhouse with an elderly pair of peasants was where the team decided to spend the night. No harm came to the occupants of the farmhouse, and the mercenaries were given a meal by the woman of the house.

Prior to first light the next morning, the excited pilot woke the mercenaries and told them to get into the Bell for takeoff. As soon as there was light to operate, the pilot took off with the Bell and the mercenaries to another location ninety minutes' flying time away. The pilot's desire to quickly get away from the area was not unfounded. Within a very short time of the bird's taking off, several local police and army units showed up. The local units were under Escobar's control, so things could have turned very bad for the mercenaries had they been caught.

The Bell landed at a preplanned refueling point, different from the one they had landed at the previous day. The mission was obviously scrubbed, and it was time for the mercs to get out of the area. All uniforms and incriminating materials were burned by the team. A number of Colombians arrived with vehicles, and the team was driven back to Cali. At one point, one of the mercenaries' vehicles were stopped by the local police but, after some tense moments, was allowed to continue on its way.

At the OH-6 crash site, the survivors were on their own. When it became evident that the other helicopter was not able to come and get them, the mercs and Colombians decided to try to walk out and get back to Cali. Only the pilot of the OH-6 was severely injured. The tail rotor of the crashed bird had torn into the cockpit and almost chopped the pilot in half. The mercenaries had done what they could for the pilot, pumping him full of morphine for the pain, but he died of his injuries within half an hour of the crash.

McAleese, Tomkins, and the other two Colombians were little more than bruised and badly banged up by the crash. Three days later, the mercs and the Colombians arrived back at Cali, having walked out of the jungle. All contact with any other Colombian forces in their area was avoided by the crash survivors, since there was no way to tell who might be under the pay of Escobar and the cartel. The mission to take out Escobar and the leadership of the Medellín cartel was over. Colombian security took the mercenaries back to Bogotá, where they boarded separate flights back to England and elsewhere.

It is considered very possible that the mercenaries' mission to take out Escobar could have succeeded, given the training and abilities of the men involved. But no additional attempts were made against the cartel by the Colombian government using outside resources. Gacha, his son, and a number of their bodyguards were killed later in 1989 in a shootout with the Colombian police. Escobar continued his operations. Some small actions were taken by members of the Colombian government, probably under Escobar's direction, to extradite the mercenaries back to Colombia, ostensibly to stand trial for their "crimes," but nothing happened to bring the mercs back to Colombia. Most of the team made themselves scarce after returning from the operation. It was obvious to all concerned that, if they were returned to Colombia, they would never live to stand trial. The mercs would have been killed long before their testimony could have caused any embarrassment to the Colombian officials who hired them.

The Rules of Engagement

International Anti-Mercenary Laws

THE ACTIONS OF BRITISH MERCENARIES AGAINST DRUG BAR-
ons in Colombia in the late 1980s probably added a lot of
impetus to the push in the United Nations to outlaw the international use of mercenaries. The Colombian drug lords may
have been simply trying to protect their own interests,
therefore pushing the convention forward; they have the
money to do so. Smaller countries just may not have liked the
idea of effective military forces being available to their opponents who could afford the costs. No matter what the final
reason, U.N. committees examined the question of international mercenaries throughout the 1980s and drafted the following convention just prior to 1990. Even if the following
legislation is passed and ratified by a majority of the U.N.
membership, which as of this writing has not yet taken place,
it would still be easy for a sovereign country to employ mercenaries as "technical advisers" or "consultants" to their existing military. It is the ease by which certain international
conventions can be bypassed that allows some countries to
agree to their ratification.

The following convention includes the applicable parts of
Article 47 of Protocol I of the Geneva Convention. The fa-

222

mous protections offered by Article 75, however, are noticeably absent, though following them is "suggested" in Article 12.

A/RES/44/34
72nd plenary meeting
4 December 1989

International Convention against the Recruitment, Use, Financing and Training of Mercenaries

The General Assembly,

Considering that the progressive development of international law and its codification contribute to the implementation of the purposes and principles set forth in Articles 1 and 2 of the Charter of the United Nations,

Mindful of the need to conclude, under the auspices of the United Nations, an international convention against the recruitment, use, financing and training of mercenaries,

Recalling its resolution 35/48 of 4 December 1980, by which it established the Ad Hoc Committee on the Drafting of an International Convention against the Recruitment, Use, Financing and Training of Mercenaries and requested it to elaborate at the earliest possible date an international convention to prohibit the recruitment, use, financing and training of mercenaries,

Having considered the draft convention prepared by the Ad Hoc Committee in pursuance of the above-mentioned resolution and finalized by the Working Group on the Drafting of an International Convention against the Recruitment, Use, Financing and Training of Mercenaries, which met during the forty-fourth session of the General Assembly,

Adopts and opens for signature and ratification or for accession the International Convention against the Recruitment, Use, Financing and Training of Mercenaries, the text of which is annexed to the present resolution.

ANNEX

International Convention against the Recruitment, Use, Financing and Training of Mercenaries

The States Parties to the present Convention,

Reaffirming the purposes and principles enshrined in the Charter of the United Nations and in the Declaration on the Principles of International Law concerning Friendly Relations and Co-operation among States in accordance with the Charter of the United Nations,

Being aware of the recruitment, use, financing and training of mercenaries for activities which violate principles of international law such as those of sovereign equality, political independence, territorial integrity of States and self-determination of peoples,

Affirming that the recruitment, use, financing and training of mercenaries should be considered as offences of grave concern to all States and that any person committing any of these offences should either be prosecuted or extradited,

Convinced of the necessity to develop and enhance international co-operation among States for the prevention, prosecution and punishment of such offences,

Expressing concern at new unlawful international activities linking drug traffickers and mercenaries in the perpetration of violent actions which undermine the constitutional order of States,

Also convinced that the adoption of a convention against the recruitment, use, financing and training of mercenaries would contribute to the eradication of these nefarious activities and thereby to the observance of the purposes and principles enshrined in the Charter of the United Nations,

Cognizant that matters not regulated by such a convention continue to be governed by the rules and principles of international law,

Have agreed as follows:

Article 1

For the purposes of the present Convention,

1. A mercenary is any person who:
    a) Is specially recruited locally or abroad in order to fight in an armed conflict;
    b) Is motivated to take part in the hostilities essentially by

the desire for private gain and, in fact, is promised, by or on behalf of a party to the conflict, material compensation substantially in excess of that promised or paid to combatants of similar rank and functions in the armed forces of that party;

c) Is neither a national of a party to the conflict nor a resident of territory controlled by a party to the conflict;

d) Is not a member of the armed forces of a party to the conflict; and

e) Has not been sent by a State which is not a party to the conflict on official duty as a member of its armed forces.

2. A mercenary is also any person who, in any other situation:

a) Is specially recruited locally or abroad for the purpose of participating in a concerted act of violence aimed at:

i.   Over throwing a Government or otherwise undermining the constitutional order of a State; or

ii. Undermining the territorial integrity of a State;

b) Is motivated to take part therein essentially by the desire for significant private gain and is prompted by the promise or payment of material compensation;

c) Is neither a national nor a resident of the State against which such an act is directed;

d) Has not been sent by a State on official duty; and

e) Is not a member of the armed forces of the State on whose territory the act is undertaken.

Article 2

Any person who recruits, uses, finances or trains mercenaries, as defined in article 1 of the present Convention, commits an offence for the purposes of the Convention.

Article 3

1. A mercenary, as defined in article 1 of the present Convention, who participates directly in hostilities or in a concerted act of violence, as the case may be, commits an offence for the purposes of the Convention.

2. Nothing in this article limits the scope of application of article 4 of the present Convention.

Article 4

An offence is committed by any person who:

a) Attempts to commit one of the offences set forth in the present Convention;

b) Is the accomplice of a person who commits or attempts to commit any of the offences set forth in the present Convention.

Article 5

1. States Parties shall not recruit, use, finance or train mercenaries and shall prohibit such activities in accordance with the provisions of the present Convention.

2. States Parties shall not recruit, use, finance or train mercenaries for the purpose of opposing the legitimate exercise of the inalienable right of peoples to self-determination, as recognized by international law, and shall take, in conformity with international law, the appropriate measures to prevent the recruitment, use, financing or training of mercenaries for that purpose.

3. They shall make the offences set forth in the present Convention punishable by appropriate penalties which take into account the grave nature of those offences.

Article 6

States Parties shall co-operate in the prevention of the offences set forth in the present Convention, particularly by:

a) Taking all practicable measures to prevent preparations in their respective territories for the commission of those offences within or outside their territories, including the prohibition of illegal activities of persons, groups and organizations that encourage, instigate, organize or engage in the perpetration of such offences;

b) Co-ordinating the taking of administrative and other measures as appropriate to prevent the commission of those offences.

Article 7

States Parties shall co-operate in taking the necessary measures for the implementation of the present Convention.

Article 8

Any State Party having reason to believe that one of the offences set forth in the present Convention has been, is being or will be committed shall, in accordance with its national law, communicate the relevant information, as soon as it comes to its knowledge, directly or through the Secretary-General of the United Nations, to the States Parties affected.

Article 9

1. Each State Party shall take such measures as may be necessary to establish its jurisdiction over any of the offences set forth in the present Convention which are committed:
   a) In its territory or on board a ship or aircraft registered in that State;
   b) By any of its nationals or, if that State considers it appropriate, by those stateless persons who have their habitual residence in that territory.
2. Each State Party shall likewise take such measures as may be necessary to establish its jurisdiction over the offences set forth in articles 2, 3 and 4 of the present Convention in cases where the alleged offender is present in its territory and it does not extradite him to any of the States mentioned in paragraph 1 of this article.
3. The present Convention does not exclude any criminal jurisdiction exercised in accordance with national law.

Article 10

1. Upon being satisfied that the circumstances so warrant, any State Party in whose territory the alleged offender is present shall, in accordance with its laws, take him into custody or take such other measures to ensure his presence for such time as is necessary to enable any criminal or extradition proceedings to be instituted. The State Party shall immediately make a preliminary inquiry into the facts.
2. When a State Party, pursuant to this article, has taken a person into custody or has taken such other measures referred to in paragraph 1 of this article, it shall notify without delay either directly or through the Secretary-General of the United Nations:
   a) The State Party where the offence was committed;

b) The State Party against which the offence has been directed or attempted;

c) The State Party of which the natural or juridical person against whom the offence has been directed or attempted is a national;

d) The State Party of which the alleged offender is a national or, if he is a stateless person, in whose territory he has his habitual residence;

e) Any other interested State Party which it considers it appropriate to notify.

3. Any person regarding whom the measures referred to in paragraph 1 of this article are being taken shall be entitled:

a) To communicate without delay with the nearest appropriate representative of the State of which he is a national or which is otherwise entitled to protect his rights or, if he is a stateless person, the State in whose territory he has his habitual residence;

b) To be visited by a representative of that State.

4. The provisions of paragraph 3 of this article shall be without prejudice to the right of any State Party having a claim to jurisdiction in accordance with article 9, paragraph 1 (b), to invite the International Committee of the Red Cross to communicate with and visit the alleged offender.

5. The State which makes the preliminary inquiry contemplated in paragraph 1 of this article shall promptly report its findings to the States referred to in paragraph 2 of this article and indicate whether it intends to exercise jurisdiction.

Article 11

Any person regarding whom proceedings are being carried out in connection with any of the offences set forth in the present Convention shall be guaranteed at all stages of the proceedings fair treatment and all the rights and guarantees provided for in the law of the State in question. Applicable norms of international law should be taken into account.

Article 12

The State Party in whose territory the alleged offender is found shall, if it does not extradite him, be obliged, without exception whatsoever and whether or not the offence was committed in its territory, to submit the case to its competent authorities for the purpose of prosecution, through proceedings in accordance with the laws of that State. Those authorities shall take their decision in the same manner as in the case of any other offence of a grave nature under the law of that State.

Article 13
1. States Parties shall afford one another the greatest measure of assistance in connection with criminal proceedings brought in respect of the offences set forth in the present Convention, including the supply of all evidence at their disposal necessary for the proceedings. The law of the State whose assistance is requested shall apply in all cases.
2. The provisions of paragraph 1 of this article shall not affect obligations concerning mutual judicial assistance embodied in any other treaty.

Article 14
The State Party where the alleged offender is prosecuted shall in accordance with its laws communicate the final outcome of the proceedings to the Secretary-General of the United Nations, who shall transmit the information to the other States concerned.

Article 15
1. The offences set forth in articles 2, 3 and 4 of the present Convention shall be deemed to be included as extraditable offences in any extradition treaty existing between States Parties. States Parties undertake to include such offences as extraditable offences in every extradition treaty to be concluded between them.
2. If a State Party which makes extradition conditional on the existence of a treaty receives a request for extradition from another State Party with which it has no extradition treaty, it may at its option consider the present Convention as the legal basis for extradition in respect of those offences. Extradition shall be subject to the other conditions provided by the law of the requested State.
3. States Parties which do not make extradition conditional on the existence of a treaty shall recognize those offences as ex-

traditable offences between themselves, subject to the conditions provided by the law of the requested State.

4. The offences shall be treated, for the purpose of extradition between States Parties, as if they had been committed not only in the place in which they occurred but also in the territories of the States required to establish their jurisdiction in accordance with article 9 of the present Convention.

Article 16

The present Convention shall be applied without prejudice to:

  a) The rules relating to the international responsibility of States;
  b) The law of armed conflict and international humanitarian law, including the provisions relating to the status of combatant or of prisoner of war.

Article 17

1. Any dispute between two or more States Parties concerning the interpretation or application of the present Convention which is not settled by negotiation shall, at the request of one of them, be submitted to arbitration. If, within six months from the date of the request for arbitration, the parties are unable to agree on the organization of the arbitration, any one of those parties may refer the dispute to the International Court of Justice by a request in conformity with the Statute of the Court.

2. Each State may, at the time of signature or ratification of the present Convention or accession thereto, declare that it does not consider itself bound by paragraph 1 of this article. The other States Parties shall not be bound by paragraph 1 of this article with respect to any State Party which has made such a reservation.

3. Any State Party which has made a reservation in accordance with paragraph 2 of this article may at any time withdraw that reservation by notification to the Secretary-General of the United Nations.

Article 18

1. The present Convention shall be open for signature by all States until 31 December 1990 at United Nations Headquarters in New York.

2. The present Convention shall be subject to ratification. The instruments of ratification shall be deposited with the Secretary-General of the United Nations.

3. The present Convention shall remain open for accession by any State. The instruments of accession shall be deposited with the Secretary-General of the United Nations.

Article 19

1. The present Convention shall enter into force on the thirtieth day following the date of deposit of the twenty-second instrument of ratification or accession with the Secretary-General of the United Nations.

2. For each State ratifying or acceding to the Convention after the deposit of the twenty-second instrument of ratification or accession, the Convention shall enter into force on the thirtieth day after deposit by such State of its instrument of ratification or accession.

Article 20

1. Any State Party may denounce the present Convention by written notification to the Secretary-General of the United Nations.

2. Denunciation shall take effect one year after the date on which the notification is received by the Secretary-General of the United Nations.

Article 21

The original of the present Convention, of which the Arabic, Chinese, English, French, Russian and Spanish texts are equally authentic, shall be deposited with the Secretary-General of the United Nations, who shall send certified copies thereof to all States.

IN WITNESS WHEREOF the undersigned, being duly authorized thereto by their respective Governments, have signed the present Convention, opened for signature at New York on. . . .

Victory and Betrayal in Ghana: The Ultimate Mercenary Story

THE PLANNING

Ghana is one of the smaller African countries on what was known as the Gold Coast in the 1800s. An estimated population of 17 million live on a little over 92,000 square miles of land, an area slightly smaller than Oregon. Like so many other African countries, Ghana has a large rift between the majority of the population that lives in poverty and the wealthy few. And, as seems almost inevitable in smaller African countries, one of Ghana's major exports is gold, with her Ashanti gold fields helping to produce over one-quarter million ounces, over 62 million dollars' worth, of gold each year.

Independence from British rule was granted to Ghana in 1957, and she became a republic in 1960. Since that time, military coups have flip-flopped the Ghanaian government from democratically elected civilian to military and back again. In 1981, Ghanaian Flight Lieutenant Jerry Rawlings turned over a two-year-old civilian government in a coup— his second—that again put him in power. He has held the position ever since, including his winning of the Ghanaian democratic elections of 1993. His strong Marxist leanings and cooperation with the governments of Cuba and others put Rawlings in the category that bore watching by the U.S. and other free-world intelligence agencies, but nothing active was done by these organizations to lead to his overthrow.

With all coups, the people who are forced out of power and wealth desire to have it back again. Ghana was no different, and there was her mineral wealth to interest outside backers in gaining influence with a new government. Godfrey Osei was one of those displaced African businessmen who wanted his property restored, with a possible raise in position not being out of the question. To gain this end, Osei followed a traditional African method of government change: he hired mercenaries to arrange a coup.

Through a variety of contacts in the underground mercenaries' network, including a close associate of the Angolan FNLA leader Holden Roberto, Osei found a mercenary capable of putting his operation together. In early November 1985, contact was initiated with an American mercenary who was "between contracts." This merc had served seventeen years with the French Foreign Legion where he became a senior NCO, a position that demonstrates no small ability.

Money was running a bit tight for the mercenary. His pay from a contract serving as a security specialist for mine owners during the Kentucky labor disputes had just about run out. But even a hungry mercenary is careful, especially if he wants to remain a living one. It was the connections through the merc "old boy" network that helped turn the man toward the new contract—that, and the fact that the contract was offering money up front.

Usually, in the mercenary business, pay is dependent on the job being completed. Reimbursement for the merc's personal costs to start the job aren't offered very often. But even with this inducement, the merc thought the offer was probably like one of a number of bad deals he had already been through. A follow-up call from the employer the next day convinced him that the job was genuine, and he moved on to a meeting in New York City.

The principal himself met the merc at the airport, identifying himself by holding in front of him a white envelope. The merc recognized the preplanned signal and introduced himself. A silent cab ride into New York followed, to an outside area in a secured building where discussions could be held and not overheard.

The principal identified himself as Godfrey Osei and stated what he wanted: an overthrow of President Rawlings, elimination of him and his family, and the securing of Accra, the capital city of Ghana, until Osei and his local forces arrived to take control—simply put, a mercenary-led overthrow of an African government and the installation of a new leader.

Over a long discussion between the two men, a general plan took shape. Osei wanted a ten- to thirty-man white mercenary force to conduct the operation with 150 to 300 Ghanaian exiles acting as a supporting attack force. Units from the Ghanaian army would also come to the support of the coup, securing Kotoka International Airport near Accra as well as strategic locations in the city itself.

The mercenaries would divide into two groups for the attack. One group would attack the Rawlings home residence, identified as "the Castle" and located on the ocean beach in Accra. Once inside the residence, the mercenaries were to kill everyone in the home, making sure that Rawlings, his family, and anyone else in the home would not be able to affect later events.

The balance of the mercenary team would attack Ussher Fort, previously Fort Crèvecoeur, built by the Dutch in 1649 and converted into a prison by the government of Ghana. Only a few kilometers west of the Castle, the prison held a number of Ghanaian businessmen and politicians imprisoned by Rawlings. Once freed and armed by the mercenaries, the ex-prisoners would join in the coup, reinforcing the mercenaries' force.

The last move by the two merc units would be to join together and capture the Ghana Broadcasting Studio (GBC), the primary broadcasting station in Accra, located just a few miles north of the beach. Rawlings had come to power himself in 1981 by seizing the GBC studios and broadcasting his own message to the people of Ghana, informing them of the change in government.

Osei saw that what had worked for Rawlings could well work for him. A message recorded by Osei announcing the overthrow of Rawlings and the installation of a new government would be carried by the mercenaries and played over the airwaves from the broadcast studio once it was secured.

Both primary targets of the mercenaries, Rawlings residence and the prison, were located on the beach within a short distance of each other. The need for a sudden attack and complete surprise indicated that the mercenaries would have to come in by sea. Small boats, most probably inflatables, would have to leave the larger mother ship that would have transported them to within striking distance. This part of the plan worried the mercenary. An encounter with the Ghanaian navy would quickly overwhelm such a vulnerable force before they ever reached the beach. But this problem was considered a nonissue by Osei. Any interference from the navy had been "taken care of."

Even with all of the assurances from Osei, the mercenary was concerned. Wild plans with huge payoffs were commonly heard in mercenary hangouts around the world. Very few of these plans ever survived the next morning's hangover. Mercenaries, boats, weapons, and equipment cost real money, not imaginary payoffs. The Ghanaian coup would be expensive, and that's what Osei was told straight-out.

Osei announced that he had $175,000 immediately in hand for the operation, with more available if necessary. This figure matched what the mercenary had originally been told was being offered for the operation by the contact who had brought Osei and him together. Now it was time for Osei to bring out the money for working capital and expenses; mercenaries expect to get paid, and it was time for some of the paying to start.

Osei got up and entered the building nearby. In a short time, he returned with a plastic bag, two inches thick and filled with U.S. bills in denominations of twenty and fifty dollars. He insisted that the mercenary count it. The total was five grand in cash.

At this point, one additional detail was unexpectedly brought out by Osei, and it didn't please the mercenary leader at all. Rawlings had sent four hundred of his best military men to Cuba for training. Sometime after December 25, these men would be back from Cuba, supposedly a well-trained and significant force. The mercenary operation had to be done by

Christmas, six weeks from the time of their first meeting.

One thing the mercenary had learned in his time with the French Foreign Legion was that in the Legion, nothing was considered impossible. Operations could be damned hard sometimes, but not impossible. The contract was accepted, and the mission planning begun.

Trust is not a common commodity in the mercenary world. The merc liked Osei but hardly trusted him completely. This general attitude had proved its worth to the mercenary during his years in the business, and it would do so again. But his troubles weren't going to be coming from the operation or even from the enthusiastic but inexperienced Osei. His problems were instead going to come from other players in the very cutthroat international mercenary business.

The first priority for the operation was securing the necessary weapons and equipment. Arms and ammunition to outfit a 150-man unit are not necessarily the easiest items in the world to shop for, especially in the continental United States. One connection the mercenary had was on the West Coast, a supplier who claimed to be able to get arms from the Mideast. But claims and deliveries are two very different things.

The merc planner had decided on Communist-bloc weapons—AK-47s, RPGs, light machine guns, and easily portable fire support in the form of light mortars. These ComBloc weapons would be easy to resupply from the stores of the Marxist Ghanaian government. He also needed ammunition, grenades, and magazines sufficient for both the mercenaries' force and the liberated prisoners or Ghanaian expatriates.

The arms suppliers were a lot more interested in where the operation was going to take place, and who was bankrolling it, than in producing the desired weapons at a reasonable price. The first offer of $1,500 each for AK-47s was quickly derided by the mercenary. He could see that the suppliers were a lot more interested in things that they didn't need to know than they were in doing business. Excusing himself from the office, the mercenary went to a public phone and called Osei, telling him in no uncertain terms that the initial $175,000 was nowhere near enough to finance the operation.

"No problem" was the answer, and not for the last time. Returning to the office, the mercenary was made another offer of $220 each for the necessary AK-47s—a reasonable enough price, but he could not reach the minimum one-thousand-gun order demanded by the suppliers. And the $3,500-to-$4,000-each asking price for antiquated RPG-2s was outrageous.

The mercenary could tell that the suppliers were either stringing him along in order to get more information or simply trying to cheat him outright. His plan for the operation was a straightforward military assault, simple weapons producing a lot of firepower from a dependable package. This wouldn't let the suppliers get the kind of inflated prices for the high-tech equipment they liked to sell, so cutting out the mercenary and connecting directly with his principal was the next-best moneymaker for them.

For the balance of the meeting, the suppliers pumped the merc for additional information. After a lot of guesswork centering around the operation's being in Africa, the suppliers offered to put the whole thing together—weapons, transport, and mercenaries—for $2.5 million.

The suppliers had their own mercenary leader to ramrod the operation, a veteran of Vietnam and Rhodesia. This situation would cut the Foreign Legion vet out of the picture, so he declined the offer of additional help and said the weapons would be enough. To secure the weapons, the suppliers extracted a $2,500 "good faith" payment from the merc before ending the conversation. He went ahead and paid, since he needed the weapons and felt that he could find these men again later, if necessary, and personally discuss the ramifications of their cheating him.

A roundabout trip back to New York, by way of Denver, got the mercenary back to Osei without leading the suppliers directly to the principal. The expenses of traveling, the good faith deposit, and the weapons' costs made Osei's mood less than happy during the meeting. The mercenary decided he might as well let Osei know what was going on all at once and told him that it was going to cost the $175,000 just to arm the operation. The boat, ancillary equipment, mercenaries' pay, and transportation costs were all yet to be calculated.

Still Osei's main concern centered around getting the operation completed by Christmas. Money was not going to be a problem, he said. After some prodding by the mercenary,

Osei dropped enough significant names to convince the mercenary that the whole operation involved the U.S. government working in the background. William Casey, head of the Central Intelligence Agency, and Robert McFarland, once head of the National Security Agency, were two of the people Osei said he had consulted regarding the operation.

This news did not come as a surprise to the mercenary. He had suspected some form of U.S. involvement; Osei was operating too much in the open for the case to have been otherwise. But dropping names that could be read from a paper was a far cry from having the direct support of a major government. Working as a mercenary rarely has any guarantees, however, and the merc accepted the statements at face value, without trusting them at all.

Osei moved to change the subject of the discussion. He started talking about why he was preparing the coup and what his background was. Once a fairly prosperous businessman in Accra, Osei had lost his trucking company when Rawlings's Marxist government decided he had too much property. Confiscation of his holdings wasn't enough, and Osei was jailed as an enemy of the people.

Escaping from the prison where he was held, the same prison he wanted the mercenaries to breach, Osei and some of his friends took over the local radio station. The attempt to convince the people of Ghana to rise up and overthrow Rawlings fell flat, and Osei was soon recaptured and again imprisoned. Actions by Swiss and other organizations won Osei his freedom and exile from Ghana to the United States.

His reasons for wanting to overthrow Rawlings were interesting to the mercenary but not of much importance. What was needed for the job at hand were the contacts Osei said had been set up for him by the people in Washington, contacts with such diverse groups as Chinese organized-crime elements and the Israelis.

Osei continued to demand that the operation be completed by Christmas. He also repeated that he wanted everyone in the Castle "neutralized," as well as anyone who shot at the mercenaries, and that the team had his full authority to do what had to be done.

Whatever authority Osei had came from the money he could

put together. And that was the part of the plan the mercenary insisted they discuss. Again, Osei stated that he wanted thirty white mercenary troops on the operation. What he was told was that the men would cost $3,000 each per month, with a $10,000 bonus at the end of the op. Those fees, combined with the air tickets for the merc team, would total around half a million dollars.

The money was available, according to Osei, from Chinese organized-crime elements in New York. The crime families were representing some banking interests from Hong Kong who wanted to move their business to Ghana. In addition to the bankers, certain Hong Kong gambling casinos were also interested in opening facilities in Ghana. The desires of all of these groups depended on Osei becoming the president of Ghana. Their influence would come directly from the monies they would be willing to front for the coup that would put him in power. This would not be the first time Osei had gone to this source to obtain funds, but that wasn't the concern of the mercenary.

With a decision made to raise more operating capital, the merc returned to Southern California. Nothing had changed with the weapons suppliers. They wanted more money up front and more details on the operation. Neither of the suppliers' desires were met by the mercenary.

With the question of the needed weapons and equipment still unanswered, the merc turned to the next part of the operation: recruiting the needed mercenaries. Osei had his own desires in the way of men—he wanted American mercenaries. This went against what the ex-legionnaire merc was looking for. The merc's opinion was that American mercenaries wanted too much in the way of equipment, planning, and support. Legionnaires were used to operating with a bare minimum—a designated target and something to shoot with. But time was running out, and Americans were available immediately.

Another New York meeting took place between the merc and Osei during the early part of December. There were two pieces of bad news that had to be delivered to the principal. One was that there was no way the team could be assembled, equipped, and on target by Christmas. This didn't seem to bother Godfrey a great deal, though it was a disappointment. The other piece of news brought a more interesting answer.

The merc said flat out that the available financing was not going to be enough. The operation was going to need more money. This, too, didn't worry Osei excessively; he had an answer for where to get the money. He was going to borrow the needed funds from his Chinese organized-crime contacts in New York. Cash in hand, at 1,000 percent interest.

While the merc had been in California trying to line up the weapons, Osei claimed that he, too, had been busy, with his contacts in the CIA. The merc was told that the CIA hadn't known that the weapons suppliers in Los Angeles were in the mercenary arms supply business. The CIA was less than pleased that a supplier they didn't know was working from the United States. This information caused the mercenary planner to reevaluate his source of supply.

A number of phone calls to the suppliers during the weeks after his New York meeting had resulted in nothing. The people in California were obviously stalling and trying to take over the operation. A source of money could be detected by the suppliers, and they wanted as much of it as they could get. Osei would have to come out to California, they said, and deal with them directly. It was obvious to the merc that the California people considered him "in the way" and wanted him out of the operation entirely.

This was enough for the merc. Shortly before Christmas, he contacted the California suppliers and told them the deal was off. Still trying to play for time, the California people said that they were working on raising 2.5 million dollars, their estimate to put on the operation and complete the deal.

Flat out, the merc told the suppliers that they were out of the operation, and he wanted his $2,500 deposit back. When he was informed that the deposit was considered earned money for the suppliers' time, things turned ugly.

You can't be thought of as a patsy in the mercenary world. Once you have a reputation as someone who can be taken advantage of, you will be, and you'll end up either out of the business, abandoned by your employer, or dead. The merc told the supplier in no uncertain terms that his money had better be available or the supplier, and his family, would not enjoy living on the planet much longer.

On top of the threat, the merc told the supplier that the Agency knew about their operation and was not happy about it at all. That was enough for the supplier. He told the merc that his money would be available in two days and to call him back. That was the last the merc ever heard of the supplier. The California people dropped completely out of sight. The merc's money was gone, and Osei accused the mercenary of stealing it.

Now the merc had to start producing, or he would soon find himself cut out of the operation. The Christmas deadline had passed, but the operation still needed to be put forward quickly. Good mercenary operations were few and far between at the time, and the merc didn't want to let this one go without giving it his best effort.

Beef, a contact the merc had made during his work in the Kentucky labor disputes, was available. The merc had no real trust in the man, but he might have the contacts the mercenary needed. As things turned out, Beef already knew about a possible operation in Ghana. He had been hired before to do some planning for it.

Some time earlier, several friends of Osei who worked in the Ghanaian gold business had approached Beef and four other mercenaries to do a feasibility study on the possibility of overthrowing Rawlings's Marxist government. The businessmen were serious enough to pay the five mercenaries $25,000 each to conduct the study and put together an operational plan. Beef's merc team had spent a month in London working on the plan, even sending one of their number to Accra, the capital of Ghana, to study the area and make contact with possible support.

The mercenary group had submitted their proposal, and that was as far as the operation went. Whether their plan was unfeasible or the backers simply wanted out wasn't announced. But when the plan was turned down, Beef and his group returned to the United States, keeping the unused portion of their expense money as a self-awarded bonus.

Money was one of the first things that Beef mentioned in regard to supplying the weapons needed for the operation. The materials would be available from the Mideast, specifically Beirut, but the cost would be expensive—several hundred thousand dollars, at least. This was too steep for the ex-legionnaire mercenary; Osei was getting reluctant to spend more money, and the merc wasn't certain what the backing was really like.

But Beef didn't want to hear the end. As far as he was concerned, the merc had come into a good deal, and they should combine forces to milk Osei of as much money as possible before breaking away. Leading his principal along was not how the merc did business. As far as he was concerned, your word was only as good as your actions. In the mercenary business, leading people along just to take their money, without delivering on your promises, was a great way to get out of the business and a good way to get dead, which also took you out of the loop.

Not willing to completely burn this particular bridge, the merc told Beef to continue working on acquiring a transport ship or other backers. Deliver either, and Beef would be brought into the job.

In January, Osei was informed that the thirty American mercenaries he wanted for the operation had been lined up, but the weapons and a ship had not yet been found. Beirut was mentioned as a possible source of the weapons. Osei mentioned during the meeting that he had contacts in Spain that might be able to supply the needed weapons for the operation. And he had a contact in London that could come up with the needed boat.

The planned coup was not the only subject Osei and the merc spoke about during the January meeting; the arrest of a number of Ghanaian nationals in New Jersey was also mentioned. The FBI had arranged a sting operation some time before the January meeting which resulted in the arrest of three Ghanaians who had been trying to buy weapons. An agent had played the part of an international arms dealer and arrested the three Ghanaians, confiscating the $200,000 in cash that they carried for buying the weapons.

Osei said that Rawlings knew the United States was being used by a number of Ghanaian dissident groups to organize a coup against his government. Setting up and arresting the three arms purchasers was simply a movement by U.S. politicians to appease Rawlings. As far as Osei was concerned, their operation was still going ahead. The merc wasn't so sure and wanted to know if the CIA was helping Osei and just what kind of support he had. As before, a noncommital answer was all that the merc could get from his principal.

Now the merc got back in touch with Beef to see if the weapons, transport, or backers were available. Beef said he had located some investors and had some possibilities on the weapons. What Beef wanted was a direct meeting with Osei. The meeting was arranged, though the merc wasn't available to attend himself. Nothing about what was said during the meeting was told to the merc, but soon thereafter the plan was changed again.

Instead of the thirty mercenaries Osei originally wanted, the number was now lowered to ten to fifteen men, to be paid $3,000 each. This wasn't a problem as far as the merc was concerned. Again, Osei stated that he would be able to get the necessary funds from his contacts in the Chinese underworld. The merc wanted to know why, if the CIA was helping with the operation, the weapons and ship didn't come from them. Osei said that the Agency would be supplying all the needed materials; all he needed the merc to do was line up the necessary manpower.

Now the merc's dislike for Beef's method of operation came back into play. Beef wanted three times the agreed-upon money per man, and the same amount as a bonus after the job was over. All this on top of special payment for Beef himself. By the time the merc found out about all of this, Beef had slipped into Osei's confidence too well for the merc to be able to shake him free. The merc told Osei to check up on Beef and Beef's supposedly well-qualified partner, Jayee, with the CIA.

Osei followed the merc's advice and contacted the CIA. Apparently Jayee was known for too much drinking and other excesses for the Agency to be pleased about his involvement with the operation. As far as the merc was concerned, this wasn't a problem. He wasn't planning on working with Jayee at all, and hoped to keep his involvement with Beef to an absolute minimum. Beef wanted too many guarantees and too much money to be of much use.

The merc was a firm believer in keeping the plan as simple as possible; that way, you could at least minimize the number of things that could go wrong. The merc didn't trust Beef or Jayee at all, and the fact that Osei no longer spoke of either man sat just fine with the merc.

By later January, the merc was told that the CIA would be taking a more active hand in the operation. After a mid-January meeting in Washington, D.C., Osei said that the CIA was sending in a handler, Teebee, who would act as a liaison between the merc, Osei, and the Agency.

The first meeting between Osei, Teebee, and the mercenary took place in a motel in Flushing, New York. The contact appeared to be genuine and seemed to have the background of a contract agent with the CIA. He also had a greater explanation for what was going on in terms of support and financing. Along with more detailed maps of Ghana, Accra, and the sea routes approaching Ghana, Teebee explained to the merc the convoluted arrangements made to get money for the operation.

According to Teebee, the Israeli Mossad was helping to secure a ship for the operation and the purchase of the arms and equipment. This was explained as an exchange of favors by the Mossad, who "owed one" to the CIA. An Argentine banker in Buenos Aires would act as the go-between, and as a cut-out for U.S. involvement in the operation. The banker supposedly owned the boat that would be rented to Osei's operation, as well as an arms company in Argentina where the weapons would be purchased. All of the weapons and equipment—150 locally produced 7.62mm FN-FAL rifles, pistols, machine guns, rocket launchers, inflatable boats, medical supplies, and ammunition—would all be available in Argentina. The use of foreign banks would insulate the U.S. from any direct involvement in the operation. The money needed would be available within twenty-four hours, and the mission would be a go.

The merc and Teebee sat down to work out the details. The boat and crew would cost $1,000 a day, $34,000 total for the estimated time of the operation. The rifles would each cost

$320 and would be supplied with ten magazines and 1,000 rounds of ammunition each. The heavier ordnance would cost about $150,000. Thirty mercenaries, per the original plan, would cost $48,000 for air travel (round-trip) to Argentina and about $310,000 in pay and bonuses after the operation was completed. The 120 Ghanaian exiles in the Ivory Coast who would join the merc's attack force would cost $60,000. All up, the operation would cost about $650,000, with an additional $100,000 for emergency and contingency funds. Three-quarters of a million dollars would buy Osei his seat as the president of a country.

Teebee and Osei left the motel to see their money people. It looked like the operation was coming off, to the mercenary, but then Osei and Teebee returned to the motel an hour later, without the money.

It was Chinese organized crime that Osei was going to see about the money, just as the mercenary had suspected from previous conversations. But the crime lords wanted an accounting for the $225,000 they had already loaned to Osei before they put up any more money. This amount was something new to the merc; he had only known about the $175,000 Osei had originally said he had available for the op. The Chinese thought Osei had simply stolen their money. Opinions had been voiced about only being able to kill a man so many times, but that including his family would increase that number.

After some explaining by Osei and Teebee, the crime lords had supposedly decided on supplying the money after all. Osei and Teebee were to come back to the meeting place after the cash was brought in. For the second meeting, they took the mercenary along.

Only a short distance from the motel was an apartment building where the meeting was to take place. When the merc entered the room, he saw three Chinese men. After some minor courtesies had been exchanged, three suitcases were placed on a table and opened. Each case was filled with hundred-dollar bills. The money was right there, and so was a new problem.

Two of the Chinese started discussing something in their own language. When the third Chinese joined in the discussion, the suitcases were closed. Something was obviously wrong. Teebee suggested that the merc go back to their motel while the problem was worked out. After returning to the motel, the merc learned that more than just a money problem was coming his way.

Teebee came back to the motel room and told the merc that their plans would have to be redone. Costs would have to be cut back from $750,000 to around $480,000. One of the Chinese had been trying to do some creative financing on his own, which hadn't worked out, and now the available funds were less. Cuts were now being suggested in the amount and type of weapons that would be available for the op, as well as in the number of men to be hired. Things appeared to be unraveling, and the merc felt that he was being cut out.

The merc's feeling became stronger when Osei showed up at the motel and asked to speak to Teebee privately outside. After the two returned to the room, the merc asked outright just what was going on. Other commitments had been made by Osei in order to ensure the mercenaries' loyalty and obedience during the op—promises such as contracts to stay on in Ghana as instructors to the new government's military as well as personal bonuses and just flat-out pay. Ghana had both gold and diamond mines, and if Osei wanted the merc and his men to risk their lives for him, they expected a cut of the wealth in return. If any of it would be left after all the dealing.

Now it looked to the merc like no bonuses would be forthcoming, or even much pay, after all of his planning and work. Only the original $3,000 promised to the merc would be coming to him. The various concessions in Ghana had already been promised to the different supporters of the operation, so no bonus could be expected from them. Teebee was just the organizer; he wouldn't be risking himself on the operation at all, so his involvement, and pay, would be "limited." This appeared to be a typical double cross to the mercenary, and his suspicions were soon proved out. At his last meeting with Teebee some weeks later, the merc was told that he was out of the operation.

Beef, the man who originally suggested that he and the merc cheat Osei, was now in on the operation. Jayee would be in charge of the actions on the ground. By this time, the merc really didn't care if he was involved in the op or not. Far too many people knew about the plan to attempt a coup in Ghana for it to remain a secret for very long. Necessary equipment was being cut back, and what was promised might not ever show up anyway. No more money at all would be coming to the merc, who was already in debt from his phone bill alone.

It was late January 1985 when the merc returned to his home and finally wrote off the entire operation. Osei was obviously listening to people who were telling him what he wanted to hear, and picking his pocket at the same time. The merc felt that by the time the operation finally got underway, it would have probably turned into a disaster for him and his men. Within only a few months, the merc heard that the operation had actually been attempted, and most of his premonitions came true in one form or another.

THE MISSION

Godfrey Osei didn't have to wait very long before he could attempt his mercenary-led coup in Ghana. Even while Osei was having his original mercenary planner work on putting the operation together, Beef was getting his own team prepared.

Beef had Jayee take the position of team commander for the operation, leading a planned group of eight American mercenaries. It was later suggested by Teebee, the team's CIA contact, that the majority of the mercenary force not be told of the actual mission objective until the team was out of United States jurisdiction and on the ground in Argentina. Even though it was supposedly a U.S. government–sanctioned operation, Teebee didn't want the men to be too concerned about the possibility of breaking U.S. laws. Of particular concern would be the laws against conspiring to overthrow another constituted government that the U.S. was not at war with, a federal felony with a reasonable amount of prison time attached to it.

The team was made up of a number of veterans of the Vietnam war; actions in Africa, the Middle East, and Central America; and various work as security or law enforcement personnel. Two of the mercenaries were retired army Special

Forces operators who were drawing government pensions. All of the men were told that the operation was sanctioned by the U.S. government, which was the only reason the two SF retirees were willing to sign on.

But the operation most of the men signed on for was not what had been planned for so many months. A simple security job, escorting a shipment of weapons and ordnance from Argentina to Ghana, was all that most of the mercs had been told was coming up. That easy a job, combined with a round-trip ticket to Buenos Aires when it was midwinter in the States and some pocket money, was all it took to get the needed mercenaries on board a flight south.

On February 12, 1986, a commercial flight left Miami bound for Buenos Aires. On board that flight were the eight mercenaries who would conduct the operation, including Jayee. In midmorning on February 13, the flight arrived in Argentina, and the men faced the first test of the ''sanctioning'' of their operation. The more superstitious of the mercs should have made note of the date.

Visas for Argentina had been placed on the men's passports in Miami without their having to do more than just hand them over. Without any fanfare, the passports were returned with visa stamps in them. Once on the ground in Argentina, the men were swept through customs without an inspection when Teebee showed up with G., an Argentinean contact. G. showed his credentials to the customs officials at the airport, and the men were waved through. It was now obvious to all of the possible doubters that the fix was in; their sanctioning was legitimate.

Operational security (opsec) was still supposedly tight. It was for security's sake that the men were transported from the airport in a closed bread truck to the hotel that would be their home for the next several weeks. Jayee paired the men up and sent them to rooms that had been secured for them by Argentine intelligence. The mercs didn't know each other and wouldn't talk amongst themselves about the operation. For all the men knew, some of them were there for another op. That first evening, they were all told just what would actually be expected of them.

It was made clear to all of the men that they could walk

out at any time. Return tickets were set, and anyone who wanted to go could be on the next flight back to the States. Jayee then proceeded to outline the general plan to the mercs. With an enthusiastic delivery, Jayee described an easy operation with minimal risk, a fast turnaround, and more money at the end of it.

For the most part, all of the mercs showed little reaction to the news of what was really going on. They would be expected to overthrow the government of an independent African country, mostly on their own but with the help of some native men. None of the men wanted to be the first to stand up and ask for his ticket home. Reputations can be fragile in the mercenary community, and the macho ethic can demand some occasional stupidity from the men who choose to live by it.

The next morning, the team had a quick but quiet breakfast and then were taken to the offices that would be their operational headquarters during their stay in Argentina. Once at the office, the mercs spread out to the available furniture and made themselves as comfortable as possible. Curious piles of material were scattered around the room, but that wasn't of first importance. Now they were introduced to their principal, Godfrey Osei, the next intended president of Ghana.

Osei began to brief them in some detail about what they were to do once they landed on the beaches of Ghana. Targets to be attacked included Jerry Rawlings at his presidential quarters. In addition to the Ghanaian political prisoners, the mercs were to release two CIA operatives who were also supposedly being held at the same location. Then the mercenary force was to capture the local broadcasting station and transmit a message to the people from their democratic liberator, Godfrey Osei.

The eight men were to be backed up by one hundred Ghanaian exiles they would pick up in Ivory Coast, on their way to the attack site at Accra. No particular resistance would be put up by the military forces in Ghana, according to Osei, and the people would welcome them all with open arms. This situation sounded all well and good to the mercenaries, not that they particularly believed it. Hearing about the details of the plan, especially the logistics, the weapons, and equipment they would be using, was much more important to them.

With no questions coming from the gathered mercenaries, Osei left the briefing, confident that he had won the men over with the simplicity of their job. Now Teebee took over the briefing, telling the men about the materials that were lined up for them to work with.

Since before the end of February, Teebee had been in Argentina, getting what the men would need and setting up their oceangoing transport. Elkay, an Argentine intelligence officer, had been performing liaison duties between Teebee and the government, making sure things went smoothly. Things had apparently gone well for Teebee, but not for the mercenaries or the operation. It was painfully obvious to the professional fighting men that Teebee didn't have a clue how to organize, operate, or equip a fighting force. And Teebee was in charge of supply.

When asked about what kind of weapons would be available to them, Teebee told the mercs that machine guns were lined up. He neglected to mention how many, what type, feed, caliber, make, or even how old they would be. When the question of Ghanaian armored forces was brought up, Teebee said that they would not bother the mercenaries. In case some Ghanaian hadn't gotten the word and showed up with a tank, the mercs wondered just what kind of antitank weapons they would have available. Teebee had gathered up rifle grenades for the mercs—not the best weapon for fighting tanks during World War II, and the basic design hadn't improved that much since then.

His ignorance of things military became even more obvious when Teebee was asked what kind of rifle grenades would be supplied. His answer centered around them being the explosive kind without much more detail forthcoming. As far as communications equipment went, Teebee felt there wouldn't be any need for such things since the mercs would only be on the ground for a few hours before the operation would be over.

Now the mercs were looking at going into an operation underequipped and with no communications to call for help in case everything went to hell. The piles of materials around the room were some of the field equipment and other ancillary gear intended for the mercenaries. The vast amount of money Teebee had spent for the equipment should have insured that the mercs would have the best of what was available. They didn't.

In the piles were plastic equipment belts, just the thing for a child playing army but not what the men wanted to carry their lifesaving equipment on in a hot, tropical environment. The ammunition pouches lying in the pile wouldn't fit on the equipment belts, the canteens would stand up to a walk in the park and little more, and the rucksacks were not any stronger than something a student would carry books in.

If quality of the personal equipment didn't raise any confidence in the mercs, the first aid equipment caused depression to quickly set in. The adhesive bandages supplied could have been found in any medicine cabinet, along with the bottles of light antiseptic—materials useful if the mercs cut themselves while shaving or if any of the men wanted to try being a blond, but not up to speed for a combat operation. And the antibiotics in the kits had been outdated before some of the mercs had even been born.

Teebee was so obviously out of his depth that the mercs were beyond even being disgusted with him. This fact was not lost on Teebee or Elkay, and they moved fast to satisfy the mercenaries about something. They took the men to another room, and it suddenly became payday when the merc force received a good part of the money they had been promised.

Between the $12,000 their leader, Jayee, received and the $5,000 to $7,000 each of the other mercs were given, the men were satisfied that something good might still be brought out of the operation. The mercs quickly sent parts of their pay back home to banks in the States, ensuring that they would have at least one thing they could depend on from this operation.

The other thing the mercs were depending on was the quality of their commander, Jayee. The merc leader had a good reputation and had seen action in many combat theaters throughout the world. Once the men had left the briefing and pay rooms, they gathered back at the hotel to decide just what they would do next. In spite of the bad beginning, the men still felt that they might pull the operation off. They had faith in their leader, and Osei still had enough financing to gather what the men really needed for the operation. At least, they thought he did.

Jayee again asked if any of the mercs wanted to back out. Again, none of the men wanted to be the first to say "I quit." Instead, they were going to break up into groups the next day and check out what other wonders Teebee had lined up for them. The ship and other supplies would be examined by some of the teams while others went through the city's shops to see what gear they could purchase to replace the crap that Teebee had tried to dump on them.

All men facing combat develop a bond between themselves that helps them face what would otherwise be a terrifying situation. The setup for the mission was not terrifying, but it was an unprofessional mess. Still, the mercs were already developing a bond, and they figured they could still pull off the op in spite of their support. That, and the fact that they had been paid and quitting would mean giving back much of the money, kept any of the men from leaving his fellows.

The evening of that first full day in Argentina, Osei invited all of the men out to dinner on him. All of the men gathered in a private dining room at the hotel and listened to Osei regale them with his plans for Ghana. Alcohol was flowing freely, but most of the mercs were not drinking very much, if at all. This was not the case with Osei, or Teebee either.

As the evening went on, Osei started talking about how he was going to disband the Ghanaian military after he took power. In spite of the fact that he had said there were military units on his side, the future leader didn't trust his fellow countrymen. Instead, Osei said, a new military would be put together, an elite unit under his direct command with the officers coming from the mercenaries with him in the room that evening.

Now was the chance for the mercenaries to get more answers about the forces they would be facing. The air force, Osei said, was not on their side, but his men in the army would close down the local airport and freeze the military assets on the ground. He went on to say that his loyal followers in the army would drive fuel trucks onto the runways of the airport and set fire to them. This would be enough to prevent fixed-wing aircraft from getting off the ground, but no mention was made about taking care of the helicopters that were also in the Ghanaian air force.

Since the mercs would be coming in by sea, they also wanted to know what was going to be done about the Ghanaian navy. Again, no problem, according to Osei. The navy consisted of a few elderly patrol boats that were on his side anyway. In reality, the Ghanaian navy, though not a real threat to a modern naval force, would have been more than a handful for the mercs to handle in an unarmed ship. At that time, the Ghanaian navy consisted of:

- Two SPEAR-class open patrol boats armed with several light machine guns
- Two ROTORK utility landing craft capable of transporting a number of troops and armed with both light and heavy machine guns
- Two PB57-class fast attack craft, 190 feet long and armed with both a 76mm gun, capable of firing eighty-six rounds per minute, and a 40mm rapid-fire gun capable of firing three hundred rounds per minute
- Two FPB 45-class fast attack craft, 147 feet long and armed with two 40mm guns, each capable of firing three hundred rounds per minute

These eight craft used some of the 900 men in the Ghanaian navy as crew, with the balance of the men mostly at the two naval bases, one at Sekondi and the other at Tema, the latter located just a short distance from Accra, the primary target of the mercenaries.

At the time, none of the mercenaries had the above intelligence. If they had had the information, the plan might have been hard to put on, since they probably would have been on their way home the next morning. Instead, they continued with their questions about what they could expect to face in Ghana.

As far as the military's reaction to the mercenaries' landing on the beach, Osei had his traditional "don't worry" answer ready. Since Rawlings was afraid of a coup, Osei said with a smile, most of the military was disarmed. When the mercs hit the beaches, the people there would just run away.

The Ghanaian military was estimated at being between ten

thousand and fifteen thousand men, with from one thousand to five thousand men in the reserves. The paramilitary forces used as border guards, and probably as guards at the targeted prison, were estimated to number around five thousand men. This was a large number of troops to disarm, leaving your borders undefended, but the mercs didn't point out this problem to Osei.

By this time, Osei was running out of steam and wouldn't answer any more questions about Ghana. The mercenaries looked to Teebee, as their intelligence officer, to answer their further concerns. Performing as competently as he had in obtaining their needed supplies, Teebee told the mercs little more than nothing. The Israelis would be giving the men up-to-the-minute intel on the situation in Ghana when they picked up the exiles at the Ivory Coast. The fact that at that point the team would be pretty well committed to the operation was not lost on the mercenaries.

The boat they would be using for their transportation was an old workboat that could easily be passed off as one of the many oil rig craft that were all over the waters off Ghana. This was the first item Teebee told the mercenaries that actually made sense to them. But their last question was one of the most important. Was the operation really sanctioned by the U.S. government?

Teebee answered that he had been in direct contact with the National Security Council (NSC) and personally worked for the CIA. There was no problem with the operation, and it had been cleared at the highest levels. The reality was that Teebee, who may have been a low-level CIA employee at one time, had approached at least one official at the NSC and outlined the proposed coup plan to him. Following that announcement, Teebee was unceremoniously rushed out of the official's office and told that the U.S. government had no interest whatsoever in overthrowing the Rawlings government. But this little bit of information didn't get back to the mercenaries until well after the operation had started. The retired SF men were not only risking their pensions; the whole group was risking their U.S. citizenship and could face possible criminal charges back in the States.

It was reasonably obvious to the mercs that the Argentine

government was backing them, so the possibility of the U.S. government being behind the operation didn't draw any suspicions. And all of the uproar the clumsy Teebee would have caused while gathering his materials, as well as the recruiting and planning done by Beef and Jayee, would have attracted the attention of at least one of the many intelligence agencies who would have been interested in the plot.

These thoughts calmed the worst fears of the mercenaries. Then Teebee, having more drinks inside him, told about why the Israelis were interested in the op. While the mercs were attacking Accra, Israeli commandos would be taking out several terrorist training camps in northern Ghana. Abu Nidal was mentioned as a possible target. Now the mercenaries had the comforting thought that they might not be facing poorly armed Ghanaian troops, but seriously pissed-off Libyans and other terrorists!

This information effectively ended the night's entertainment. The mercs went back to their rooms, each man with his own thoughts. The next morning, they broke up into teams to try to make up for Teebee's failure in equipping them. Some of the men would sort through the equipment that was already in their operational headquarters and decide if any of it was suitable for the mission. As it turned out, almost nothing Teebee had purchased, at great expense, was of any use to the mercenaries. Almost everything had to be replaced, and the men had to go out and buy the materials themselves, with the money that they had on them.

No specific information about the operation had come from Jayee, so thoughts about equipment had to be general and based on the mercs' own experience. But these men had been around for some time in the fighting business and had learned to depend on their own knowledge before. While another team of mercs sought out their communications requirements, some of the men went out to check on the weapons and the ship.

Following their Argentinean contact, Elkay, the mercs went to a government weapons warehouse to check on the hardware selected for them by Teebee. Surprisingly, most of the weapons seemed very worthwhile, except for the hardware Teebee deemed unnecessary.

For their basic weapons, the mercs had 150 of the Argentine

version of the FN-FAL rifles. This 7.62×51mm battle rifle was familiar to the mercs, as it was to the over ninety countries that had adopted it as their standard rifle. Capable of selective fire and fed from a twenty-round magazine, the FAL was heavy, but powerful for its weight. The flash hider on the end of the FAL's barrel would also act as a rifle grenade launcher, which meant that each of the mercenaries could launch their "heavy firepower" if necessary.

The heaviest support weapon available to the mercenaries were their four Argentine-made MAG light machine guns. This weapon was also a well-proven design, rugged and powerful, in use by nearly as many countries as the FAL rifle. The MAG fired the same 7.62×51mm round as the FAL, feeding the ammunition from a flexible metal-link belt. A quick-change barrel allowed the MAG to continue firing in support of an assault, with the barrels being easily swapped when one became overheated.

For handguns, there were six Browning Hi-Power 9mm pistols available, another weapon the mercenaries were very familiar with. The thirteen-shot semiautomatic pistol was also well known throughout the world and had a deserved reputation for reliability. Three 12-gauge short-barreled, pump-action shotguns were included with the weapons. The shotguns would be useful in guarding prisoners, and particularly valuable if the fighting turned close-up and personal. The last three small arms in with the others were a bit of a pleasant surprise to the mercs.

Three Argentinean PA3-DM (since renamed the FMK) submachine guns were sitting with the mercenaries weapons. The 9mm selective-fire submachine guns could be fired on single shot or full automatic and were fed with a forty-round magazine. Normally, the submachine gun is desired because the short, easily handled weapon contains a good deal of firepower for its size. But these particular weapons weren't short or handy, which didn't make them any less desired by the mercenaries. What made the sub-guns long and unwieldy were the silencers attached to the barrels, almost doubling the overall length of the guns.

Silenced weapons would be very useful to the mercenaries in taking out any sentry who might otherwise announce their presence before they were ready. But the PA3-DMs were one of the few bright lights in their weapons inventory. There were no mortars, no rocket launchers, and almost no heavy weapons of any kind. Crated up were boxes of hand and rifle grenades, cans of small-arms ammunition, and little else.

The four hundred hand grenades were native-produced Argentinean GME-FMK2-MO high-explosive fragmentation grenades. The antipersonnel FMK2s had round, cast-iron bodies that would break up into hundreds of high-velocity fragments when they exploded. Each of the sixteen boxes of grenades held twenty-five FMK2s, which could not be considered too many when you included the expected one hundred Ghanaian exiles who had to be armed along with the eight mercenaries. For heavy firepower, all the mercenaries had were one hundred FN high-explosive rifle grenades. The rifle grenades could take out a light armored vehicle, but only if the firer was very good or very lucky—or waited until the target was too close to miss.

For each of the MAG-58 machine guns, there were three thousand rounds of belted ammunition. Each FAL rifle had one thousand rounds of ammunition. There was plenty of 9×19mm ammunition for the submachine guns and pistols, but none of the special subsonic ammunition that would make the suppressed PA3-DMs even quieter when fired.

According to Elkay, that was everything that had been ordered by Teebee. All of the ammunition was plain metal-jacketed ball; no armor piercing and no tracers were included. Since the operation was expected to be conducted at night, tracers would be very useful. Elkay was told to order the tracers by the mercs, whose opinion of Teebee was dropping by the minute.

No cleaning equipment could be located in the supplies. All of the weapons were brand-new, fresh from the factory, but even the best weapons have to be tested and cleaned. The MAGs didn't have any spare barrels either—so much for their being used for sustained covering fire.

But the weapons could be test-fired on board the boat, sights could be checked and realigned easily at that time. The men weren't on their way yet, and they still might have time to correct the deficiencies in their arsenal before they left. The weapons weren't a disaster; that situation could be dealt with.

Jayee and Teebee would have to be talked to, and Osei would have to cough up some more money.

For all of the disappointment the mercenaries had about the weapons, it was nothing compared to the feelings held by the merc team who went to check out the boat. For the estimated three-week ocean trip to Ghana, Teebee and Elkay had obtained a World War II–vintage Liberty ship, a rusting hulk of a transport vessel that had only been expected to last a few years when it had been built almost fifty years earlier. Covered with rust and bird excrement, the ship looked like it was being held up by the dock rather than just being tied to it.

Jayee and several of the mercenaries went on board the crumbling ship. Rust flaked off wherever their hands touched. Going up to the bridge, the mercs could see that the vessel had been stripped of anything valuable, and the remainder left to decompose. All of the instruments and controls necessary for conning the vessel were either gone or useless. It would take weeks of work and a lot of money to make the ship barely capable of navigating the South Atlantic.

Then the mercenaries found something that made all the expected work and expense unnecessary. When the men went down to check the engine room, their inspection was a short one. There was no engine to drive the ship, just marks and garbage on the deck to show where it had been. Their ship wasn't transportation; it was in such bad shape, it couldn't be used for target practice by a competent navy. It would probably sink as soon as it was pulled away from the dock.

All of the mercs were less than happy when they returned to their headquarters. The other supply teams had seen the obvious when they went out to obtain communications equipment and proper supplies. Teebee had been badly price-gouging Osei, cheating him out of his operating funds and shorting the mercenaries on the equipment needed for the operation. After discussing what they had learned, the team decided that their worst shortfall was the nonexistent ocean transportation and the lack of heavy weapons.

Teebee explained that they were not going to settle for the dilapidated Liberty ship, but, for the available money, the choices were poor and little was available. As for the weapons, what they had was all they could get. The mercenaries would just have to settle for that. At this point, Jayee told the men in no uncertain terms that they could still back out of the operation, but his tone gave his opinion about anyone who quit or kept complaining.

This was a bad situation for the mercenaries to have to deal with. Not only were they being lied to and cheated by their supply officer, their leader was acting like anything but a leader. But most of the mercenaries were used to working with less than they wanted. And they still hung on to the stubborn belief that Jayee would pull everything together.

So for days in Buenos Aries, the mercs continued to work together to get the equipment they needed, to test and adjust what they obtained, and to listen to nightly pep talks from Osei. For all of their work, the problems just weren't going away. Transportation to Ghana still wasn't on-line, and Jayee was acting more and more like a martinet. Instead of answering questions from the men, he just indicated to them that he was in charge and to get on with their work. No detailed plans were discussed, and no briefings were given.

One problem the mercs didn't have was dealing with and interpreting intelligence on the target site. No intel was coming in to them at all. Contact with the Ghanaian expatriates hadn't been made by the mercs. Where Rawlings had his forces placed was unknown. Even their landing sites and rendezvous points hadn't been determined. This was a situation that could quickly get the whole team killed in Ghana.

One of the mercs came up with a plan that was finally agreed on by Jayee. The merc, who was experienced in gathering information, would return to the United States. Once there, he would gather all available information on the target site and send it back to the team in Argentina. After that, the merc would continue on to the Ivory Coast and make contact with the exiles who were supposed to be going in on the op with the mercs. That would put the mercenary in a position to determine a location where the exiles could be picked up, and also put him within range of the target site in Ghana.

Entering Ghana as a tourist, the merc could gather intel on the targets for the merc force and send back what information he could gather. When the mercs actually made their assault, the in-country man would act as a beach guide, bringing the mercenaries in to the proper landing site quickly and with little fanfare.

The only problem was, the team couldn't let Teebee know about the merc going back to the States. The men didn't trust Teebee at all and figured he might do something to harm the group if he figured they were going around him. A story about the mercenary's family being ill and his having to return home was put out and apparently accepted by Teebee. Now at least the team had a man they trusted trying to get the information they desperately needed.

At this point, Beef, who had recruited most of the team, suddenly showed up in Buenos Aires. Supposedly, he had been working back in the States, trying to gather financial backing for the operation. Now he was in Argentina with no news for most of the team.

The time continued to pass, and the mercs were constantly told that everything was fine. The operation was approved of by the U.S. government, the needed equipment would be available, and the ship would show up in time. A number of the mercs even went with their leadership, Jayee, Beef, and Osei, to a villa in the outskirts of Buenos Aires where a barbecue was being held for all foreign guests of the government.

Arriving at the villa, the mercs noticed that different tables were set up for different national groups. Canadians, Swedes, South Africans, and others were at the party, along with Cubans and East Germans. As the party went along, a spokesman went around to all of the different tables and announced who was there, introducing them to the guests at large. When he arrived at the mercenaries' table, he announced the presence of the next president of Ghana, a guest of the Americans. So much for opsec.

Teebee had the end of his mercenary career finalized just a few days after the party. Even Osei believed he had been cheated when the Argentine civilian who had been selling the team their radios explained how he had been double-billing the team. The inexpensive two-way radios that Teebee had been buying for the team suddenly cost more than the best model on the market. The extra cost was being kicked back to Elkay, with a share going to Teebee.

Suddenly Osei was no longer much of a friend to Teebee.

In spite of his best try at calming Osei down, it was obvious that Teebee's time was up. Within just a few days, Teebee suddenly vanished from Argentina. The gutsy little cheat still tried to get more out of the deal, calling Osei from the United States a few days later. Osei refused to meet with Teebee anywhere and slammed the phone down, ending the conversation. Osei quickly put in a call to Ess, another of his American "CIA" contacts, in New York, who supposedly had Teebee working for him. Complaints about the miserable ship, Teebee's disappearance, and the constant theft of his money poured out. Ess calmed the future president of Ghana and assured him that not only would Teebee be taken care of, but a ship would soon be available.

Osei amused himself by describing to the mercenaries—those who would listen, anyway—all of the fun things he had in mind if Teebee could be brought to Ghana after the coup. Torturing a prisoner to death was long an accepted tradition in parts of Africa, and Osei saw no problem in bringing this same tradition to Ghana for a selected individual. The mercs simply continued to get ready for the operation, glad they weren't in Teebee's shoes.

Within a very short time of the call to Ess in New York, Elkay announced to the mercs that a seaworthy ship and crew were available. The ship was a 120-foot oceangoing tug more than capable of transporting the mercs, their equipment, and the Ghanaian exiles to the target beach. The op was a go, and the mercs had only a few more days to get ready.

Ten Zodiac inflatable boats were obtained for the beach assault, each with an outboard motor and capable of carrying ten men. The boats and motors cost about $32,000, some $24,000 less than the price quoted to Osei by the now-missing Teebee. Outside of the major purchases, such as the Zodiacs, the mercenaries were buying their equipment out of their own pockets. Jayee assured the men that they would be reimbursed for every receipt they turned in after the operation had gone down.

At that point, some intelligence materials started to show up from the merc who had gone back to the States. Jayee still hadn't given the team a detailed briefing or even outlined all the parts of the plan. The mercs only had a rough idea of what the plan was for attacking Ghana, but by this time a kind of superstition had settled in with the men that everything would go. Jayee was a professional warrior, and he would pull everything together.

The weekend of March 1, 1986, saw the mercs on the dock, preparing to embark on their mission. A large number of Argentine military and intelligence officers showed up with trucks carrying the weapons and supplies. Containers of weapons and ammunition, all labeled GODFREY OSEI, ACCRA, GHANA, were unloaded from the trucks by local troops and carried on board the ship. Even the tracers the mercs had asked for had been supplied in place of some of the regular ammunition.

Osei was there to see the mercs off, and it was obvious to all that he was less than comfortable around the water. Looking a little worse for wear, Osei told the mercs that he would be meeting with them in just a few weeks in the Ivory Coast. And he again mentioned his disappointment that Teebee would not be available in Ghana to entertain the new president.

Jayee received the last of his money, in order to pay the necessary bribes to the locals who were arranging for customs, passport stamps, and other necessities. Equipment was loaded and stowed away in conex containers secured to the deck. Finally, the ship cast off, and Jayee, Beef, and the eight mercs were on their way across the South Atlantic to Africa. In three weeks, there would be a new government in charge in Ghana.

Besides the possible Ghanaian forces the mercs would have to face at their target, another enemy showed up, one the mercs couldn't fight at all. The weather started turning bad almost as soon as the ship had left the harbor. Combat-experienced professional warriors are not necessarily salty sailors. As ten-foot waves crashed over a deck that was only two feet above sea level at the stern, the mercs found other things to occupy their time rather than preparing for the operation. Dramamine and their bunks had a lot more appeal to the seasick mercenaries than anything else on the pitching ship. Landing on the beaches at Accra, or anywhere else, sounded very good to the miserable men.

After three days, nature's onslaught eased up, and the storm finally blew itself out. The ship had struggled to make headway against the storm, and the team was running behind schedule. If any of the men went with Jayee on another operation, he would have to make it an airborne insertion, something the mercenary leader heartily agreed with.

Now the men settled into a routine that would make the most of the time they had. After they got up early in the morning, an hour's worth of PT was led for the group by Beef. Then they had a hearty meal, and the Zodiac boats were attended to. All of the boats were spread out on the deck, assembled, inflated, and launched into the water. Now the low back deck of the oceangoing tug was working in the mercenaries' favor, but new problems were showing up. Even with the ship dead in the water, it was difficult to launch the rubber boats and get them underway. Doing it at night, with a bunch of inexperienced and probably seasick exiles on board, would be an even more difficult problem.

The plan, such as it was, was now told to the mercs. The team would land at Accra at 0200 on Sunday, March 23. The intention was to take advantage of the fact that the day before was scheduled as payday for the Ghanaian military. The mercenaries were hoping that much of their possible opposition would be too drunk to resist them, just in case Rawlings had decided to let them keep their weapons after all.

No specific timing had been decided on for picking up the Ghanaian exiles in the Ivory Coast. That would come when their merc in-country had given them the details over the ship's radio. The ship would stop at the rendezvous point to pick up the Ghanaians, probably the day before the operation was launched. With the troops on board, the ship would move to and anchor a mile or so offshore at Accra, and the mercs would ferry the troops to shore with the Zodiacs.

With all of the men on shore, after a probably harrowing boat ride in the dark over several miles of open ocean, the mercs would be ready to launch their assault. The team would break up into groups, each one to assault a specific target. One team would attack Rawlings's residence, eliminating him as their primary target. Another team would attack Ussher Fort Prison and release the political prisoners as well as the captured CIA men. Two other groups would move inland, capture the radio station, and take control of the local armory just across the street from the station.

All of this was known to the team, but they still hadn't been given a detailed briefing by Jayee. Normally, prior to any mission's being launched, an operational order (op order) is given detailing every contingency of a plan. Men would be told exactly what their individual jobs would be, and who would take over their assignments if they were injured or missing. Friendly and enemy forces would be described, including how to tell the former from the latter. A person would be designated to take over command if the leader fell, to automatically maintain the chain of command.

All of this information would normally be only a part of a full op order. But only a few weeks out from the target, the mercs still hadn't been given the necessary basics. Even emergency evacuation procedures and rendezvous points—how the mercs would get the heck outta Dodge and back together— hadn't been put out. But the men still had faith in Jayee, and they continued to prepare for the op.

Once they were in international waters, weapons could be broken out and tested. When their heavy weapons, the MAGs, were broken out, the mercenaries had another unpleasant surprise. Only two of the four MAG light machine guns were in the crates. A search of all the containers didn't produce the missing weapons.

When the mercs tested the two machine guns, one of the weapons broke apart, its stock group falling to pieces from the shock of firing. Now the mercs were down to only one machine gun for the entire force. All of the crates had been checked, and even those boxes were causing trouble.

A clerk in a shipping office back in Buenos Aires followed his normal procedure and contacted the foreign recipient of a government shipment of arms. Each of the crates of weapons and ammunition the mercs were holding was clearly marked as going to Ghana for Godfrey Osei. The clerk simply told the proper authorities in Ghana that their shipment was on its way.

Of course, the authorities in Ghana hadn't ordered a shipment of weapons, at least not from Argentina. And Osei's name was well known to the Rawlings government. Suddenly, all of the Ghanaian military forces found themselves on alert.

Possible enemies of the state were rounded up and secured, and a warning went out to all of the navy forces and neighbors of Ghana to be on the lookout for the 120-foot ship that was carrying the shipment of arms.

Of course, all of this wasn't the bad news the mercs were now hearing. What they were learning instead was that at that time of year, the waters off Ghana were normally rough with heavy running seas. Six-foot surf could be expected on the beaches at Accra at any time, with little advance warning. Well-trained aquatic troops such as the U.S. Navy SEALs might be able to land under such conditions, but it would kill most of the mercenaries and their Ghanaian allies without a shot being fired.

Now Jayee got in touch with the mercenary back in the States, using the ship's radiotelephone. The plan was changed, and the merc would have to get trucks and drivers, and meet the landing force five miles down the beach from their original site. Charts on board ship indicated that much calmer waters could be expected at that landing point. The merc in the States agreed to Jayee's orders and would get the needed transport in place.

The trouble with the modified plan was that the mercenary back in the United States hadn't been able to get a visa to visit Ghana yet. When the paperwork finally was approved, the man would arrive too late to arrange for anything for the mercenary force. They were going to be on their own.

What existed of the plan started to fall apart, and it fell apart in a hurry. The captain of the transport ship could see what some of the problems were, and he wanted no part of them. The tug wouldn't get any closer than five miles from the shore at Accra. Nothing the mercenaries could do, including threats, would change the captain's mind.

On top of his refusal to move closer to shore for the operation, the captain wouldn't continue with the voyage to Africa unless more money was paid into his accounts back in the States. Jayee quickly got onto the radio and in touch with his contacts in the States. Money was approved for the captain— up to $100,000, even though he had only asked for $50,000. But Jayee told the captain and the other mercs that the additional money had been refused. The operation was off.

All of the mercs were disappointed, and it showed. Even Jayee's talk about keeping the equipment and weapons, and planning a later op with another boat couldn't brighten the situation for the team. All of their work was for nothing. The ship turned back for South America and, a week later, pulled into Rio de Janeiro, Brazil.

AFTERMATH

By March 10, the tug with the discouraged mercenaries pulled into and anchored in Rio harbor. The trip back to shore had been considerably easier than the trip out had been. But Rio had not been the destination of the ship; no visas had been procured, customs permits for the cargo didn't exist, and docking facilities hadn't been arranged.

Pulling into Rio harbor in the middle of what they were told was a harbor pilot's strike, the mercenaries found that no foreign ships were being allowed to land. So within sight of the shore, the mercs had to remain on board their ship for the time being.

A representative of the shipping company that owned the tug they were on was waiting on shore to meet with Jayee and arrange the necessary paperwork for the cargo, a berth for the ship, and transit visas for the mercenaries so that they would be allowed to travel to the airport and catch flights back to the United States.

Elkay had also come up from Argentina to meet the mercenaries' ship and try to talk them into another attempt at completing their mission. Elkay even told Jayee that he had another captain and crew ready to go right back out and transport the mercenaries and their equipment back to the Ivory Coast and then to Ghana.

Jayee didn't want to hear anything of what Elkay had arranged. As far as he was concerned, the mercs' mission was over. Jayee had made other arrangements that didn't include Elkay for the disposition of the firearms. The attempted mission had ended, and nothing that Elkay could say would change Jayee's mind. Within a few days, Elkay returned to Argentina, supposedly to inform Osei of the news.

The rest of the mercenary force had remained on the ship

while Jayee had his meeting. They had put their fate in the hands of their leader and were not particularly happy about the situation. The captain of the ship had gathered up the mercenaries' passports, so they weren't in a position to go anywhere on their own. The conex containers holding their weapons and equipment had been secured by the captain with official customs seals from Argentina. The men had to sit on the ship in enforced idleness, their weapons illegally in a foreign country and they themselves in Brazil without visas, or even passports for the moment. This was not a situation to instill confidence.

After about four days had passed without any real news from Jayee, the mercs decided to take some action on their own. Using one of the inflatable boats originally intended for their assault on Ghana, the eight mercenaries left their ship and headed to shore.

The men's intent was to contact the American Consulate in the city and arrange for their own transportation back to the States. The first step in this plan was to get in contact with a member of the consulate. After locating a public telephone, the men called the consulate and were put in touch with the available duty officer. A cursory explanation of their situation resulted in the duty officer's refusing to make any decisions and kicking the mercs' problem upstairs to his boss, the American consul in Rio. But the consul wasn't immediately available, and the men had to call back in a few hours, when the official would be available.

Now the men had to lounge about the dock area of Rio, attempting to blend in with the people while killing several hours. None of them had their passports and, even if they did, the passports didn't have entry stamps for Brazil. They could be immediately arrested and charged with entering the country illegally. If their ship was searched, it would take little more time to have the mercenaries charged with some form of gun smuggling. Those charges would ensure a lengthy stay in Brazil as unpopular guests of the government.

Finally, enough time had passed that the mercenaries were able to call back to the consulate and speak to the American consul himself. The men explained their situation sufficiently to swing the consul over to their side. Now, without passports and in a foreign country illegally, they heard the consul tell them that their problems could be solved. All they had to do was return to their ship and wait to be contacted. The mercenaries had put their faith in a State Department career diplomat whose job was to look out for American interests abroad. The only problem was that the diplomat hadn't told the mercs exactly whose interests had priority, the mercenaries' or those of someone above him in the State Department or CIA.

The mercs returned to their ship for a hopefully short stay. Though the mission had gone badly and was finally abandoned, they had effectively beaten the odds and were now looking forward to home. And, because they had thought of it beforehand, at least some of their pay was in banks back home.

A small naval patrol boat approached the mercenaries' ship as several of the men were up on deck relaxing. The appearance of the boat with a number of long-haired, bearded civilians aboard did little to raise the mercenaries' suspicions. One of the men was below taking a shower when what turned out to be a boatload of Brazilian federal police pulled up alongside the oceangoing tug.

Fifteen heavily armed plainclothes police swarmed on board the tug, quickly securing the mercs and forcing them to lie down on the deck. The soap-covered mercenary who was in the shower was quickly brought on deck wearing nothing more than a towel, pushed along by a shotgun-wielding policeman.

As the tug was moved to the police docks, the mercenaries were searched, their money, watches, and valuables going into the pockets of the policemen doing the searching. When the mercs were handcuffed together and all sitting on the deck, the police broke open the weapons and equipment containers. Excitement among the police was obvious to the mercenaries. Many of the weapons and other ordnance never made it to the police property room. Pistols slipped into pockets, and all three of the suppressed PA3-DM submachine guns disappeared. Once at the police docks, a number of weapons cases were loaded into private cars that bore no police markings.

Meanwhile, the eight mercenaries were bundled into transportation and moved through the streets of Rio de Janeiro. Stripped of everything, including most of their clothes, the mercenaries were unceremoniously dumped into cells, with

Jayee and Beef going into one cell to segregate them from the other six mercs, who were placed in a cell together.

The six mercenaries found themselves in a twelve-by-fifteen-foot cell, illuminated by a single bulb caged in the ceiling. The only thing the men could do was wait, and decide on their cover story together. The men decided that the original story that had brought them to South America in the first place, that they were to escort a shipment of arms to Ghana, was the easiest one to stick to.

The duty officer from the American consulate came down to see them one day early in their imprisonment. He had little more to say than that it was probably just a visa problem and would soon be cleared up. That was the last word the six mercs had for over three weeks. The American consul had been to see Jayee and Beef a number of times during those weeks, but the other mercs never heard of the meetings until later.

Living conditions were about as bad as could be expected, perhaps worse. Beds were concrete slabs with no bedding. The water- and scum-covered cell floor bred insects and disease, both of which racked the mercenaries. They subsisted on a diet of bread, rice, and beans. Sanitary facilities were a well-used hole in the floor, and water was supplied through a rusted steel pipe, running when the guards felt like turning it on.

Brazil has a law on the books that men can be held for up to twenty-one days and then must be released or charged. The American consul finally came to speak to the six mercs and tell them that everything would be all right. As far as the diplomat was concerned, the problem was only one of visas, and the mercs wouldn't even need a lawyer. In addition, the consul said that he had no control over what the Brazilians did with criminals in their own country. The mercenaries were left in the cell. The consul, the man charged with the well-being of American citizens on foreign soil, didn't even mention that they were in the twenty-fifth day of their incarceration and that they should have been released four days earlier. The men were effectively dumped by the U.S. government.

Forty-five days later, ten weeks after their arrest, the mercenaries were told that they were going on trial. Up until that point, the men had hoped that what they had been told was true, that it was just a visa problem and they were going home.

Now the realization set in that they were going someplace, but it wouldn't be home. Given their own clothes from on board the ship, the mercs were allowed to shower and clean up prior to their court appearance. The one merc finally finished his shower, over two months later.

A fast appearance before a Brazilian judge, and a large number of news media cameras and reporters, went by before the mercenaries had any idea of what was actually being done with them. The Portuguese spoken in the courtroom had been only roughly translated for them. Without knowing the charges against them or putting in a plea of guilt or innocence, the mercs found themselves quickly hustled back to their cells.

Two more weeks passed before the mercs were again cleaned up and taken into court. Now they learned that gun-smuggling charges had been brought against them. The judge in front of the mercenaries put on a show of rage and histrionics, mostly for the benefit of the many television cameras in the courtroom. The mercs were screamed at as being the scum of the earth, with no respect for Brazilian law or even the country. What had been done with the mercs had little resemblance to what was actually Brazilian law, but they had no real way of knowing that.

Police witnesses were brought forth, and they swore to the abbreviated list of weapons the mercs were charged with possessing. An apparently friendly army officer was brought out past the mercs, but he did little more than say that the weapons were not ordered by the Brazilian military. Every time the mercs' appointed attorney tried to bring up a defense, he was put back in his place by the judge who said there was no defense.

Finally, the sham of a trial was ended, and the mercenaries returned to jail. After about a month passed, the men were finally sentenced. Jayee and the captain of the tug both received five years in prison, one year over the maximum proscribed by Brazilian law. Each of the other mercenaries received four-year sentences.

The men had been completely abandoned by their country. In fact, the consul had probably turned them in to the Brazilian authorities himself. What *was* true was that the consul had never informed the mercs' families about what had happened to them; they found out about the mercenaries' plight through news reports on television and in the newspapers. The mercs had been discarded by the U.S. government, and effectively flushed away by powers in the Brazilian government as well.

THE IMPRISONMENT

Though the mercenaries didn't realize it, since they had no grounds for comparison, they were receiving the same treatment usually reserved for the worst of Brazilian criminals. The Aqua Santa—Holy Water—prison was surrounded by the slums of Rio. From this central processing place, the mercs would be sent on to their long-term facility to serve out their sentences. Normally, foreign prisoners were sent on to relatively easy prisons, but that was not going to be the case with the mercenaries. Aqua Santa's warden told the mercs that the American consul had really done a number on the men. Instead of following normal procedures, the mercs were going to be sent to Helio Gomez, a prison normally reserved for only the most hardened criminals.

Aqua Santa was not quite a prison built along the lines of American penal practices. Daily survival was something that had to be worked at, and the merc prisoners set themselves to learning what they had to in order to keep on living. Medical treatment was something reserved for the outside world; it didn't exist in the prison.

Diseases and parasites not often found even in the jungle were rampant in the prison population. Malnutrition added to the general misery. Food came most often in the form of a thin, gray gruel with bits of unidentifiable material suspended in the mess. You ate what was available, and you made do, or you died. But it was hard to stay upbeat when even the other prisoners thought the mercenaries looked like they were in bad shape.

Some things improved slightly for the mercenary prisoners. Families and other supporters back in the States had found out where the men were. The contents of some packages that were sent to the mercs survived the ravages of the guards to actually get to the men they were intended for. Money, hidden in some of the packages, could be used to bribe certain guards. Who could be bribed or trusted was one of the lessons the mercs learned.

Some extra food and materials could be obtained, and every little bit went toward helping the men survive another day.

The mercenaries spent only a month in Aqua Santa. In August, they went on to the lesser comforts of Helio Gomez. Separated from the civilized world, Helio Gomez had developed a civilization of its own, one where the mercs had to again learn the rules. The filth and disease of Aqua Santa were carried over and multiplied at Helio Gomez with torture, rodents, and prison gangs thrown into the mix. Medicine and more food were available only to those who could afford to pay for them. Nothing was free except for the misery.

No contact was heard from the American consulate. The only support the mercs received were the infrequent packages from their families and friends back in the States. The mercs had to blend in enough to survive their imprisonment, however long that might be. The main gang in the prison was known as the Red Commando, and the mercs developed contacts and friends in that group. The leader of the gang took on most of the mercenaries as his own charges and saw to it that they learned what they needed to know.

It was pointed out to the mercenaries that they had been sent to Helio Gomez on purpose. Contacts the gang leader had on the outside confirmed that the mercs had been ordered away by "the highest authority"—either someone influential or some government wanted the mercs to just go away for a long time. Most of the very few foreign prisoners who were sent to Helio Gomez did not survive long. The mercs had been effectively given a death sentence.

The mercs "paid" for the protection and guidance they received by instructing the Red Commando members in how to conduct military operations. Tactics, weapons—both how to build and how to use them—and other skills were accepted by the Red Commando as payment. One additional edge the mercenaries had was that they didn't use drugs or take advantage of the other vices that were common in the prison. In combination with their position as foreign mercenaries, their way of living helped give the mercenaries something of a special status among the prison population.

But not all of the mercenaries were cooperating with each other. Jayee was still suspected to have sold out the merc team for his own ends. His own bad luck and greed may have been all that landed Jayee in Helio Gomez along with the rest of his men. What the other mercs did notice was that Jayee seemed to be able to buy better food and medicine than the other mercs.

The other mercs suspected Jayee of simply selling them out in order to better his own position. Jayee constantly said his money and other valuables had been taken from him by the federal police during their arrest. But the mercs suspected Jayee of holding back some of the funds he had been given by Osei at their last meeting, funds that were desperately needed by the other mercs for food and medicine.

After they had finally nursed their suspicions long enough, the mercs searched Jayee's possessions. Inside of packs of cigarettes, the mercs found $2,000 in hundred-dollar bills. With the mercs' suspicions apparently confirmed about Jayee's sellout, the story quickly made the rounds of the prison grapevine. Jayee's "accidental" death was offered to the mercs by their friends in the Red Commando, but the offer was turned down. Jayee was now abandoned by the mercs he had originally been the leader of.

The normal dangers of prison life were not all the mercs faced in Helio Gomez. Word came to the men that another government wanted to punish them further. Argentina was making noises about extraditing the mercs to face charges regarding customs violations and failure to make proper payments on their materials. The mercs suspected that elements in the Argentine military and intelligence communities wanted to completely eliminate their connection with the Ghana coup attempt. The easiest way to erase the final connection would be to get the mercenaries into the Argentine criminal justice system and have them vanish completely, probably into the jungles with a bullet in each of their heads.

By early October, a new development raised the possibility that the mercs' freedom might be at hand. The mercenaries' trial had been reviewed by a Brazilian court of appeals, and their convictions had been overturned. According to the court, the men had directly broken no Brazilian laws, and there was no reason for them to remain in prison.

Quickly gathering up their meager possessions, the mercs were moved to another location on the prison grounds to be out-processed for release. But instead of freedom and a trip home, the mercs walked into the hands of the waiting Brazilian federal police.

In addition to their case being reviewed, the Brazilian Supreme Court was examining Argentina's request that the mercenaries be extradited to their country. Until the decision was made, the mercs would remain in prison.

Shackled together, the mercs were driven off to a federal prison in Rio. Freedom for the men had lasted less than a few hours. Again, the mercenaries had no way of knowing what their fate would be. Seven weeks later, they were again shuttled to another location.

The men were suddenly awakened in the middle of the night and told to prepare to be moved. Again shackled and put into a police van, the mercs expected the worst. What was being done to them fit the scenario of men who disappeared during the night. When the van stopped at the Rio airport, the mercs were only slightly relieved that they weren't at a jungle execution site.

Instead of being killed outright, the mercs were put on board a civilian aircraft. Until they were told differently, some of the mercs were sure that they were being extradited to Argentina. They learned instead that they were being moved to another federal prison, this one much deeper inside Brazil, near Brasilia, the country's capital.

The new prison was still not at U.S. standards, but it was a vacation spot in comparison to Helio Gomez or Aqua Santa. The mercenaries were given clean clothes to wear, sanitary facilities that allowed the men to clean themselves, and clean cells with bedding. Outside exercise was allowed, giving the men some of the first sun they'd had in a long time. Even their meals had improved considerably. With the better treatment, the physical and mental condition of the mercs also improved rapidly. But the reason behind their new treatment was still a question. The question wasn't long in being answered.

A public broadcasting crew from the United States had come to see the mercenaries and record at least part of their story. The Brazilians wanted the audience back in the United States to know just how well the prisoners were being treated in their confinement.

But along with their good treatment and public appearance came some bad news for the mercs. Near the middle of December, the decision of the Brazilian Supreme Court was announced. The mercenaries were to be turned over to the Argentine government. The men were being extradited.

THE ESCAPE

That decision was the last straw for most of the mercenaries. Jayee was not included in the men's plans, Beef chose not to be involved, and one of their number was too sick to join in, but an escape plan was now going into effect.

The mercs had been assembling an escape kit for months, and only through great effort and luck did they manage to keep their supply cache from being discovered. Money, food, local civilian clothing, medicine, and tools were all part of their kit. An escape network intended to get the men back into the United States had been put in place, but that network began in Bolivia, over seven hundred miles to the west.

Several things were working in favor of the mercenaries: their own audacity, luck, and skills, and the fact that the new prison's guards were particularly lazy. The mercs assembled their kit and prepared their escape route from the prison building. Secreted hacksaw blades were used to cut through the locks on the mercs' cell doors as well as the ceiling bars in the cell block's shower. Dummys were made up to make their bunks look like the men were still sleeping in them. Cuts in the ceiling bars and cell-door locks were disguised with a paste made from toothpaste, metal cuttings, and dirt. Finally, everything was in place for the men to make their move—and that's when the riots broke out.

In Brasilia, the people were rioting. The reason for the riot was unimportant to the mercs. What *was* important was the increase in the guard population, the lockdown of the prisoners, and the new patrols put into place. Now the mercs spent the nights watching the increased guard force patrol the prison with men and dogs. At any time, the mercenaries' preparations could have been discovered in a general search. But the men's luck looked like it was going to hold. The riots died down, and their own plans went unnoticed.

As the riots broke, the town—and the prison—quieted down. For the first Sunday after the riots ended, the least effective of the guards pulled duty. Nothing in the guards' demeanor or routine indicated to the mercs that anything had changed. Now was their best chance to escape.

Later that Sunday night, the mercs kept the guards occupied with constant chatter and requests. One of the men remained in the shower room, taking one of the longest showers of his life but also keeping the guards from changing their shift. Finally, the guards just told the mercs to leave them alone, and they watched the men make a show of locking themselves in, with the damaged cell locks still unnoticed.

Now the merc in the shower pulled the ceiling bars free with a strong yank. The four men who decided to go prepared their escape kits and dummies. The cell doors were opened, and the men began to make their break for freedom.

Using an almost traditional prisoner rope made of knotted bedsheets, the mercs began to lower themselves from the prison-block roof. Prior to moving, one of the men had lain on the roof and noticed that a light rain had started to fall. All of the guards and dogs were staying under cover from the weather. In addition, the spotlights intended to show the prisoners were now working in their favor. Instead of illuminating the prison, the lights were pointed away from the buildings, shining outward toward the farther wall, blinding the guards and destroying their night vision as well.

The mercs were able to climb down from the roof of their building between two of the searchlights. The open gate in the inner prison compound's wall was fifty meters away. Past that gate were other prison buildings, another wall, a gate, and escape. Their sick compatriot within the prison pulled back the knotted-sheet rope after the men were on the ground. Disassembling the rope, the merc remade the beds that the sheets had been taken from and made sure everything looked normal. The guards might not notice anything amiss until the next morning, giving the mercs six or more hours for their escape.

Now came the time for the most audacious part of the plan. The mercs put on their civilian clothes and stuffed all of their other gear into the small tote bags they had gathered. The tote bags were much like the bags the guards used for carrying their weapons and gear home after their shifts were over, and that was part of the mercs' plan.

Many of the guards and Brazilian police moved through the outer gate all of the time. It was only around ten at night, so there was still plenty of movement through the gate. With the rain picking up, the first two mercs walked to the first guard shack and through the gate beyond. The fact that the guards on duty were smoking marijuana was surprising even to the jaded mercs.

Once through the first gate, after waving to the bored guard, the mercs had to pass through the main gate in the outer wall. This gate was more heavily guarded, with a dog as well as men, but the guards paid no notice to the mercs as they walked past. Even the dog didn't care. A few nerve-racking minutes later, the second pair of mercs met up with their teammates at the chosen site, a hospital across the street from the prison.

Now that they were out of the prison, the escape plan was much more loosely organized. The men used a salvaged map from an old paper to give them direction, and they used a portion of their funds to hire a cab that drove them several hundred kilometers from Brasilia. One of the mercs broke off from the group, intending to use his own contacts to get himself out of the country. He succeeded in returning to the States a month or so later.

Through various means, the mercs stole their way across the Brazilian countryside. About five hundred kilometers from Brasilia, the men had to hole up for the night and wait for a bus that would be available the next morning. To avoid hotel check-ins, because of their lack of papers, the mercs made use of a local brothel to hide, a place where identities were not considered important.

The mercs had taken the time to prepare properly for their escape. Smooth-shaven and short-haired, the men looked little like the pictures of the hairy, scruffy foreign mercenary escapees shown on Brazilian television. Even the off-duty policeman in the bar paid no attention to the mercs.

Arriving at their planned site almost two days later, the nearly exhausted mercs met with a contact who had made arrangements for them. A light plane took the mercs to within a short distance of the Bolivian border. A cooperative cab driver, considering the mercs nothing unusual, knew the methods for getting people across the border with little official interference. After a harrowing cab ride, the mercs made their way into Bolivia without incident. Ten months after their imprisonment began, the mercenaries were free of Brazil.

But Bolivia still had to be dealt with. The Bolivian escape network, though, operated in the mercenaries' favor, and they soon found themselves in La Paz, waiting for another American contact.

The publisher at *Soldier of Fortune* magazine had been following the mercs' plight, and men at the magazine had been actively helping the merc team as much as they could. In a final act of generosity, the publisher himself handed one of his staff the several thousand dollars the mercs needed in cash to get back home to the States. On December 23, the staff man risked Bolivian customs with all of the cash stashed on him. Meeting with the mercenaries, he handed over the cash to some very grateful, and impressive, men.

Bluffing their way past an airline clerk and an embassy official by dropping the names of some important officials, the mercs boarded a flight for the United States. On Christmas Day, the mercs walked onto U.S. soil at Miami Airport. Even their lack of passports wasn't a problem now—they were finally home and alive.

Jayee and the other mercenaries back in the prison were eventually extradited to Argentina. After several months had passed and thousands of dollars were paid for bail, the men were given their passports and sent back to the United States.

Ghana remained a Marxist government under the direction of President Jerry Rawlings. Godfrey Osei was not heard from again, and may have been considered an embarrassment by the governments and people who supported him.

The mercenaries involved with the coup attempt learned the most valuable lesson that can be known by a merc: know what you are getting into, and prepare for the worst. Most mercenaries are not hired because they are the best fighting men available. They are hired because they are as expendable as any other weapon.

Sources and Suggested Reading

MERCENARIES IN HISTORY

Greek Mercenaries in Persia

Adcock, Sir Frank. *Greek and Macedonian Art of War.* New York: Berkeley, 1957.

Anderson, J. K. *Military Practice and Theory in the Age of Xenophon.* New York: Berkeley, 1970.

Xenophon. *March Up Country.* Ann Arbor: University of Michigan Press, 1958.

Hannibal in Italy

Cottrell, Leonard. *Hannibal, Enemy of Rome.* New York: Da Capo Press, 1992.

Dupuy, Ernest R. and Trevor N. Dupuy, ed. *The Harper Encyclopedia of Military History, 4th Edition.* New York: HarperCollins, 1993.

Heroditus. *The Persian Wars* (several translations are available).

May, Major Elmer C. *The Art of Ancient Warfare.* West Point: United States Military Academy, 1970.

The Fine Art of Contract Negotiation. The Game of Survival, and Mercenaries Triumphant

Contamine, Phillippe. *War in the Middle Ages*. Cambridge, MA: Blackwell Publishers, 1984.

Deiss, Joseph Jay. *Captains of Fortune: Profiles of Six Italian Condottieri*. New York: Crowell, 1967.

Oman, Charles William Chadwick. *A History of the Art of War in the Middle Ages*. Mechanicsburg, PA: Stackpole Books, 1924.

Procopius, translated by H. B. Dewing. *History of the Wars, Vol. 3: The Gothic War*. Cambridge, MA: Harvard University Press, 1922.

The Hessians in America

Hibbert, Christopher. *Redcoats and Rebels*. New York: Avon Books, 1991.

Leckie, Robert. *George Washington's War*. New York: HarperCollins, 1993.

Tuchman, Barbara. *The First Salute: A View of the American Revolution*. New York: Ballantine Books, 1989.

Wheeler, Richard. *The Voices of 1776*. New York: NAL Dutton, 1991.

Death With Honor

Murray, Simon. *Legionnaire*. New York: Times Books, 1978.

Ryan, James W. *The French Foreign Legion's Greatest Battle: Camerone*. Westport, CT: Greenwood Publishing, 1996.

Faithful unto Death

Jordan, David P. *King's Trial: Louis XVI vs. the French Revolution*. Los Angeles: University of California Press, 1981.

TWENTIETH-CENTURY MERCENARIES

Combat in a Strange New World and A Meeting of Honor

Fraser, David. *Knight's Cross: A Life of Field Marshall Erwin Rommel*. New York: HarperCollins, 1993.

Keegan, John. *The Second World War*. New York: Penguin Books, 1990.

Mallin, Jay, and Robert K. Brown. *Merc: American Soldiers of Fortune*. New York: Macmillan Publishing Co., Inc., 1979.

The Lost Cause

Porch, Douglas. *The French Foreign Legion*. New York: HarperCollins, 1991.

Young, John Robert. *The French Foreign Legion: The Inside Story of the World-Famous Fighting Force*. New York: Thames and Hudson, Inc., 1984.

Mercenary Knight of the African Skies

Hempstone, Frederick A. *Mercenaries and Dividends: The Katanga Story*. New York: Praeger, 1972.

Seagrave, Sterling. *Flight/Soldiers of Fortune*. New York: Time-Life Books, 1981.

The Crusade against Castro

Asprey, Robert B. *War in the Shadows*. New York: Doubleday & Company, 1975.

CIA Field Information Reports. June 12, 1962, to October 1964.

Buyer and Seller of Men

CIA documents re: John Banks, 1971–1973.

Dempster, Chris and Dave Tompkins. *Fire Power*. New York: St. Martin's Press, 1980.

Civilian Irregular Defense Group

Moul, Dinh. "Montagnard Mercenary at the Battle of Lang Vei." *Vietnam Magazine* (April 1998).

Fawcett, Bill, ed. *Hunters and Shooters: An Oral History of the U.S. Navy SEALs in Vietnam*. New York: Avon Books, 1996.

AMERICAN SOLDIERS OF FORTUNE

Revolution over China

Boyington, Gregory. Interview with the author. *International Air Expo*, Brown Field, Otay Mesa, California. May 1986.

Seagrave, Sterling. *Flight/Soldiers of Fortune*. New York: Time-Life Books, 1981.

Larger Than Life

Boehm, Ray. *First SEAL*. New York: Simon & Shuster, 1998.

CAT Bulletin (Febuary 15 and July 1, 1950).

CAT Bulletin 7, no. 6 (June 1954).

Soldier, Jurist, Patriot

Mallin, Jay and Robert K. Brown. *Merc: American Soldiers of Fortune*. New York: Macmillan Publishing Company, 1979.

The Unknown Mercs

Mockler, Anthony. *The Mercenaries*. New York: Macmillan & Company, 1969.

Wise, David and Thomas B. Ross. *The Invisible Government*. New York: Random House, 1974.

The Cuban Second Front

Meyer, Karl E. and Tad Szulc. *The Cuban Invasion: A Chronicle of Disaster*. New York: Praeger, 1962.

Today's Legionnaire

Debay, Yves. *The French Foreign Legion Today*. Osceola, WI: Motorbooks International, 1992.

Porch, Douglas. *The French Foreign Legion: A Complete History of the Legendary Fighting Force*. New York: HarperCollins, 1991.

An American in Angola

CIA documents re: George Bacon, 1969–1972.

Hoare, Mike. *Congo Mercenary*. New York: Robert Hale, 1967.

July, Robert. *A History of the African People*. New York: Charles Scribner & Sons, 1970.

MODERN MERCS

Coal Miners' Mercenaries

MacKenzie, S. W. "Rent-a-Gurka: Crown's Finest Fighters for Hire." *Soldier of Fortune* (March 1994).

Pate, James L. "Guerrilla War in the Hills: Mercs Come to Appalachia." *Soldier of Fortune* (September 1986).

The Cocaine Wars

Adams, James. *The Financing of Terror*. New York: Simon and Shuster, 1986.

Rosie, George. *The Directory of International Terrorism*. New York: Paragon House, 1986.

Direct Action in Cali

Ehrenfeld, Rachel. *Narco Terrorism*. New York: Basic Books, 1990.

Killyane, Richard. "Target Medellín: Brit Mercs Mount Air Assault on Drug Lord's Lair." *Soldier of Fortune* (December 1984).

The Rules of Engagement

Drenowski, Dana. "Merc Work: Does the Geneva Convention Apply?" *Soldier of Fortune* (December 1984).

Drenowski, Dana. "More Mercs and the Law." *Soldier of Fortune* (April 1985).

The actual text of the international convention was downloaded from a United Nations website: *http://www.un.org/*

Victory and Betrayal in Ghana: The Ultimate Mercenary Story

Balor, Paul. *The Manual of the Mercenary Soldier*. Boulder: Paladin Press, 1988.

Coleman, John. "Soldiers of Misfortune Part 2: American Mercs Board a Slow Boat to Ghana." *Soldier of Fortune* (May 1987).

Coleman, John. "Soldiers of Misfortune Part 3: Capture, Jail, and the Great Escape." *Soldier of Fortune* (June 1987).

Duvall, Pierre. "Soldiers of Misfortune: Best-Laid Plans of Mice and Mercs." *Soldier of Fortune* (April 1987).

Ghana, the Land of Gold. Government pamphlet.

Hobart, Major F. W. A., ed. *Jane's Infantry Weapons, 1975*. London: Jane's Yearbooks.

Index

289